Learning for Little Kids

Learning for Little Kids

*A Parent's Sourcebook
for the Years 3 to 8*

by Sandy Jones

Houghton Mifflin Company
Boston   1979

Also by Sandy Jones
Good Things for Babies

Library of Congress Cataloging in Publication Data
Jones, Sandy.
 Learning for little kids.
 Includes index.
 1. Education, Primary—Handbooks, manuals, etc.
I. Title.
LB1523.J66   372.24′1   78-8890
ISBN 0-395-26296-8 **ISBN** 0-395-27210-6 pbk.

Printed in the United States of America

M 10 9 8 7 6 5 4 3 2 1

The author is grateful for permission to reprint the following:

"Mathematics for the Very Young" by Louise Ellison (*Parents*' magazine, July 1969); "Daddy Tells a Story" by Sidney
A. Stutz (*Parents*' magazine, June 1971); "How Children
Learn about Sex and Birth" and "Talking to Your Child
about Sex and Birth" by Anne C. Bernstein. Reprinted by
permission of *Psychology Today* magazine. Copyright ©
1975 Ziff-Davis Publishing Company; "When Pets Die"
from Linda Jane Vogel, *Helping a Child Understand Death*
(Philadelphia: Fortress Press, 1975), pp. 32–39. Copyright
© 1975 by Fortress Press and reprinted with the permission
of the publisher; "Investigate Your Backyard Beasties" by
Stephen W. Kress, reprinted from *Instructor*, copyright ©
October 1975 by The Instructor Publications, Inc., used by
permission. "How to Talk to a Scribbler" by Joseph J. Sparling and Marylin C. Sparling. Reprinted by permission
from *Young Children*, Vol. XXVIII, No. 6 (August 1973), pp.
333–341. Copyright © 1973, National Association for the
Education of Young Children, 1834 Connecticut Avenue,
N.W., Washington, D.C. 20009 "The Sense of Wonder"
from pp. 42–45, 49, 52 of Rachel Carson, *The Sense of Wonder*. Copyright © 1956 by Rachel L. Carson. By permission
of Harper & Row, Publishers, Inc.

Photo credits are as follows:

Lakeshore Curriculum Materials Company, copyright 1977,
pages 9 (bottom), 66 (bottom right), 176 (left), 179 (right),
180, 191 (bottom left), and 213 (top left); Fun-da-mentals,
page 20; Glen S. Cook & Son, page 72 (top left); Dennis E.
Conners, page 100 (bottom left); Public Health Services Ad-
ministration, Department of Health, Education and Welfare, page 110; Community Playthings, Rifton, N.Y., pages
148 (top left), 221 (top left), 223 (bottom left); Shindana
Toys, Inc., © 1977, page 214 (bottom left); Children's Television Workshop, © 1974, page 215 (left); Parker Brothers,
page 218 (top right).

The illustration on page 51 (bottom left), is reprinted with
permission from Action for Children's Television.

Photographs by Erika Stone appear on pages ii, x, 14, 34,
39, 40, 52, 74, 82, 90, 102, 128, 152, 166, 169, 182, and 192.

Line drawings by Sally L. Wright appear on pages 3, 13, 36,
37, 57, 84, 140, 151 (top left), 171, 173, 186, 187, 188, 194,
196, 199, 204, 205, and 207.

To my husband, Paul, who has given himself unselfishly to both Marcie and me so that this book could be written.

Foreword

The purpose of *Learning for Little Kids* is to offer parents (and teachers) a compendium of things to do and ways of sharing life with a young child. There are no theoretical treatises on the cognitive development of the young child, just down-to-earth discussions about everyday matters. The products in the book have been chosen because they have value in helping a child learn rather than just keeping a youngster busy. The articles, mostly by parents, are meant to be practical and helpful.

Little children are beautiful! Their freshness and curiosity are awesome to me. I suppose that if I didn't have an ongoing love relationship with my beautiful five-year-old, I wouldn't be so inspired to spend two years thinking about young children and longing for all youngsters to have their parents take time out from the rush of life to sit down and share.

Children can bring adults a sense of renewal. They can help us realize our true roots in the human race — how we came to be where we are and what role our own parents played in that. Being Mommy or Daddy to someone can restore us to tenderness. It can help us be turned on to the simple things in life: the beauty of our world and its small pleasures, like a snail crawling across the sidewalk or the luxury of pouring water in the bathtub. If we can just take time to enjoy the gifts that young children bring to us!

Adults have something to give to young children, too. We can nurture them and support them as they try out their wings. We can help them create things with their own hands so that they feel strong and good about themselves. We can teach them in gentle ways about the realities of human living. It's a good role — unappreciated by society as a whole but very, very important.

I don't picture you reading the book from cover to cover, but I see you dipping in where something interests you and adapting ideas to your own situation.

Time for thank yous: to my husband, Paul, who has given the gift of time to me by cooking meals and sharing child care so that I could write, and to Susan Doering and her daughters, Andrea and Stefanie. Paul, Marcie, and I have "house shared" with Susan during the year I was writing *Learning for Little Kids*. Our cooperation freed me to do the research and work that the book needed. To my editor, Anita McClellan, who supported me in a beautiful way while I struggled to become a writer. And to Marcie, who set herself up a little desk next to mine to work on gluing, cutting, and other very important tasks while I worked on mine. ("Mommy, why do you want to write an old boring book, anyway?")

The pronouns "he" and "she" have been alternated chapter by chapter to recognize both sexes of children. Although I've done my very best to make the sources and prices of products and books up to date and accurate, sometimes human errors may occur and sometimes companies decide to drop products that don't sell for them. I hope that you will not meet with frustration as you follow up on the catalog portion of the book, just keep in mind that mail-order businesses and prices are rapidly changing these days.

Please feel free to write me if you've got ideas to share or suggestions for change. I would love to hear from you, and I will answer you as quickly as I can. Address your letter to Houghton Mifflin, Two Park Street, Boston, Massachusetts 02107.

Yours in the spirit of love,

Sandy Jones

Contents

Teaching Self-Care and Safety

Because children are so small, and in many ways so helpless, their drive for independence asserts itself strongly as a counter to the inevitable dependence that they must accept. My husband's grandmother, at the opposite end of life's spectrum and forced to be dependent when she didn't wish to, asserted herself in the same way Marcie does: "I'll do it *myself!*" She complained that when you reach ninety-two you "ain't worth a nickel with a hole in it." The wise parent senses her child's need to feel mastery over her world and provides as many opportunities as she can for the child to do things for herself.

One of the most direct ways to help a child feel good about herself is to lead her into caring for herself: shampooing her hair, brushing her teeth, choosing what to wear, dressing herself, tying her own shoes. The instructions are gentle ones — no harsh words or force — taking the opportune moment to demonstrate and providing ample praise for success. It's tempting to try to take over these tasks when you're in a hurry — but your child's loud protests will quickly teach you to respect the private territory of the self that you and your child have established together.

REDESIGNING THE INDOOR ENVIRONMENT

Children are small people living in a world designed for large people. The chairs, the stairways, the sinks, the toilets, the beds, the shelves — all of the house has been arranged for the comfort of people over four feet tall. A child must continually adjust herself to this in the same way that a handicapped person must adjust herself to the architectural barriers built by the nonhandicapped majority.

While adults meet eye to eye, children must meet adults from way down below. The overall effect of the giant world and tall people robs the child of a sense of mastery over her world. The child-care rooms in Russia have raised platforms that allow children to be at adult eye level if they so desire. At first the reasoning behind making children artificially taller seems absurd, but when you realize how unyielding the adult world is to the child even within her own home, a single concession such as that one seems like a thoughtful understanding of the child's dilemma.

Where do you begin readjusting a home to make it more comfortable for a young child? Her bedroom. Adults take walls for granted. But to a child, walls are for kicking when you're mad or tense, for bouncing balls off of, for putting art work on, for watching shadows in the night. Making use of wall space for play shows good planning. Put a blackboard, bulletin board, and an unbreakable mirror at child's eye level. If you use wallpaper, select paper that has many bright and intriguing patterns.

Don't use a toy chest for storing toys. Toy chests have accounted for countless injuries to children's fingers and in some cases for the deaths of young children when the heavy lids have come smashing down on their necks. Not only that, but toys in a chest are in such a jumble that a child is frustrated and distracted from play when she attempts to find a particular toy.

The best solution is open shelves with compartments. This way a child can practice sorting toys as she cleans: "the trucks go here, the dolls here, and the books here." Multicolored shelves are exciting to look at. With contact paper and plywood you can turn part of the shelf into a dollhouse or a play garage.

A good way to keep your child's room from turning into a junk heap is to rotate toys and books every few weeks. Store extras in a box in the closet. Keep the shelves pared down to a few good toys. Display the books open and standing on the top of the shelf so that your child can readily see their covers.

Colorful plastic or ceramic clothes hooks can be screwed into the wall at a child's height for hanging up clothes. A small wooden shelf on the floor with compartments for shoes, gloves, and other winter accessories will help to maintain order.

Beds should be low to the floor, easy to get in and out of, and without wooden sides or sharp corners that a child could hurt herself on. One couple I know has built bunk beds for their children from two cubicles with shelves and lighting built in at either end and curtains that can be drawn for privacy, so that each child has a secret inner world to escape to. It seems to me that children would welcome a sense of being enclosed.

Other features of a room for a child: a carpeted space near the books with a child-sized chair or pillows for reading on. A smooth area, perhaps covered with linoleum or other stain resistant surface for painting, rolling trucks, and other messy play. Other ideas: a record player with a record rack, open shelves or easy-to-operate drawers for clothes storage, a low pole in the closet for hanging clothes.

Think about bringing the high ceilings down to your child's level by using bright mobiles, Chinese kites, or with a puff of brilliantly patterned fabric. A child-sized desk or table and chair is a valuable place for cutting, gluing, and pounding away on an old typewriter.

Do you have space for a child area in your kitchen? Children naturally want to be close to where their parents are, particularly when they are waiting to eat. Perhaps you can buy or construct a small table for drawing projects and snack-eating with a shelf to store your child's own kitchen toys: a potato masher, an old pot, wooden spoons, and other paraphernalia. It's thoughtful to store dishes, glasses, and silverware (plastic ware for snacks and lunchtime) on the lower shelves of the kitchen cabinets so that your child can help set the table and get water for herself.

A sturdy, nonslip stool is an excellent investment to help your child become more self sufficient. One in the bathroom helps in reaching the sink, and one in the kitchen for getting water and helping with food preparation.

DRESSING

Preschoolers love to change clothes. What is this fascination with putting things on and taking them off? Partly it's important practice in muscular control — "my arms here, my legs there." Perhaps, too, it's an enchantment with the mystique of clothing . . . a primitive delight with the possibility of changing one's self with the change of clothes. At any rate, you'll begin to feel that you have a genuine clotheshorse on your hands. You'll probably need to alter your concept of what's clean and what's dirty, reshelving clothes from the floor as long as they're not visibly soiled. A costume box is a good way to siphon off the clothes-changing drive.

Take care to buy clothes that enable a child to dress herself. Knit shirts with ample head holes are preferable to shirts with small buttons. Pants with elasticized waistbands are easier to manage than those with zippers and snaps. Marcie has two hand-me-down skirts made of a soft, washable knit fabric with elastic waists. They have become her day-to-day favorites, probably because they're so easy to pull on and off.

Shoes have a special significance to a child. If you doubt that, try throwing a child's shoes on the floor when you're angry, and you'll see that your child takes it as a most insulting gesture. Shoes are symbols of independence, close friends in the process of walking and running. Don't be misled by eager shoe salesclerks into thinking that you ought to buy stiff leather lace-up shoes with artificial arches and slick soles. In reality, the child's ideal shoe is flexible and soft. It can be slipped on and off easily by the child herself. Slip-on sneakers with a good tread are excellent except in very cold weather. A child can also manage buckle fasteners on shoes much earlier than shoelaces.

As with all other skills calling for muscular control by young children, "the bigger the better" rule applies to learning to tie shoelaces.

How to Tie Your Own Shoe Laces

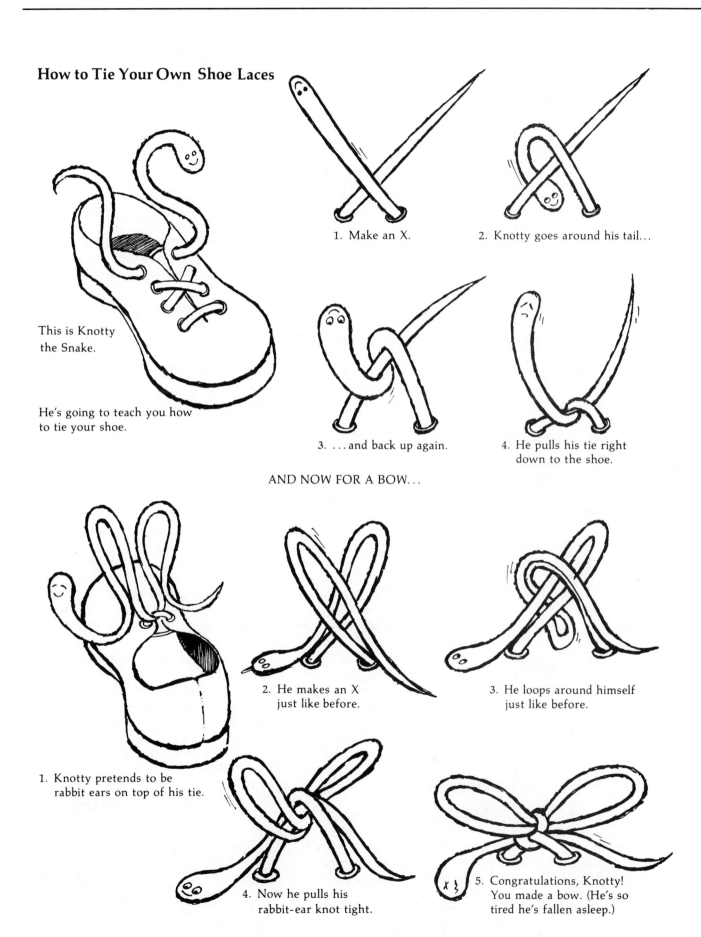

This is Knotty the Snake.

He's going to teach you how to tie your shoe.

1. Make an X.

2. Knotty goes around his tail...

3. ...and back up again.

4. He pulls his tie right down to the shoe.

AND NOW FOR A BOW...

1. Knotty pretends to be rabbit ears on top of his tie.

2. He makes an X just like before.

3. He loops around himself just like before.

4. Now he pulls his rabbit-ear knot tight.

5. Congratulations, Knotty! You made a bow. (He's so tired he's fallen asleep.)

Tying should begin with a big sash or cord around the child's waist fastened in the back with a safety pin so it won't slip down. If you want to make a belt for teaching tying, have the left side one color and the right side another so that the over-under sequence can easily be seen. You can even make a snake's head on one side so that the belt will have personality: "Sam the snake is crawling over his tail. Two times makes a knot." Allow plenty of time for practice, and back off if your child seems frustrated. Bow tying is much harder for youngsters to master. The easiest method is to make loops on either side that are tied just like a knot.

BRUSHING AND FLOSSING TEETH

The first step in good toothbrushing is learning where the teeth are. Using a mirror, see if your child can tell the difference between the biting teeth in the front of her mouth and the larger chewing teeth in the back. Teach her where the different surfaces of her teeth are — the front, the back, and the top.

Let her practice brushing the front, the back, and the tops of her teeth with toothpaste on her finger. After she has a feel for where the different parts of her teeth are, she's ready for a toothbrush. Dentists recommend a small-sized brush with soft, plastic bristles that have been rounded off at the tips. Some feel that an electric toothbrush does a better job than a young child can do with her limited muscular coordination. Ask your dentist to recommend a brushing method. Some prefer a gentle back-and-forth motion at the gum line followed by a rotation of the brush downward, while others feel that any brushing movement is satisfactory.

Plaque-disclosing tablets can help in teaching your child good brushing habits, and in maintaining them. The tablets contain a harmless dye that sticks to the plaque (a sticky substance where decay causing bacteria thrive) coating the teeth. You'll be able to demonstrate clearly where the child has missed brushing. The tablets are available at most drugstores. A small piece of one tablet is adequate for most children. It will take a few sessions with the tablets to set up a habit of thorough brushing. They should be used at least weekly to maintain a good cleaning technique.

Flossing is an important daily practice, too. Often it's easier for children if the ends of the floss are tied together so as to form a 10-inch circle. Your dentist is the best person to demonstrate flossing. You and your child should brush and floss together, since imitation is an excellent teacher.

SAFETY

Our children are subject to many more risks than we or our parents were because of the speed and sophistication of our lives. Even though we are getting disease more under control as the result of our sophisticated medical knowledge, accidents are increasing. The National Safety Council estimates that in an average year, 4300 youngsters under five years of age die from accidents in their homes. For every child killed, another four suffer permanent injury.

It's natural that as parents we want to protect our children from being hurt needlessly. Yet, in our age of anxiety, it's hard to know what is realistic protection and what is hovering overprotection. On one hand, we want our children to enjoy the sense of mastery that comes from scaling trees and other risky leaps and jumps that children love to do, but we also want to hold them back for fear of injury. Sometimes we're unintentionally more protective toward our daughters. When I was a child, my brother got to climb and roughhouse while I was taught that this was unladylike. The threat of injury was amplified for me, even if unconsciously. I suppose that we all will have to listen to our instincts in judging the safety of any situation. My friend Gloria watched her son climb to the top of a giant geodesic tube dome in a local park. He lost his balance at the top and fell. She later said she wished she had listened to her own warning signal and had stopped him earlier.

AUTOMOBILES

Crossing a street is probably the first major lesson that children must learn about the hazards of our present-day life. The automobile is everywhere. Never before have so many children had to contend with the constant intrusion of these metal machines — in front of the house, in shopping centers. Often, nowadays, pedestrians are seen as enemies or obstacles by impatient drivers. You can make signs to help your child learn to read the "walk" and "don't walk" signs. Explain that car drivers can't see small children well. You can teach your child about red lights and green lights, how to wait for the cars to stop, how to watch for cars with signal lights blinking, or cars that are in the process of turning. If your child has to walk to and from school, you can accompany her until you feel comfortable about her safety in dealing with cars. A bright safety vest or reflective belt will help to make her more visible.

Some basic rules that you should impress upon your child:

1. Stop at the curb before crossing any street.
2. Always cross the street holding hands with an adult.
3. Always look both ways for cars. (Jason's mother was surprised to see him looking up and down — "both ways" in his vocabulary.)
4. Listen for the sound of cars.
5. Be careful about walking behind parked cars. Can you hear the car's motor running? Is there a person in the driver's seat? Are the red or white lights on the back lit, meaning that the car might back up?

6. Don't chase a ball out into the street. (You might want to roll a ball into the street, and then teach your child that she is to come and get an adult to retrieve the ball for her.)

When you feel that your child is ready to begin making judgments about crossing streets, you should let your child "cross" you both, so that you can check to see that she has mastered the basic rules. Make your child go back again if she's been careless.

Your child should always sit in the back seat of the car for safety. A child less than four years old or forty pounds in weight should have a car seat. (For the most up-to-date information on what seat to buy, check *Consumer Reports* available in most public libraries.) A child over four years old should use the adult seat belt with a small, baby-sized pillow padding the child's abdomen where the belt crosses. Always check to see that the doors are locked before starting the motor.

BICYCLES

The U.S. Consumer Product Safety Commission estimates that in the fiscal year of 1973, 371,000 people suffered bicycle related injuries serious enough to be rushed to a hospital emergency room. Kids between five and fourteen accounted for over 250,000 of those injured. The death list reads like this: boy, eight years old, runs into a wall and dies from a broken skull; boy, nine years old, falls from a bicycle onto the street and breaks his neck; girl, six years old, is hit by a car while on a bicycle and dies from head injuries.

Understanding the safety risk, you've decided that you still want to buy your child a bicycle. Look around your neighborhood to see that there is a safe, car-free place for your child to ride. Responsibility for the decision of whether to expose your child to the risks of traveling on busy streets or bumpy sidewalks is ultimately going to be yours.

The Bicycle Institute of America has some suggestions for selecting and maintaining an appropriate bike for your child. Choose a bicycle that is the right size for your child. The greatest cause of accidents on bikes is improper fit. When your child is straddling the bike both feet flat on the floor without shoes, there should be at least an inch of clearance between the crotch and the frame of the bicycle. A child shouldn't use the same bike as her parents, nor should parents buy a large bike expecting the child to grow into it. If a bicycle is too large, a child is more apt to have accidents because her feet slip off the pedals, she can't get on and off the bike easily, and she can't maintain good control over it. This doesn't mean that you will have to buy a bike every year to accommodate your child's growth. The seat and handlebar can be raised as she grows, but it's important to begin with a well-fitted bike.

The Institute suggests that you start with a lower-priced model since you can't predict in advance how much your child will be using her bicycle, or how enthusiastic she will be after the initial excitement wears off.

The Consumer Product Safety Commission has these tips for parents in the market for a child's bicycle:

• Be sure that the bicycle has safety equipment, including a reflector or a red taillight that can be seen from 300 feet, a light in front of the bike that can be seen from 500 feet, and a warning device such as a bell or horn.

• Buy additional light-reflecting materials to put on the front and rear fenders, the handlebars, the pedals, and chain guard to make the bike more visible.

• Foot slippage is a frequent cause of accidents. Look for pedals with ridges or some form of skid-resistant surface to prevent shoes from slipping off. (You may have to purchase these pedals separately.)

You should also check your child's bicycle periodically to make sure that:

• All nuts, bolts, and clamps are tightly secured.

• The light is kept clean and bright with good batteries.

• The pedals spin freely.

• Worn pedals and spokes are replaced immediately.

• The mirror is not broken or cracked.

• The tires are properly inflated.

• The chain is frequently cleaned and lubricated with light oil.

• The seat is adjusted to the size of the child so that her leg bends only slightly with the ball of the foot on the pedal at the bottom of the stroke. (Don't allow your child to raise the seat to a height that inhibits her control of the bike.)

Some of the hazards of children's bicycles are sissy bars, a long tubular metal backrest that makes getting off the bike difficult, the lack of a chain guard causing children to entrap bare toes or fingers (shoes should *always* be worn for bike riding), and a knobbed gearshift box located on the front crossbar of the bike.

To teach your child to ride, choose a quiet, car-free area like a parking lot or a schoolyard. Lower the saddle until your child can touch the ground comfortably and easily. (After she has learned to balance, the saddle can be raised to the proper level described above.) This provides your child with the feeling that she can recover her balance to keep from falling. Be sure your child wears heavy pants to protect her knees from inevitable falls. Hold on to the back of the saddle of the bike and run *behind* the bicycle, out of sight. Going down a slight incline is easier. Tell your child to look straight ahead while pedaling as hard as she can. Reassure her that you will hold the bicycle up, so that she needn't worry about falling. Ride in a straight line at first. Gradually, you'll be able to decrease your balancing help to the point that your child won't know when you are or are not supporting her.

You should set up definite rules about where your child is permitted to ride and see that they are obeyed. As your child becomes more proficient at bike-riding, warn her about the dangers of potholes, glass, and gravel on the street, of people opening doors from parked cars, of attempting to do tricks such as riding without using her hands, or doing wheelies. Remind her never to let children hitch rides with her on her bike and never to ride double with anyone else. She should obey traffic rules: Always ride with friends in single file on the right-hand side of the road, stop at stop signs and intersections, and use hand signals for turns.

FIRST AID

A SAFETY CHECK LIST FOR PARENTS

_____ I store bleach, kerosene, liquid detergent, insect poisons out of the kitchen and on a high shelf where my child can't reach them.

_____ I never put leftover gasoline or other chemicals and poisonous liquids in jars or glasses that might make them look drinkable.

_____ I keep vitamin pills, iron pills, aspirin and other medicines, and denture cleansing tablets out of reach. I don't carry medicines in my pocketbook or coat pocket unless they're in child-proof containers. I flush unused prescription drugs down the toilet every six months.

_____ I turn all of the pot handles on my stove toward the back so that they won't be pulled over by mistake. I don't allow my child around the stove without being

right next to her. I'm extremely careful when boiling or frying foods.

_____ None of the electric cords to the coffeepot, the toaster, the blender, or other appliances are hanging down so that they could be pulled over accidentally. I've warned my child not to use a knife or other metal object to pry toast from the toaster.

_____ I always keep a screen in front of the fireplace and don't allow my preschooler to poke at the fire.

_____ I am always present when my child is around water — the bathtub, a wading pool, lakes, ponds, even big mud puddles, since kids can drown in only two inches of water. I've inspected neighborhood pools to be sure that they're child-proof, and I've begun working with my child on basic water safety.

_____ I keep knives, pointed scissors, needles, pins, thumbtacks, matches, and cigarette lighters out of the reach of my child.

_____ There are no frayed or damaged electrical cords in my house. No sockets are overloaded. All unused outlets are covered with plastic "dummy" plugs.

_____ All second-story windows have well-fitted screens in good repair so that my child won't accidentally fall out.

_____ All clotheslines are higher than my child can reach so that there's no danger of her running into them or getting entrapped in them.

_____ I make my child stay indoors when I use the lawn mower since it may hurl child-level objects or cut feet and hands. I never put gasoline in the mower while it's in the basement or garage, where it might be spilled and ignite.

A BASIC FIRST-AID KIT
- 3 by 3-inch sterile gauze dressings
- Box of plastic strips in an assortment of sizes
- Roll of ½-inch adhesive tape
- Small bottle of Mercurochrome or other mild antiseptic
- Box of baking soda, or Adolph's unseasoned meat tenderizer for bee and other insect stings.
- Tweezers and needles for splinters (young children can operate tweezer scissors themselves)
- Syrup of ipecac to induce vomiting in case of poisoning
- Calamine lotion for poison ivy and other itches
- Thermometer
- Ice bag
- Rubbing alcohol

Have the telephone numbers of the following persons posted by the telephone:
- Doctor
- Ambulance
- Poison control center
- Police department
- Fire department

HINTS FOR TEACHING FIRST AID AND SAFETY TO YOUR CHILD

Help your child memorize her name, your name, her home address and phone number. If you're going into a crowd where you might be separated from each other, pin this information on her clothing or use a press-on label.

Teach her how to dial for help in an emergency — "O" for operator, or your city's help number.

Plan an alternative fire exit from upstairs and practice crawling to it. Decide exactly where you will all meet outside. (Buy a smoke alarm if you haven't already got one!) Practice with your child what to do in case her clothing catches on fire. Lie down and fold your arms over your head to keep the flames away from your face.

Rolling over will help cut off the air and put out the fire. *Never run!* That only makes the fire burn faster.

Teach your child how to treat simple burns with an ice cube, how to wash her hands gently after a cut, how to put on an adhesive bandage without touching the sterile pad. (I prefer Curity Curad bandages since they are less painful to remove than most others.)

Often children become anxious at the sight of blood. Talk about how blood carries nourishment to muscles and skin. Reassure her that an injury to the body is going to start healing right away and a scab will cover the hole in her skin. A healthy respect for scabs can help hold her back from scratching them off out of curiosity.

If a child gets something in her eye, caution her not to rub it. Sometimes it helps to rub the *other* eye. Try rinsing the eye with water, or pulling the top lid down over the bottom lid to help the eye rinse the object out.

Bee sting remedies: A seventy-six-year-old beekeeper suggests scraping straight down with your thumbnail to remove the stinger without breaking the poison sack. He then uses vinegar to neutralize the poison. Another remedy that's been suggested for bee, hornet and mosquito bites is to make a paste from Adolph's unseasoned meat tenderizer and water and apply it directly on the sting.

Remind your child always to call you if she breaks glass. Put broken glass into a sturdy paper bag before throwing it away so that no one will get cut by slivers in the trash. Children should be cautioned never to carry a glass, a pair of scissors, or a knife themselves.

Parents all over the United States are now taking free Cardiopulmonary Resuscitation (CPR) through their local heart associations and adult education courses. Through the course you will learn how to give mouth-to-mouth resuscitation as well as how to apply pressure on the sternum to stimulate a heart that has stopped beating.

BOOKS FOR MAKING CHILDREN'S FURNITURE AND INDOOR EQUIPMENT

CHILD-SIZED FURNITURE

Children's Rooms and Play Yards
The Editors of Sunset Books and *Sunset* Magazine
Lane Publishing Co., Willow and Middlefield
Roads, Menlo Park, CA 94025 ($1.95)
Written for the home craftsperson, the book
suggests ideas for toy storage, for playhouses and
play yards, and a variety of unusual beds for
children. Items that look simple but practical: an
easel for two, box blocks made of plywood and
fastened together with an aluminum corner post,
and sandboxes of all descriptions.

Preschool Equipment for a Multi-Use Center
Stone Mountain Educational Projects, Inc., Roaring
Brook Farm, Conway, MA 01341 ($3.50 paperback)
Directions for making wooden indoor play
equipment that folds away when not in use. A shelf
with two fold-up "wings" that make easels, a
combination shelf-workbench for wood projects, a
wooden housekeeping set that includes a play stove
and refrigerator, a rocking boat. My favorite piece is
a puppet theater playhouse made from plywood
with a carpeted floor inside, a window for puppet
shows and a door that opens and shuts. The entire
project is estimated to cost a little over twenty
dollars.

Preschool Guide
Colorado Association of Future Homemakers of
America
Order from:
Mrs. Leah W. Little, State Bursar, Colorado Assn. of
Future Homemakers of America, Box 413,
Johnstown, CO 80534 ($3.00 paperback)
Gives measurements and instructions for making a
toy shelf, a three-sided wooden box with a center
shelf that can be used as a chair for a small child or
as a low table, a driving board with a wooden
steering wheel, a doll bed, an ironing board, a
portable climbing structure, and a low, circular
table.

Making Children's Furniture and Play Structures
Bruce Palmer
Workman Publishing Co., 231 East 51st Street, New
York, NY 10022 ($3.95)
Innovative play structures made from slotted
corrugated cardboard, fiberboard, and hardboard.
Simple stools, chairs, and tables, a shelf, a dome, a
puppet theater, a playhouse and a make-believe
airplane.

Child-Sized Chair
A flexible all foam chair for reading or playing on.
It's washable, flame-retardant, stain-resistant and
nontoxic. Comes in dry-look, wet-look or hide-look
finishes. Colors: lemon yellow, orange, red, gold,
olive green, ultramarine blue, black, or white.
Manufactured by:
The Carter Company, 186 Alewife Brook Parkway,
Cambridge, MA 02138 ($32–$79, depending on the
finish)

Fat Mat
A great recliner for a young child to read and play
on. Foam-filled with wipe-clean vinyl finish. Size:
16 × 34 inches. Yellow or avocado green. Order
from:
Lakeshore Curriculum Materials, 8888 Venice
Boulevard, Los Angeles, CA 90034 ($28.50 + 15%
shipping and handling. CA residents add 6 or 6½%
sales tax)

SAFETY AND HEALTH INFORMATION

"First Aid for Little People"

Johnson & Johnson, Consumer Services
Department, New Brunswick, NJ 08903 (Free)
Aimed at the young school-aged child, this helpful
brochure discusses how to treat cuts and scratches.
How to tell when a person's not breathing. Suggests
getting adult help. And offers basic first-aid
measures.

"Preschool Children in Traffic: A Parents' Guide for Action"

Local American Automobile Associations (Free)
A series of brochures that teach preschoolers from
two to six years of age about street crossing. The
fifteen-page guidebook for parents has practical
suggestions for training your child about traffic
along with factual information about "typical"
pedestrian accidents involving young children. The
brochures for reading to young children are explicit
and well illustrated: "When I Go Outside"
(toddlers), "I Listen and Look for Cars Coming"
(two- and three-year-olds), "How I Cross a Street"
(four- and five-year-olds), and "Traffic Signal
Lights" (six years old and up). Another excellent
free brochure for parents is entitled "Parents,
Children and Traffic: What Is the Solution?"

"Your Child and Household Safety"

Dr. Jay M. Arena
Chemical Specialties Manufacturer's Association,
Suite 1120, 1001 Connecticut Avenue, N.W.,
Washington, DC 20036 (50¢)
A fact-filled booklet with a chapter of safety advice
for parents of three- to five-year-olds. Includes
principles of first aid, treatment of poisons, animal
bites, and gas inhalation.

"Panic or Plan?"
"Your Child's Safety"

Metropolitan Life Insurance Company, One
Madison Avenue, New York, NY 10010 (Free)
Two brochures on safety preparedness. The first
gives parents the chance to rehearse correct
responses to emergency situations. The second
discusses teaching safety rules and suggests
appropriate, safe play materials by age.

"The Children's Hospital Accident Handbook"

Department of Health Education
The Children's Hospital Medical Center, 300
Longwood Avenue, Boston, MA 02115 (35¢)
Discusses the causes of accidents in children, citing
a Children's Hospital study that demonstrated that
accidents to young children most frequently occur
when they're hungry, hyperactive, or when the
family is under stress from tension, illness, or
pregnancy. Practical suggestions for treating
common childhood accidents — insect bites,
nosebleeds, burns, abrasions, fractures, and head
injuries.

"Young Children and Accidents in the Home"

U.S. Department of Health, Education and Welfare
Order from:
Consumer Information Center, Pueblo, CO 81009
(65¢)
Describes the major causes of accidents that involve
young children. A safety checklist by age of child,
accident-causing situations, a fold-out first-aid chart
for posting on the medicine cabinet.

"Tuffy Talks about Medicine"

Aetna Life and Casualty
Order from:
Film Librarian, Public Relations & Advertising
Department, Aetna Life and Casualty, 151
Farmington Avenue, Hartford, CT 06115 (Free)
Tuffy is a dog and friend to Steven, who makes the
mistake of taking medicine from his brother's
friend. A coloring book.

"A Guide for Teaching Poison Prevention in Kindergartens and Primary Grades"

U.S. Department of Health, Education and Welfare
Order from:
Consumer Information Center, Pueblo, CO 81009
($1.00)
An excellent source for teachers of young children.
Suggests games, imaginary play, a puppet show,
worksheets for children all on the theme of
preventing poisoning.

"D Is for Dentist"

American Dental Association, 211 E. Chicago
Avenue, Chicago, IL 60611 (Free)
A question-and-answer comic book for school-aged
children. Describes the dentist's chair, brief
mention of a device (unnamed) for cleaning the
teeth to remove the decayed part of the tooth and
filling up the hole. One child admits that her tooth
hurt when it was being repaired. Stresses the
importance of fixing teeth when the "holes" in them
are still small.

"Cleaning Your Teeth and Gums"

American Dental Association, 211 E. Chicago
Avenue, Chicago, IL 60611 (Free)
A small brochure with color photographs giving
specific directions for using disclosing tablets,
dental floss, and teaching the proper technique for
brushing.

"A Visit to the Dentist"

American Dental Association, 211 E. Chicago
Avenue, Chicago, IL 60611 (Free)
A brochure in picture-book form with simple
language. No mention of the drill. Reminders about
not eating sweets between meals.

"Your Child's Sight: How You Can Help"
"Home Eye Test for Preschoolers"

National Society for the Prevention of Blindness,
Inc., 79 Madison Avenue, New York, NY 10016
(Both Free)

Ways of telling if your child has vision difficulties. "Excessive rubbing of the eyes, shutting or covering one eye, difficulty with close work, frequent blinking, squinting or frowning, undue sensitivity to light, inflamed or watery eyes, recurring styes and itching and burning of the eyes may be signs of eye problems, and indicate the need for a professional eye examination." The Home Eye Test is available in Spanish or English and consists of a chart to help parents discover "lazy eye" early enough to acquire corrective treatment.

"Your Guide to Oral Health"
American Dental Association, 211 E. Chicago Avenue, Chicago, IL 60611 (Free)
An informative brochure discussing fluoride, and proper tooth care. The causes of cavities, oral diseases and abnormalities. A valuable reference.

"Parents Want to Help"
American Dental Association, 211 E. Chicago Avenue, Chicago, IL 60611 (Free)
A bright, colorful fold-out poster with information on caring for teeth, suggestions for a sound diet, ages for eruption of baby and permanent teeth.

Blue Bugs Safety Book
Virginia Poulet
Children's Press, Inc., 1224 W. Van Buren Street, Chicago, IL 60607 ($5.25)
A very simple reader with large print to help in teaching your child basic safety rules and warning signs — "Stop," "Enter," "Exit," "Danger," "Poison," "Walk," "Don't Walk." Can be mastered even by a three-year-old.

Your Child's Teeth
Stephen J. Moss
Houghton Mifflin Company, Two Park Street, Boston, MA 02107 ($3.95, paperback)
A practical, informative guide to dental care, the book gives information on protecting teeth from cavities, gives emergency treatment suggestions, tells how to care for your child's teeth through adolescence. Diet suggestions are given and old wives' tales dispelled. An excellent reference book.

"Sparky Membership Kit" (SPY-9A)
National Fire Protection Association, 470 Atlantic Avenue, Boston, MA 02210 (50¢)
Sparky, a Dalmatian and a firefighter, helps teach young children about fire safety. The membership kit includes a plastic firefighter's badge, an inspector's handbook that tells children how to identify fire hazards in their houses, and a membership card for Sparky's Fire Department.

PRODUCTS FOR SELF-CARE AND SAFETY

Cuddly Kitty
Cuddly Kitty has a zippered pocket on its back that will hold small treasures. It has snap-on legs, button-on arms, and a head that hooks on to its body. The bright red vest is for lacing up, the belt for buckling. A fine pet for practicing self-dressing skills. Made of soft, furlike materials, it measures 15½ inches long with an arm span of 11 inches. Instructions are included.
Developmental Learning Materials, 7440 Natchez Avenue, Niles, IL 60648 ($8.00)

Scotchlite Rescue Marker
A brilliantly reflective marker to place on the window in order to designate a child's room in case of fire. The marker is self-adhesive, weatherproof and long-lasting. From the "Catalog of Child Safety."
Safety Now Co., Inc., Box 567 / 202 York Road, Jenkintown, PA 19046 (50¢)

Step-Up Stools
Sturdy molded plastic stools for use in the
bathroom. The 3-inch high stool is for boys to use
while standing at the toilet. The 6-inch stool is
excellent for reaching the sink and other objects in
the house. Write for ordering information.
Stephen Shanan Co.; 10107 Westview, 211,
Houston, TX 77043 (3″ stool, $7.95; 6″ stool, $9.95 +
postage and handling)

Light Switch Extension
Gives a young child the security of being able to
control darkness. Also removes the danger of falling
from chairs and stools. The extension fits directly on
top of a regular ''up and down'' light switch. All
that's needed for installation is a screwdriver to
change the top screw of the light switch plate. Your
child pushes the clear plastic rod up to turn the light
on and pulls it down to turn the light off. Plastic cap
at the light switch comes in beige, green, or yellow.
Stephen Shanan Co., 10107 Westview 211, Houston,
TX 77043 ($2.95 postpaid)

Learning Book Pattern
A book with things to snap, lace, button, and zip.
You make it from instructions and the pattern.
Excellent for 2- to 4-year-olds.
Order from:
Patterns, Box 57 R. R. #1, Blue Hill, NE 68930
($3.25 postpaid)

Note: Not all manufacturers and publishers will accept single orders for a product or book. Always write to them first, before sending money, to be sure that they will take your order. Make sure you've got the most recent price, including shipping and handling charges. If the company is in your state, then you may need to include state sales tax as well.

Preparing Children to Be Free People

2

The lifestyles of American families are changing rapidly. So are the roles that people play within the family. As children, we were conditioned to think of a family as a father and mother, a blue-eyed older brother, a younger sister and one dog living for decades in a small cottage surrounded by a neat picket fence. Perhaps that was the middle-class white American dream back then but it certainly did not address itself to children who were not white, who lived in a city apartment, whose mother worked, or whose father lived elsewhere. The result was the alienation of many Americans who could not identify with what was being characterized as *the* American family.

Today it is commonly recognized that many marriages end in divorce with the result that one parent becomes the family breadwinner as well as both mother and father to the children. Couples are having fewer children. Adoption has become an increasingly acceptable method for starting and expanding a family; nearly 90,000 children are adopted annually. Millions of families change their places of residence every year. Picture books that portray children of the 1950s or the 1960s seldom speak to the needs and lifestyles of the mobile children of the late 1970s and the changing roles of their parents. This chapter will help you find books and materials suitable for your child's particular needs.

BEYOND SEXISM

Sexism is a new concept for most of us. When we were little few people ever gave thought to the way in which little girls were treated differently from little boys. After all, our parents and teachers said little girls were supposed to be pretty and demure, and "boys will be boys" — tough and aggressive.

Not until we realized what was being done to the minds and hearts of men and women — the way in which they were categorized, stereo-typed and made to play rigid predetermined roles — did we become aware of how crucial the early years were in determining how boys and girls and later men and women would define themselves.

One trouble with putting girls in organdy and lace and making them be docile is that it prevents them from being free children able to take risks and feel the strength of their bodies. One trouble with expecting boys always to be aggressive, climb trees, and play with trucks is that it leaves them no room for the tender, nurturing soft qualities that are so admirable in fathers. What's needed is a middle ground that allows children to grow both ways.

Ultimately, we want our children, boys or girls, to be able to follow their inner feelings. To become what seems natural, comfortable, and good to them. If fixing cars, doing things that require strength is enjoyable to our daughter — then why shouldn't she have the freedom to pursue what fulfills her most? If our son loves children, or likes to cook, why can't he enjoy what brings him pleasure? We're so frightened about being judged by other people. What would the neighbors think? What will the teachers think? Wise parents don't raise their children according to what others think, but according to what they feel is right within themselves.

We must face up to the fact that as adults we're intimidated by masculine and feminine roles. Women try to be the perfect homemakers, the perfect wives, the perfect mothers. Men try to be the perfect providers, the pillars of strength, fathers of authority and wisdom. By playing roles rather than *being what we really are,* we leave ourselves open to the bitter realization that we are puppets rather than real human beings.

At some point in our lives we have to do away with lies and false definitions that have been passed on from preceding generations. As women, we have to affirm that make-up and clothing don't define our worth, that the tidiness of our house is not a gauge of our value as people, that we can have new roles and take responsibility for our own lives and still feel good about ourselves. As men, we must break through the macho concept, go beyond the John Wayne role model to accept tenderness, love, and occasional inner feelings of weakness. As parents we must transcend rigid and authoritarian stances in child rearing to accept our own and our children's humanness.

Once we have asserted ourselves, we can begin to think in terms of freedom for our children, letting our daughters climb trees and play with trucks, giving our sons dolls to play with. Rather than ruining our children by not forcing them into the roles of the past, we are giving our children the flexibility necessary to become people defined by human qualities rather than gender.

What are the human qualities we want for our children? The ability to be self-sufficient when necessary and yet able to accept realistic dependency needs. To be well-developed physically: able to be strong as well as gentle. To have a clear sense of the self: knowing one's own limitations and yet accepting and liking his or herself. Being honest and open about one's feelings, being able to say when you're hurt or when you're angry; unrepressed, able to make decisions knowing exactly where you're at inside. Understanding membership in the whole human race, not just as part of a race, a sex, a job, a region, a nation. All of these qualities boil down to an inner poise, a self-assuredness that transcends shallow role definitions.

This inner poise is the ultimate gift that parents can give their child. It comes from responding sensitively to the child's needs in the early years, from accepting the child as he is. Having empathy about what it's like to be a child and yet with enough adult perspective to be able to offer guidance and limits when they seem called for. This kind of parent relies on intuition rather than shallow rules and regulations. It is a recognition of the reality of two human beings sharing a moment in time together — one small and very dependent, the other large and a bit more self-sufficient but, nonetheless, both equally valuable persons.

FOSTERING A CHILD'S DIGNITY

There's been a great deal of talk in recent years about disciplining children. A "well-disciplined" child is thought to be a credit to the parent who has not spared the rod and spoiled the child. Yet this authoritarian rule neglects a child's self-esteem and dignity, which emanate from within. A parent fosters a child's self-esteem, not by punishment and forcing a child to see his weaknesses, but by judicious guidance and helping the child to see his own strengths.

A parent who respects the child's dignity:
• Calls the child by name and does not yell at the child or abuse him with words or with actions.
• Takes some time each day to focus full and undivided attention on the child. Allows himself or herself to be fully absorbed with the child.
• Gives the child the opportunity to make decisions on every level, from choosing what to wear to having a voice in the family's use of time.
• Stoops down to the child's level whenever possible to speak eye to eye rather than talking down to the child.
• Talks with the child rather than at him.
• Acknowledges the child's frustrations and feelings rather than denying them or punishing him for them.
• Protects the child from overextending himself when he or the parent is tired or hungry.
• Uses positive redirection rather than threats or punishment.

• Gives reasons for actions rather than expecting the child to accept everything on authority.

• Offers nurturance and love when needed and allows the child to regress and move backward in times of stress as well as forward with self-assertion in confident moments.

• Tries to give the child chances to test himself and to learn new skills.

• Is open and honest about his own feelings and why they exist with no double standard for feeling and acting. If a parent's angry, he says he's angry and tells the child why. If he feels like crying, he cries and explains his sadness.

• Respects the child's right to say no: not to want to go somewhere, not to wish to eat something, not to like a person or a situation.

If a child has been treated with dignity and respect, he will treat others that way, too. One parent's relationship with one child can reflect on many other human beings, in the present as well as the future. This is what makes individual parenthood have such tremendous meaning for the entire human family.

ANALYZING CHILDREN'S BOOKS FOR RACISM AND SEXISM

The Council on Interracial Books for Children (1841 Broadway, New York, NY 10023) lists some rules that parents can apply in judging whether a children's book is sexist or racist.

• Check the illustrations. Look for stereotypes — oversimplified generalizations about a particular group, race, or sex, which usually carry derogatory implications. Avoid books that in any way demean or ridicule a character because of sex or race. Analyze the action in the book. Are the males the activists and the females the inactive observers?

• Check the story line. Do nonwhite persons have to exhibit extraordinary qualities such as excelling in sports or academics in order to gain acceptance and approval? Are the achievements of girls and women based on their own initia-

tive and intelligence, or are they due to their good looks or their relationship to boys or men? Could the same story be told if the sex roles were reversed?

• Are minorities and their settings contrasted overtly or implicitly in an unfavorable way with white middle-class suburbia? Are other cultures oversimplified and their people presented as quaint natives in costume?

• What are the relationships in the story? Do only the whites control the power, hold the leadership and make the decisions? Do nonwhites and females only play supportive roles?

• What effect will the book have on a child's self-esteem? How will it affect your daughter's self-image when she reads that boys perform all the brave and important deeds? What if she's not fair of skin and slim of body, as is so often the norm? If your child is black, what effect will it have on him or her to be continuously bombarded with the color white as the ultimate in beauty, cleanliness, virtue, and the color black as evil, dirty, menacing?

• Is the author qualified to write a book with a minority theme? If the author isn't a member of the minority being written about, is there anything in his or her background that would specifically recommend him or her as creator of this book? (Example, a man writing a book dealing with the feelings and insights of women.)

• Watch out for loaded words and phrases. Racist ones like savage, primitive, conniving, lazy, superstitious, wily, crafty, docile, backward. Sexist ones such as all masculine pronouns or "man" words like *forefather, fireman, brotherhood of man.*

To the Council's list I would add a cautionary note to avoid books that portray older citizens as ineffectual, quaint but never in charge or independent. Check for stereotypes that place older women in the kitchen baking and older men working solely on hobbies or as bumbling and absentminded. Older persons should be portrayed neither as witches nor as all-wise

PICTURE BOOKS PORTRAYING BOYS AND GIRLS, FATHERS AND MOTHERS IN ALTERNATIVE ROLES

Christina Katerina and the Box
Patricia Gauch
Coward, McCann and Geoghegan, Inc., 200
Madison Avenue, New York, NY 10016 ($4.99)
Imaginative Christina makes a castle, a clubhouse, a racing car and a mansion from an empty refrigerator carton.

City in the Winter
Eleanor Schick
Macmillan Publishing Co., Inc., Riverside, NJ 08075 ($5.95)
Jimmy stays with his grandma while his mother goes to work. They spend a long snowbound day together feeding the birds, making a barn from a cardboard box and cooking soup.

Did You Ever?
Paula Goldsmid
Lollipop Power, Inc., P.O. Box 1171, Chapel Hill, NC 27514 ($1.75, paperback)
Girls and boys together knock a nail and wash a whale.

Girls Can Too, a Book of Poems
Lee B. Hopkins, Editor
Franklin Watts, Inc., Subs. of Grolier, Inc., 845 Third Avenue, New York, NY 10022 ($4.90)
Poems telling about active and spirited girls and in some cases proving their superiority to boys.

Go and Hush the Baby
Betsy Byars
Viking Press, Inc., 625 Madison Avenue, New York, NY 10022 ($4.95)
Will tries to entertain his baby brother with songs, magic tricks, and stories while Mother paints and bakes.

Grownups Cry Too
Nancy Hazen
Lollipop Power, Inc., P.O. Box 1171, Chapel Hill, NC 27514 ($1.75, paperback)
When Stanley was young he thought only little kids cried. As he grows up he learns that everybody cries sometimes.

Hattie, the Backstage Bat
Don Freeman
Viking Press, Inc., 625 Madison Avenue, New York, NY 10022 ($4.95)
Hattie zooms across the stage scaring everyone in a mystery play.

gods but as human beings with all the fallibilities and strengths of people in every other age group. If a child learns early to be open to experiencing friendships with older persons then there's hope for our own generation to be allowed to function fully and strongly as long as we desire it and to be treated with kindness and dignity in our own maturity. Our love for the human race is not complete until it encompasses all ages, races, and varieties of humankind.

Hurray for Captain Jane
Sam Reavin
Parents' Magazine Press, 52 Vanderbilt Avenue,
New York, NY 10017 ($5.50)
An adventure story with beautiful illustrations
about Jane who fantasizes that she is the first lady
captain of an ocean liner.

Martin's Father
Margrit Eichler
Lollipop Power, Inc., P.O. Box 1171, Chapel Hill,
NC 27514 ($1.75, paperback)
Martin spends the day with his dad doing the
laundry, making sandwiches and playing games.

Mommies at Work
Eve Merriam
Scholastic Books, 904 Sylvan Avenue, Englewood
Cliffs, NJ 07632 (95¢)
A first book about mothers who work but always
come home. A good comfort book to begin
preparing a child for a mother's new role.

Mothers Can Do Anything
Joe Lasker
Albert Whitman and Co., 560 W. Lake Street,
Chicago, IL 60606 ($4.50)
Humorous illustrations portray mothers in all kinds
of jobs — being principals, taxi drivers, lion tamers.

Nancy's Back Yard
Keith Eros
Harper & Row, Pubs., Inc., Keystone Industrial
Park, Scranton, PA 18512 ($4.95)
Children play out their dreams of fiery dragons,
Cinderella, feeding monkeys, riding a giraffe and
deep sea diving.

Noisy Nancy Norris
Lou Ann Gaeddert
Doubleday and Co., Inc., 501 Franklin Avenue,
Garden City, NY 11530 ($4.95)
Active, joyous Nancy loves to make noise but finds
that people don't always like it.

Noisy Nora
Rosemary Wells
Dial Press, 1 Dag Hammarskjold Plaza, 245 E. 47th
Street, New York, NY 10017 ($4.95)
Nora, a middle mouse child, has to wait while Mom
and Dad take care of the other mouse children. She
decides to run away. Deals with the theme of anger.

Petronella
Jay Williams
Parents' Magazine Press, 52 Vanderbilt Avenue,
New York, NY 10017 ($5.50)
An exciting adventure story about Petronella, a
brave heroine who seeks her fortune and a prince.

The Sheep Book
Carmen Goodyear
Lollipop Power, Inc., P.O. Box 1171, Chapel Hill,
NC 27514 ($1.75, paperback)
A farmer shears her sheep, prepares the wool, and
knits a sweater.

The Sunshine Family and the Pony
Sharon Lorre
Seabury Press, Inc., 815 Second Avenue, New York,
NY 10017 ($5.95)
An alternative lifestyle is pictured with a group of
friends living together in the country. Both sexes
share work and play.

What I Want to Be When I Grow Up
Carol Burnett
Simon & Schuster, Inc., Rockefeller Center, 630 Fifth
Avenue, New York, NY 10020 ($5.95)
Young children love the zany pictures of Miss
Burnett as a lepidopterist, a rock singer, and a skin
diver. Children's drawings of what they'd like to be
are included. Even if it's too early to start thinking
about careers, the full-color comical pictures are fun
to look at.

William's Doll
Charlotte Zolotow
Harper and Row, Pubs., Inc., Keystone Industrial
Park, Scranton, PA 18512 ($4.95)
Father says no when William wants a doll, but his
wise grandmother understands that a doll will help
William to learn to care for his baby just as any
good father would do.

SOURCEBOOKS FOR PARENTS AND TEACHERS ABOUT CHANGING ROLES FOR CHILDREN AND ADULTS

Children Are People: An Annotated Bibliography
Judy Brunger-Dhuyvetter, P.O. Box 2428, Stanford,
CA 94305 ($1.00)
A bibliography of excellent children's books. Gives
age ranges, sources for ordering. Books are divided
by fiction and nonfiction.

**Growing Free: Ways to Help Children Overcome
Sex-Role Stereotypes**
Association for Childhood Education International,
3615 Wisconsin Avenue, N.W., Washington, DC
20016 ($1.00)
A collection of articles including, "Building Positive
Futures: Toward a Nonsexist Education for All
Children," "Reinventing Sex Roles in the Early
Childhood Setting," and other articles relevant to
parents and teachers of young children.

Non-Sexist Education for Young Children
Barbara Sprung
Citation Press, A Division of Scholastic Magazines,
Inc., 50 W. 44th Street, New York, NY 10036 ($3.25)
A book to help teachers of young children in setting
up an environment that allows freedom of roles for
young children. Suggests activities such as making
family books and using puppets to talk about
mothers going to work. Reviews nonsexist toys and
puzzles and suggests picture books.

We Can Change It!
Susan Shargel and Irene Kane
Change for Children, 2588 Mission Street, Room
226, San Francisco, CA 94110 ($1.00 + 25¢ postage
and handling)
A bibliography of books for children preschool level
through the third grade, showing them in
adventurous, confident, sensitive roles. Books with
short, simple texts are divided from those with
longer texts. An excellent discussion of how adults
can intervene in children's stereotyping of each
other.

BOOKS FOR YOUNG CHILDREN TO FOSTER CULTURAL AWARENESS

Caron Chapman of Learn Me, Inc., a nonsexist
learning-materials store, has helped me compile the
following list. All of the books are available from
Learn Me, Inc., 642 Grand Avenue, St. Paul, MN
55105, at list price plus 15 percent for postage and
handling.

BLACK

A is for Africa by Jean Bond. African life and
culture told with color photos for letters of the
alphabet. Ages 7–10. ($6.00)
Black is Beautiful by Ann McGovern. Black-and-
white portrait of black objects to counteract the idea
that black symbolizes evil and white, beauty. (95¢)
Black Is Brown Is Tan by Arnold Adoff. A black
mother, white father, and brown children live a
loving life together. Watercolor illustrations. ($4.95)

Color Me Brown by Lucille Giles. Biographical
coloring book of famous black Americans. ($2.00)
Country of the Black People, Book One, by Corene
Caselle. Picture book history of the Ghana Empire
of 800 years. Third World Press. Ages 6–8. ($3.00)
Dragon Takes a Wife by Walter D. Myers. Harry
Dragon visits hip Mabel Mae Jones for advice on
how to lose his fear of fighting. Humorous,
humanistic black fairy tale. Ages 5 and up. ($6.50)
Evan's Corner by Elizabeth S. Hill. Evan, a black
child, finds a private corner in his crowded
apartment. ($1.45)
Ezra Jack Keats Books. Amusing stories about black
boys in the city but not a girl to be found. *Hi, Cat;
Goggles; Snowy Day.* ($1.25 ea.)
I Want to Be by Dexter Arnold and Pat Oliver.
Black-and-white photos and text depict black
children in occupations from A–Z — architect to
zoologist. Nonsexist, too! Ages 4–10. ($2.95)
Jackie by Luevester Lewis. Story of a black child.
($1.50)
Jambo Means Hello: Swahili Alphabet Book by
Muriel Feelings. A book with gentle black-and-
white watercolor illustrations. Includes a map of
East Africa where Swahili is spoken. ($6.00)
Josephine's Imagination by Arnold Dobrin. A
Haitian girl who invents and then sells her broom
dolls. Colorful watercolor illustrations. Ages 3–6.
($1.50)
Li'l Tuffy and His ABCs by Jean P. Smith. Great
alphabet coloring book, using black references to
culture. ($1.50)
Moja Means One by Muriel Feelings. Swahili
counting book, companion to *Jambo* ($1.75)
Playtime in Africa by Efua Sutherland. Well-written
descriptions of children in Ghana with stunning
photos. Ages 4–6. ($6.95)
Runaway Slave by Ann McGovern. The story of
Harriet Tubman told simply and forcefully. Ages 6–
12. (95¢)
Some of the Days of Everett Anderson by Lucille
Clifton. A poem a day describing what Everett does
in a week. Ages 3–6. ($1.25)
A Weed Is a Flower by Aliki. Picture story of the life
of George Washington Carver. (95¢)
Why Mosquitoes Buzz in People's Ears by Verna
Aardema. African tale involving many jungle
animals illustrated with large, colorful woodcuts
based on African motifs. Caldecott Award. ($2.75)

ASIAN

Children of Viet Nam, Indochina Resource Center.
Story and coloring book. Ages 5–11. ($1.25)
A Crocodile's Tale by Jose Aruego. A Philippine
folk story of the boy who frees a crocodile from a
trap and must then convince the crocodile not to eat
him. ($1.95)
Crow Boy by Taro Yashima. A Japanese story of
how Chibi overcomes his shyness in the last year of
school. Ages 4–7. ($1.25)

Don't Tell the Scarecrow and Other Japanese Poems, Issa, et al. Two to four line Japanese poems. Simply illustrated. (95¢)

Funny Little Woman by Arlene Mosel. Tale from Old Japan where the women who liked to laugh had to use wits and courage to escape from the Oni. Caldecott Award. ($7.95)

In a Spring Garden by Richard Lewis. An excellent collection of simple Japanese Haiku. Illustrated by Ezra Jack Keats. ($1.75)

Momo's Kitten by Mitsu Yashima and Taro Yashima. A Japanese-American finds and cares for a mother cat and her kittens. (95¢)

Stonecutter: A Japanese Folk Tale by Gerald McDermott. A Japanese folk tale of the man who always wanted to be something more "powerful." Illustrated with collages reflecting motifs in traditional Japanese prints. ($5.95)

Umbrella by Taro Yashima. Story of a Japanese girl who lives with her family in New York. Ages 4–8. ($1.25)

SPANISH

Amigo by Byrd B. Schweitzer. Amigo, a prairie dog, thinks he has trained his pet Francisco, a Mexican boy. Gentle. Ages 4–7. (95¢)

Jo, Flo, and Yolanda by Carol De Poix. How Spanish surnamed triplets are alike and different. Ages 4–8. ($1.75)

My Mother the Mail Carrier/Mi Mama La Cartera by Inez Maury. Five-year-old Lupita, with her working mother, experiences life in this bilingual picture book with a smooth Spanish text. A strong mother and daughter. ($3.50)

NATIVE AMERICAN

Arrow to the Sun, a Pueblo Indian Tale by Gerald McDermott. Uses Pueblo art with vibrant color. The author-artist tells the story of Boy searching for his father — Lord of the Sun. Illustrates Indian reverence for the source of life, Solar Fire. Caldecott Award. ($8.95)

Indian and Free by Charles Brill. Photo portrait of contemporary life on a Chippewa Reservation. Photos from Red Lake, Minnesota. Outstanding book! ($10.00)

Trees Stand Shining by Hettie Jones. Native American poetry illustrated with beautiful watercolors. Ages 4 and up. ($1.75)

SOURCEBOOKS FOR PARENTS AND TEACHERS ON CULTURAL AWARENESS

Cultural Awareness for Young Children at the Learning Tree
Earldene McNeill, Judy Allen, and Velma Schmidt
The Learning Tree, 9998 Ferguson Road, Dallas, TX 75228 ($9.95)
The cultures of black, Eskimo, Mexican, Native American, and Asian peoples are presented for young children through crafts, costumes to make, cooking and art experiences. An extensive review of children's books concerning each culture. Example: The unit on black culture suggests ways to make an African village from refrigerator cartons. Recipes are given for preparing yams, fried bananas, peanut stew, and other African dishes as well as a "soul food" dinner. There are directions for making a Masai collar necklace, clay beads, and tribal masks. Children are taught basic Swahili words, are taught to make rhythms and instruments. A superb resource, especially for working with groups of young children!

CHOOSING CHILD CARE

In the family of our mothers' day the father went to work and the mother stayed home to care for the children for at least the first five years and usually until the children were grown. Families used to live close together, too, so there was always a relative, maybe a grandmother or an aunt, who could pinch-hit for the mother if she *had* to go to work.

New work opportunities permit women to have *meaningful* jobs, ones that feel challenging, that leave room for decision making. Being a mother is meaningful work, too. But being a twenty-four-hour mother with no extended family for help and support may feel like an imprisonment.

About the time a child is three, we mothers begin to want some life of our own, private goals besides those of putting down another meal or vacuuming the rug. Our child seems ready for change of scenery, too. He's restless, whiny, and having continual battles of will with us. Or perhaps we don't have a choice and work is a necessity that must be faced soon.

A good child-care arrangement can offer a child the stimulation of new friendships with children the same age. It can give him new chances to experiment with materials not available at home. Best of all, it can give him a chance to prove his own self-sufficiency.

That's not to say that young children don't need an important parent figure and much home nurturing, but at the same time, a mother who feels fulfilled and excited about her life instead of bored and angry is going to have more to give to her child. It's the quality of interactions with the child — the intensity with which a parent can focus on the child in a given moment — that has the greatest impact on the child's sense of security and confidence about himself and his world.

How to find good child care? You could have a baby sitter come into your home — expensive, and sometimes unreliable. You could take your child to someone else's home — cozy, secure, but maybe not stimulating enough. Or you can look for a child-care center — not so secure and cozy, vaguely like an institution, but with easels to paint on, blocks and all kinds of toys to play with.

The decision is not an easy one. It's layered with vague feelings of guilt — committing your child to a place when you should be home taking care of him. The pain of loneliness and separation. Wondering what he's doing, if he's happy, if he's crying. Wondering if your child's being judged, if the teachers think he's too spoiled or too shy. Those first negative feelings give way to trust and pleasure if things work out well.

People who care for children in their homes often advertise in the classified section of the newspapers under "Positions Wanted." If you live in an apartment or have a community bulletin board, you might post a notice: "Child care needed from 8:00 A.M. until 4:00 P.M. weekdays. Three-year-old girl. Prefer your home. Must be in the Riderwood area. Call: 333-3333." Or you can place an ad in the paper. Look for a care-giver who is sensitive to children, perhaps one who has children himself or herself. The house should be clean and relatively in order. There shouldn't be more than four children in the group. There should be a variety of toys and a swing set or other play equipment in a fenced-in yard. Does the person plan activities just for the children to do? Does the person seem energetic and pleased with what he or she's doing? Does he or she have a child-sized table and chairs or other signs of accommodation to the needs of little children?

The best way to find good child-care facilities is through word of mouth from other parents. You can also look in the Yellow Pages under "Schools — Nursery and Kindergarten," or under "Day Nurseries." Sometimes community organizations such as the American Association of University Women, or the National Organization for Women publish directories describing child-care programs in a community. The headquarters of the United Fund or the Department of Social Services may have a telephone "Information and Referral Service" that will help you. Look in the Yellow Pages under "Social Service Organizations." The reference department of the library may also be a good source for finding the copy of a local child-care directory if your community has one.

One very important factor in whatever child care you choose: the center should be close to your house or to your work. It's just too stressful to have to drive thirty minutes out of the way to deliver and pick up a child.

There are some terms that you need to become familiar with as you begin your search.

Day Care or Day Nursery   Cares for children for six to eight hours a day. Serves lunch and snacks. May have all ages of children from babies to five-year-olds. Usually won't take a child for less than all day, although some are more flexible about when you drop off or pick up your child. Sometimes too many kids for the number of teachers results in tension and chaos.

Nursery School   Usually has only a morning program for two to two and a half hours. Children are grouped by ages. May be commercially operated on a franchise or supported by a church. Usually has good equipment and teachers, but their hours may be wrong for your needs.

Parent Co-op   A group of parents operate this type of school together. They hire the teacher to suit their needs. They buy or make the equipment. Mothers or fathers are expected to give time to the school as teacher's aides. Monthly meetings are held to work out the hassles of operating the school. Usually just morning or afternoon hours. They're hard to locate

because they seldom advertise. They usually use church facilities, which may be a clue for locating them.

Playgroup   Usually means a cooperative arrangement among parents in a neighborhood. Children meet once or twice a week in different houses for several hours. Parents take turns being in charge for the day. The purpose is to provide time out for parents and to give children a chance to play with others in a group setting.

If you plan to work all day, then day care or a day nursery will be the best answer for you. Be sure to check about the policy of caring for a child who is sick. If you can find a part-time job then you will be interested in the programs with shorter hours.

Have you thought of applying for a job with a partner as equally qualified as you to split the salary and share the eight-hour working day or to alternate working days? You may find a good deal of resistance to the idea from employers so you'll both need to work out a sales pitch that proves to them that you can work cooperatively and that the two of you will bring more expertise to the job than either of you alone would. You'll also need some overlapping working hours to coordinate your responsibilities. Arrange to substitute for each other too when one of your children is sick.

When it comes time to select child care, visit the center without your child and stay for the day or half the day. If the teachers seem defensive about this, that's a good enough reason to dismiss that school, since it's very important that you feel welcome any time.

Signs of a good school:

• The teacher relates positively toward the children — and calls them by name.

• Care-givers are quiet and gentle, rather than loud and obtrusive. They handle conflicts firmly while explaining their actions — no yell-

ing or using terms like "you're a bad boy (girl)."
• One adult for every five to seven children.
• The kids are very busy and enjoy what they're doing — different kids doing different things in small groups.
• The center has lots of indoor space and outdoor equipment to climb and play on.
• The playthings are stored at child level. Materials include blocks, dolls, easels for painting, a record player, child-sized furniture, something to climb on, picture books, perhaps fish in an aquarium or furry creatures in cages.
• The room is arranged in sections so that each area has a specific kind of activity — playing house, music or reading, art, noisy play, quiet play, blocks.

Bad signs that should make you think twice about a child-care center:
• The children are regimented with enforced sitting in chairs. Children have to ask permission to go to the bathroom, or are cajoled to eat even when they're not hungry.
• A television.
• Long enforced naps when a child is considered naughty for not going to sleep.
• Avoid teachers who yell at children, spank them, and who dominate the room continually so that children are not given any opportunity to make decisions about activities.
• Check the atmosphere of the room. Are the children tense, quarreling or fighting?
• Watch out for chaotic conditions in which anything goes — a child can hit another and the teacher doesn't interfere. There should be a conscious plan on the part of the staff for each day with goals for individual children.

Let your child have a month to get used to going to a center before you begin to work. One crisis at a time. Go with your child the first day regardless of whether other parents do. It's about as important for you as it is for your child. Your child can come to you and touch base to gain confidence for meeting new people and doing new activities. You will see how your child is doing. You can confirm that you're doing the right thing and provide yourself with peace of mind to carry you through the times when your child doesn't want to go. Try to learn the names of the other children. This will be a great help later when your child announces: "Mommy, I don't want to go to school today." Learn the care-givers' first names and make friends. Your friendship will be the best psychological asset you can have.

The ultimate test of any child-care situation is your own child and how he feels about it over a long period of time. Every child has days when he doesn't want to go to school. That's normal and to be expected. But if your child shows strong day-to-day resistance to school, you ought to talk to the teacher about it, and you ought to consider seriously trying a different situation. Perhaps he needs a class that's more relaxed, or perhaps there's a classroom bully who makes him uncomfortable.

If your child is showing strong reluctance to child care, you need to look at yourself, too. Are you unconsciously signaling your child by being uptight when you take him to school? Are you encouraging your child to cling to you because you haven't resolved your own guilt or ambivalence about child care? When you can clear your own head enough to identify the positive things that school is doing for your child you can almost always overcome a child's resistance by your own day-to-day optimism about the experience.

(See page 26, Guides for Choosing Day Care.)

DIVORCE AND CHILDREN

Dr. Mavis Hetherington and her associates at the University of Virginia have conducted extensive studies of the dynamics of the family unit during the first two years after divorce. She found that there was a high level of family disorganization during the first year after divorce:

Routines were irregular, feeding time was off, even delivery of children to nursery school was affected. The first two months after divorce, the father and mother both seemed to go through a period of euphoria and relief, with some moments of feeling helpless and distressed. At the end of the first year, both parents reported feelings of depression and anxiety — many felt that the divorce was a mistake. Mothers who kept the children most often felt shut in like prisoners. As one mother put it: "There's no time out in the parenting game." Fathers, on the other hand, felt isolated and shut out of the family. Finally, after two years, families restabilized and mothers and fathers began to feel more positive in their outlook toward their futures.

The greatest stress during this time seems to come between the mother and her young sons. In Hetherington's study, affections lessened. Boys were found to ignore their mother's requests, to whine, to act aggressive and to be more dependent. Some mothers called the scene "declared war." And one described her situation with her sons as "like being bitten to death by ducks."

Children are likely to feel quite angry about divorce. They blame their parents for what has happened, in the same way that a child blames a parent who has died. Underneath the anger is a deep fear of being deserted. It's most important to reassure your child that *he* is not being divorced. That you will care for him and stay with him because you belong to each other.

Children have different ways of showing anger. Some internalize it, become too nice, and too cooperative. Others become agitated and roam around looking for trouble to get into or objects to break. Rather than denying that your child is feeling anger, it's better to face it head on. "Look, you're really mad with Daddy and me for what's happening." Then you can try to offer some outlet for those intense feelings: "I want you to hit this pillow to show me

how mad you are. I'll pretend I'm the pillow and yell like you're hurting me. Wow! You really *are* mad at us, aren't you?" Maybe you can't take any more anger right now, you're feeling pretty hurt yourself — then it's time to go for a long walk with your child to ease some of the tension and pain.

A child needs to be reassured that he wasn't the cause of the break-up. Preschool children believe that they can wish events into happening. There have probably been times when he wished to get rid of his mother or his father. Now it seems to have happened, and he secretly thinks he's responsible. Or, perhaps, he feels he's finally been so bad that the departing parent couldn't take it anymore. It's valuable to clarify, over and over if necessary, that "Mommy and Daddy are living separately because they will be happier in separate lives. This decision has nothing to do with thoughts you may have had or ways that you have acted. We think you're a fine child and we both love you very much. And we both will be your mommy and daddy forever and ever."

It's helpful to keep the child's environment as unchanged as possible during this time of stress. Often the impulse is just the opposite — to move away, to change everything in order to start a new life. A parent's departure is a profound and stressful change for the child and is best managed with all the other aspects of his life kept the same: the same house, the same friends, the same neighborhood.

Suppose you do move, and everything does change. Then planning and structuring your everyday life can help to provide predictability and security for your children. You should establish routines: getting up at the same time each day with adequate time to get dressed and to eat a good breakfast before starting the day. Planning a week in advance what you're going to be eating and having a "grocery shopping day," a "laundry day," a "house cleaning day." Even if you think you can't afford it, paying someone to come in once a week to do the heavy cleaning can work wonders to relieve you of the burden of household chaos. A simple cooperative arrangement with neighbors in which you get one evening a week off from your kids in exchange for you giving them one night of your time can help to break the adult's feeling of entrapment.

Try to find some support for yourself during the lonely, trying first year. Perhaps the answer lies in joining a church or a group such as Parents Without Partners. Maybe even a temporary therapy arrangement can help you to work through your anger and loneliness. Can you keep channels of communication open between you and your spouse? If you can comfort each other during the year of untying, it will be your best source of support.

It's best not to linger on thoughts of how it could have been.

As Phyllis Fleishman said in an interview published in *Momma Handbook: The Sourcebook for Single Mothers,* "If we are going to maintain authentic relationships, in actuality we don't really have a choice. We do the best we can to make sure we're getting along well with the person we start to live with. But we cannot simply choose to have it stay that way. People develop, change, and sometimes move away from each other. At that point, then, there is no choice . . . to stop growth is not only harmful for the adults but for the children as well. The only good relationship for a child is one where the child is involved with people who lead honest lives." Life goes forward, never backward. You and your children may emerge even stronger and more together than before the divorce. That's worth looking forward to.

GUIDES FOR CHOOSING DAY CARE

Child Care Handbook
Order from:
American Home Economics Association, 2010 Massachusetts Avenue, N.W., Washington, DC 20036 ($4.00, paperback)
Describes the difference between Montessori, Piagetian programs, the open classroom, and other pedagogic philosophies. Gives an idea of a good curriculum. Extensive bibliography on day care, books for and about children, and on films about day care. A glossary of terms relating to child-care facilities.

Choosing Child Care: A Guide for Parents
Stevanne Auerbach and Linda Freedman
Order from:
Parents and Child Care Resources, 1855 Folsom Street, San Francisco, CA 94103 ($3.00 + 50¢ postage and handling)
A very practical handbook for evaluating child-care facilities. Questions to ask the staff when you first call. A checklist for the physical facilities, for assessing the emotional climate of the center, the learning climate, and the social climate. Gives parents a way of rating different programs toward making a final decision.

"Checking Out Child Care: A Parent Guide"
Jane R. Gold and Joan M. Bergstrom
Day Care and Child Development Council of America, 1012 14th Street, N.W., Washington, DC 20005 ($1.00)
Brochure giving tips for assessing care-givers, the environment, and danger signals of a bad program.

The New Extended Family, Day Care That Works
Ellen Galinsky and William H. Hooks
Houghton Mifflin Company, Two Park Street, Boston, MA 02107 ($6.95, paperback)
An excellent guidebook for parents who wish to study up on the varieties of child-care programs. Gives basic guidelines for evaluating a program and thorough descriptions of fourteen different centers around the United States. After reading this book, doing your homework, you should be able to choose a child-care arrangement with confidence.

BOOKS FOR PARENTS ABOUT DIVORCE

Daddy Doesn't Live Here Anymore
Rita Turow
Greatlakes Living Press, 21750 Main Street, Matteson, IL 60443 ($8.95)
An immensely practical handbook dealing with the common questions, problems and reactions of children concerning divorce. Some of the chapter titles include: "Whose house does the child go to for holidays?" "What do you call a new stepparent?" and "How do you provide your child with adult companionship if the other parent doesn't come around anymore?"

Momma Handbook: The Sourcebook for Single Mothers
Karol Hope and Nancy Young, Editors
A Plume Book/New American Library, 1301 Avenue of the Americas, New York, NY 10019 ($3.95, paperback)
A compendium of articles, poems, and sharing among women who have experienced divorce. In the section on "Kids and Us" is a valuable collection of interviews with Phyllis Fleishman, Director of Modern Playschool/Play Mountain Place, discussing divorce and anger in children, handling sibling rivalry, and other very practical topics.

Part-Time Father
Edith Atkin and Estelle Rubin
Signet/New American Library, 1301 Avenue of the Americas, New York, NY 10019 ($1.75, paperback)
An excellent, sensitive book about divorce and how it affects fathers. How to tell children about divorce, how to arrange visits, tackling the problems of alimony and remarriage.

BOOKS FOR CHILDREN ABOUT DIVORCE

A Private Matter
Kathryn Ewing
Harcourt Brace Jovanovich, Inc., 757 Third Avenue, New York, NY 10017 ($5.95)
Marcy's father lives far away and she rarely hears from him. When a kind couple moves in next door, she begins to pretend that the husband is her father. Eventually she has to accept the fact that a neighbor can't take the place of her real father.

Emily and the Klunky Baby and the Next-Door Dog
Joan M. Lexau
The Dial Press, 1 Dag Hammarskjold Plaza, 245 E. 47th Street, New York, NY 10017 ($4.95)
The stresses of a newly divorced mother, her young daughter, and her baby are portrayed. Emily, a four- or five-year-old, decides to run away to Daddy but gets lost in the neighborhood.

Me Day
Joan M. Lexau
The Dial Press, 1 Dag Hammarskjold Plaza, 245 E. 47th Street, New York, NY 10017 ($4.95)
Rafer lives with his mother and his brother. It's his birthday and he didn't get a letter from his dad. His mother gets a call, and tells Rafer to go to the fruit store. To his delight his dad is waiting for him.

Divorce Is a Grown Up Problem
Janet Sinberg
Avon Books, 959 Eighth Avenue, New York, NY 10019 ($2.95, paperback)
A simply stated explanation book about divorce for a preschool child. The book focuses on the feelings young children experience during this family crisis. There are some helpful, practical suggestions for parents and an annotated bibliography of books for children and parents.

Mushy Eggs
Florence Adams
G. P. Putnam's Sons, 200 Madison Avenue, New York, NY 10016 ($4.69)
Two young brothers, who live with their working mother, are attached to a kind Italian baby sitter named Fanny who must leave them to go back to Italy. Focuses on the love that young children can develop toward their care-giver and their sorrow at losing her.

My Dad Lives in a Downtown Hotel
Peggy Mann
Camelot/Avon Books, 959 Eighth Avenue, New York, NY 10019 (95¢, paperback)
Joey's convinced that if he only behaves better his dad, who lives in a hotel room, will forgive him and come back home. He's so ashamed about his parents' separation that he won't tell even his best friend about it.

Talking about Divorce: A Dialogue Between Parents and Child
Earl A. Grollman
Beacon Press, Inc., 25 Beacon Street, Boston, MA 02108 ($2.95, paperback)
A book for parents to read to a child. The parents' guide at the end of the book has a frank discussion about how to handle an upcoming separation with your child. Information on how to locate child-guidance clinics, support groups, a lawyer. Reviews books for children and adults.

The Boys and Girls Book about Divorce
Richard A. Gardner
Bantam Books, Inc., 414 E. Golf Road, Des Plaines, IL 60016 ($1.95, paperback)
Although the book is aimed at nine- to twelve-year-olds, some portions can make good read-to-me fare for younger children. The book is a "how-to" manual for kids in getting along with grownups going through divorce. It centers on the child who stays with the mother. The book tries to help the child see that he's not to blame and suggests ways of using his anger constructively.

SUPPORT GROUPS FOR DIVORCED PARENTS

Parents Without Partners, Inc., 7910 Woodmont Avenue, Washington, DC 20014

National Organization for Women (N.O.W.), 1957 E. 73rd Street, Chicago, IL 60649

Divorced Catholic Group, % Paulist Center, 5 Park Street, Boston, MA 02108

Divorce Lifeline (A Presbyterian Organization), 1013 Eighth Avenue, Seattle, WA 98104

MOMMA, P.O. Box 5759, Santa Monica, CA 90405

MOVING

Frequent moving has become a style of life for many young families. Each move brings a feeling of stress and dislocation until the family is able to readapt. Old friendships have to be broken and new ones made. It's not unusual for a child or an adult who has had to undergo frequent moves to be cautious about making friends because of the recent pain of separation from old friends.

How can parents of young children help make moving as untraumatic as possible?

• Let your child share in choosing a new house. If the distance is too far, then try to remember to take a photograph of the new house so that your child can visualize where he will be going. A picture of a neighborhood child about the right age can help a great deal in easing the transition from one location to another.

• Give your child packing tasks, too. Let him pack his toys, tape the box closed, and even label the box with a Magic Marker.

• Pack a suitcase or bag of favorite books and toys to stay with your child in the car.

• As you pack boxes around the house, try to leave living areas intact so that family routines are the least disturbed. Save kitchen packing until last, since eating is the one activity that will go on in the house until you leave it. Pack an "emergency" box for transition meals in your new home and mark it well: knives, forks, can opener, plates, glasses (just enough for each member of the family), paper towels, a pot and a pan, instant coffee, canned juice, maybe a can of ravioli, a jar of peanut butter and some crackers. Be sure you can put your finger on it the minute you arrive.

• Spread packing over a number of weeks rather than trying to do it all in a few days. Begin collecting boxes in advance. Look for those that are sturdy and have tops. You'll always need about twice as many boxes as you think you will. Good places to find them are

liquor stores, department stores, and from neighbors who've recently moved in. Boxes are particularly plentiful midweek when stores are stocking their shelves for the weekend. Pack books first and in small boxes since they are extremely heavy. Then move on to the least needed things in the house, saving the most needed things until last.

• Think positively about the packing process. You're clearing out many unnecessary extras and simplifying your life. (Give unwanted clothes and shoes to the Salvation Army or Goodwill Industries.) You're opening the possibility of new friendships, going to a new job with a new and better salary, there will be new places to visit and new things to see.

• It's probably better not to have young children around on moving day itself, since they can become very distressed by seeing their room emptied and their prize possessions being carted away. If possible, maybe you or your spouse could go ahead with the children to avoid the chaos of the last day.

• Face leaving openly. Don't try to sneak off without proper good-byes. Let your children have a chance to say good-bye to their friends, and maybe leave a toy with them. Saying good-bye is painful — but the pain is less long and agonizing when it's expressed openly. Admit the fact that you hate to leave and that you sure will miss your friends — it helps your child to accept his feelings as well.

• Make up a story about moving for your child and illustrate it, even if it's just with stick figures. Tell him about the boxes, the big truck that's going to carry things to a new home, leaving old friends behind but finding new ones. Try to describe the new home as accurately as possible so that your child can conceptualize where he will be going. Nylint makes a sturdy metal toy U-Haul truck that is good for imaginary moving play.

• Have you thought of a good-bye ritual? Rituals help people in other life crises, why not in moving? One possibility would be to plant a tree in the yard before you go if the weather permits. Explain to your child that you are leaving the tree as a reminder of having lived in this place. If possible, tell him that you and he will come back once in a while and the tree will still be there, growing bigger and bigger. "Then we'll be able to say, when you were a little child, you used to live here. Before you moved you planted this tree so that you could leave something behind that people would enjoy." (Janice May Udry's book, *A Tree Is Nice,* goes along with this theme perfectly.)

• Remember that it takes six months to settle into a new home. That time is needed to adjust to a new situation, to find the grocery store, the bank, a dentist, and all of the other necessities of life. Up until that time, you'll find yourself besieged with fears about the safety of your child. These won't go away until you establish friendships with neighbors and can feel comfortable about where your child will play.

• Take the bull by the horns. Get out and knock on your new neighbors' doors until you meet everyone around you. It's painful and you may feel self-conscious, but it's the best way in the world to begin to feel secure about where you live. Perhaps there's a neighbor with kids the same age as yours. As you break down the barriers, you'll be surprised at how familiar the new situation really is, and how people are basically alike wherever you go.

• Try to plan some special family events during those first few stressful months to help renew a feeling of togetherness: a trip to a museum, a picnic in the park, even a walk or ride to an ice cream store one evening.

(See Books for Children about Moving, page 30.)

FACING ADOPTION

It's important for an adopted child to know about his origins. Sometimes parents don't intend to keep their child's adoption a secret, but they find talking about it so uncomfortable that they put it off until it creates enough anxiety within them to become a skeleton in the closet. Discussing adoption may mean having to face up to the painful reality of being unable to bear children, and the thought of your adopted child's unknown mother.

The word "adopted" needs to be practiced until it feels comfortable. Think about it. You and your spouse adopted each other, didn't you? Rather than thinking of the word in a negative manner, think of it as a positive — grown-up people deciding to choose another person to complete their family, attaching themselves to that person, acceptingly and lovingly. John Ciardi speaks of marriage as a choice each day to marry the loved one. So it is with you and your child. You are choosing to adopt and love your child daily, just as a natural mother and father are.

How to teach your child about adoption? As in all other teaching, it's best done off the cuff, spliced into daily episodes and conversations. Picture a mom and dad hugging and a tot coming into the room and trying to snuggle in between. "We adopted each other, Jim, because we love each other so much and we want to live together every day. We adopted you, too." Hugs and kisses for everyone.

A special scrapbook with baby pictures and family pictures helps. It will be most valuable to your child later if you note special events and observations: "Today you took your first step. We were so proud of you!" You also will want to record the details of your first meeting and how you both felt about the event.

The term "first" parents seems like a good way of phrasing "natural" parents to a child, because it suggests something that has happened in the past and is now over. You should be honest with your child about what you know of his previous parents as he gets older and more curious. Always try to tell the natural parents' story in a positive way, picturing them as caring about their child's welfare. To disparage his natural parents only hurts your child's feelings about himself in the long run.

Naturally, being adopted puts a big question mark in the child's mind about who his natural mother and father are and what they look like. Adopted children often build up elaborate fantasies about this element of their past. Perhaps they wonder about people that they see on the street. In times of family conflict, they may use their fantasies to escape a temporary unhappiness. Most of us as children at one time or another probably hoped we were adopted because we were having to come to grips with our parents' limitations and hoping for an alternative that would allow us to escape into a world where everyone was happy and loved each other all the time.

Helping your adopted child express his fantasies will enable him to gain better control over them. Perhaps you can play house together, setting the stage for your child to act out his ideas about adoption. Or, if your child asks questions about his original mother and father with a troubled look on his face you can gently ask him what he's thinking. Confirm that you understand how he must feel by repeating what he has communicated to you. If it's true, you may want to add that you'd probably feel that way, too. It's important to sense when your child has had enough of such talk. Then, you can follow his lead into some other subject or activity.

If you give your young child acceptance, love, and plenty of reassurance that once adopted he won't be "unadopted" later, you will have done all that you can to provide him with a secure base for growing up. It may be that he will hunt for his biological roots when he becomes an adult, as many adoptees are doing, but once his curiosity is satisfied, he will be able to move into life as his own person with a clear image of himself — the gift that you gave him.

BOOKS FOR CHILDREN ABOUT MOVING

Moving Away
Alice R. Viklund
McGraw-Hill Book Co., 1221 Avenue of the Americas, New York, NY 10036 ($3.00)
Although the ending is a bit too ideal — a child moving to a place with a garage to roller skate in, a stream, a pear tree in a yard filled with birds — the book does present a realistic picture of packing boxes, the echo of an empty room, watching furniture go into a big truck, and the sadness of good-byes.

Moving Day
Tobi Tobias
Alfred A. Knopf, Inc., Subs. of Random House, Inc., 457 Hahn Road, Westminster, MD 21157 ($4.95)
A little girl and her teddy bear must move. Described sorting out possessions, packing boxes, putting things on the van, saying good-bye to familiar places, the long drive and finally settling into a new bed.

New Neighbors
Ray Prather
McGraw-Hill Book Co., 1221 Avenue of the Americas, New York, NY 10036 ($4.95)
The story of Rickey as he attempts to make friends in his new neighborhood.

Sad Day, Glad Day
Vivian L. Thompson
Scholastic Book Services, 904 Sylvan Avenue, Englewood Cliffs, NJ 07632 (75¢, paperback)
An honest portrayal of a child's fears and feelings about moving.

A Tree Is Nice
Janice May Udry
Harper and Row, Pubs., Inc., Keystone Industrial Park, Scranton, PA 18512 ($3.95)
Points out how nice trees are for climbing and enjoying in childhood. The full-color illustrations of children and trees are exceptionally pleasing to the eye. At the end of the book, children are encouraged to plant trees themselves.

BOOKS FOR CHILDREN ABOUT ADOPTION

Abby
Jeannette Caines
Harper & Row, Pubs., Inc., Keystone Industrial Park, Scranton, PA 18512 ($3.79)
Abby is an adopted black preschooler with an older brother, Kevin, who is not adopted. Very simply stated story of a brother and a sister. Excellent for a very young child.

Adopting Baby Brother
Barbara Gilchrist Taber, P.O. Box 5061, River
Station, Rochester, NY 14627 ($2.50 + 25¢ postage)
Barbara Taber has published this book herself. It is
the story of an interracial adoption — a black baby
boy adopted into a white family with two girls, one
black and one white. Color drawings.

And Now We Are a Family
Judith C. Meredith
Beacon Press, Inc., 25 Beacon Street, Boston, MA
02108 ($4.95)
Children's simple drawings and childlike printing
tell the story of adoption as a parent would tell it to
a child. The focus is on a child who was born out of
wedlock.

I Am Adopted
Susan Lapsley
Bradbury Press, Scarsdale, NY ($4.95)
Charles is adopted. There are nice color drawings to
explain the meaning of the word "adoption" to
neighborhood children or school friends.

Chinese Eyes
Majorie Ann Waybill
Herald Press, 616 Walnut Avenue, Scottdale, PA
15683 ($5.95)
Becky, an adopted Korean first-grader, is taunted by
older boys who call her "Chinese eyes." She is hurt
and confused by it, but an understanding mother
helps her feel proud of her eyes.

The Chosen Baby
Valentina P. Wasson
J. B. Lippincott Co., 521 Fifth Avenue, New York,
NY 10017 ($5.95)
Peter's parents want to adopt a baby. Mrs. White,
the social worker, chooses a baby that is just right
for the family. Later, when Peter gets older, his
mother and father adopt a baby sister, Mary. Warm,
loving drawings by Glo Coalson capture the
excitement and joy that an adoptive couple and
their relatives feel about the new baby. No mention
of the baby's previous parents.

The Family That Grew: Book II
Florence Rondell and Ruth Michaels
Crown Publishers, Inc., 419 Park Avenue S., New
York, NY 10016 ($4.95 for vols. I & II)
One of two volumes. Volume I discusses adoption
from the adoptive parents' point of view. This story
is aimed at the young adopted child.

My Journey Home
Jackie Patridge
Organization for a United Response (OURS), 3148
Humboldt Avenue, S., Minneapolis, MN 55408
($2.00)
Helps to explain why a family would adopt a child
from Korea. Simply written story with photographs
of Korea and spaces to add your own child's photos
and pictures.

The Ordinary Miracle
Joan McNamara
Adoptalk, 6 Madison Avenue, Ossining, NY 10562
($1.75 + 25¢ postage and handling)
Two stories about adoption, one focusing on
different kinds of families and one on how a child
came to be adopted. The latter can be used with
almost any adoption situation.

Is That Your Sister?
Sherry Bunin and Catherine Bunin
Pantheon Books, Div. of Random House, Inc., 457
Hahn Road, Westminster, MD 21157 ($4.95)
A story written by a six-year-old child about her
and her younger sister's adoption. The adoption is
across racial boundaries, so that she is faced with
people who notice that she doesn't resemble her
parents.

BOOKS FOR ADULTS ABOUT ADOPTION

The Adoption Adviser
Joan McNamara
Hawthorn Books, Inc., 260 Madison Avenue, New
York, NY 10016 ($9.95)
A handbook for couples considering adoption with
up-to-date information about agencies,
independent adoptions and international adoptions.
Excellent state-by-state directory of adoption
resources and support groups for adoptive parents
and a bibliography for children and adults about
adoption.

"You and Your Adopted Child" (#274)
Eda J. LeShan
Public Affairs Pamphlets, 381 Park Ave. S., New
York, NY 10016 (35¢)
Mrs. LeShan, a child psychologist, and mother of an
adopted daughter, discusses many of the issues that
adoptive parents face: fears before getting the baby
or child, the uneasiness of telling a child that he is
adopted, the normal temperamental differences
between children.

PARENT SUPPORT ORGANIZATIONS

Organization for a United Response (OURS), 3148
Humboldt Ave., S., Minneapolis, MN 55408
Publishes handbooks, aids and a newsletter. Note
cards and adoption announcements are for sale.

National Council of Adoptive Parents Organization,
P.O. Box 543, Teaneck, NJ 07666
Newsletter *National Adoptalk* deals with issues of
national concern in adoption, foster care, and child
welfare.

Child Welfare League of America, Inc., 67 Irving Place, New York, NY 10003
Concerned with day care, foster care, adoption, and other services to children. Publishes *Child Welfare*, a professional journal concerned with child welfare services. The free publications catalog lists seventeen publications on adoptions.

TOYS THAT FOSTER AWARENESS OF A CHILD'S SELF AND OF NEW ROLES

Job Inset Puzzle
Eight wooden puzzle parts show people in eight different occupations. They are designed with knobs for easy manipulation by your children and for those with inadequately developed fine muscle control. The puzzle promotes career awareness. Blacks, whites, and Spanish-Americans are represented with women shown as a police officer, an office worker, and a doctor.
Developmental Learning Materials, 7440 Natchez Avenue, Niles, IL 60648 ($4.50)

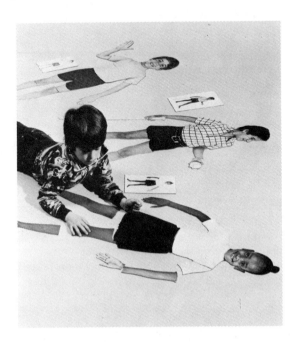

Body Puzzles
Giant child-sized puzzles of children themselves. Each puzzle has a different number of die-cut pieces printed in full color on die-cut heavy board. The puzzles measure 4 feet long when completed. The pieces emphasize the interrelationship of body parts. Solution cues that contribute to body concept include matching clothing, skin color, recognizing major body parts, and discerning the size and shape of less easily identified parts. Each puzzle comes in a sturdy box with a photo of what it will look like when completed. Available as: white boy (thirty-one pieces), black girl (twenty-five pieces), Spanish-American boy (nineteen pieces).
Developmental Learning Materials, 7440 Natchez Avenue, Niles, IL 60648, ($6.00)

Women Workers
Workers selected to fit into block play, the set includes a postal-service worker, a businesswoman, a carpenter, a police officer, a doctor, and a maintenance worker. The figures are cut from thick plywood and stand on their own. The complete set is available with either black or white workers. From the "Special Education Materials" catalog. Price subject to change.
Childcraft Education Corp., 20 Kilmer Road, Edison, NJ 08817 ($6.95 + $1.95 shipping and handling)

Note: Not all manufacturers and publishers will accept single orders for a product or book. Always write to them first, before sending money, to be sure that they will take your order. Make sure you've got the most recent price, including shipping and handling charges. If the company is in your state, then you may need to include state sales tax as well.

"When I Grow Up I Want to Be"
Children dress felt figures of a man and a woman to identify careers. The clothing for each profession fits both the man and the woman. Thirty-six occupations are represented for use on a felt board. Practical Drawing Co., P.O. Box 5388, Dallas, TX 75222 ($8.95 + 15% shipping)

Robot
Down with "Old Maid" and up with "Robot"! Full-color plastic coated cards depict careers in a nonsexist, multiracial way. Nineteen occupations are presented with a man and a woman doing the same job on each card. A variety of game plans is included.
Fun-da-Mentals, Box 263, South Pasadena, CA 91030 ($3.00. CA buyers add 6 or 6½% sales tax)

Language Skills

3

Shinichi Suzuki, founder of the Suzuki method of teaching violin to very young children, tells of his astonishment at the fact that all young children speak their native tongues with perfect fluency. The children of Osaka speak the difficult Osaka dialect, the children of Tohoku the Tohoku dialect. "I felt I had made a tremendous discovery. If a child cannot do his arithmetic, it is said that his intelligence is below average. Yet he speaks the difficult Japanese language — or his own native language — very well. Isn't that something to think about?"

We seldom appreciate the magnificent job that we have done in teaching our children the English language. We haven't been conscious of being language teachers, yet from the time our children have been babies we have repeated words to them, talked to them, and corrected their mispronunciations and faulty syntax. As with all complex learnings, the skill has taken years, bit by bit, conversation by conversation, during brief moments surrounded by other activities.

ACTIVITIES TO ENCOURAGE LANGUAGE DEVELOPMENT

If you haven't looked into children's books since you were a child, you'll be surprised at how colorful and exciting they are for preschoolers these days. Why not start the library habit by going to the library every few weeks with your child? Most libraries have liberalized their rules to allow children to be their natural, rowdy selves. Many have story hours for young children, and some even have records and toys that can be checked out. One library has a bedtime story hour for children at seven o'clock. The stories the librarian reads are the gentle, drowsy types. Children are encouraged to come with their pajamas on.

Build or buy a low shelf for your child's book collection. Paint it a bright, appealing color. Make a reading corner in your child's room and furnish it with pillows of all different sizes and bright fabrics. Think of ways that the two of you can enjoy books in out-of-the-ordinary places. Take a walk together and bring a book to read under a tree. Keep several books in the car for travel. Take books along when you'll have a long wait, in the doctor's office, doing the laundry, or in traffic. You may find your child pretending to read. She is developing a strong desire to learn to read, and shouldn't be discouraged from listening to her own voice and getting a feel of what reading aloud is like.

Use the telephone. A toy phone is good for imaginary conversations. Once your child has learned to recognize the numbers one to ten she can begin to make real calls to Mommy or Daddy at work if you give close supervision to see that the numbers are dialed correctly. A plastic shield that fits over the telephone dial to enlarge the numbers is available in some office supply stores. If you have an extension phone, let your child have the unplugged phone to practice dialing and play conversations.

Record players and inexpensive tape recorders are excellent devices for enriching a child's language experiences. A child can record her own stories using her voice with a tape recorder. Records can often be bought inexpensively at rummage and yard sales.

Take mini field trips and visit the kitchen of a restaurant, the firehouse, the animal shelter, a car-repair garage, the back room of a bakery, a dairy farm, or a hospital (call the public relations department to find if tours are offered.) When you return home, write down what you saw and draw pictures to illustrate.

Poetry and rhymes seem to appeal to a young child who's already excited with the possibilities of sound and word combinations. Your library should have plenty of poetry books for young children. Mother Goose rhymes are great. When your child is familiar with them you can play games like: "Can you finish this rhyme? 'Mary had a little lamb . . .'" or you

Making Big and Little Letters and Numbers

Can You Dial the Telephone?

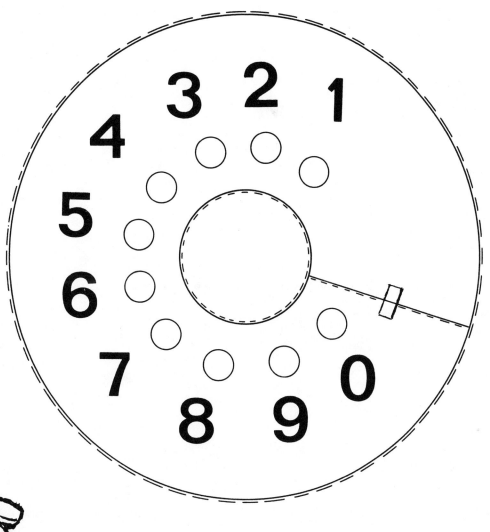

Cut out this dial and tape it to your telephone.

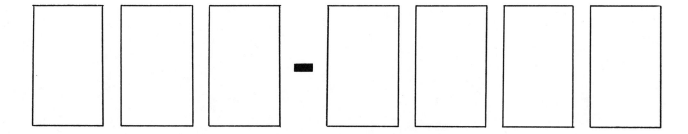

What's your favorite telephone number?

Cut out the telephone dial on the other side.

can beat out the rhythm to see if your child can recognize it. Fingerplays are a good way of acting out rhymes while helping to develop hand coordination. Do you remember the "Eency Weency Spider" or "Here's the Church, Here's the Steeple"? Another rhyming game is "I'm thinking of a word that rhymes with 'cat' and you wear it on your head. It's a _____."

An old workable typewriter or a beginner's printing set can be valuable in reinforcing letter and word concepts. Other ideas for making alphabets: make sand letters from cutout sandpaper or sand-dotted letter shapes made of liquid glue on paper. Glue cotton, dried beans, rice, or paper chips in letter shapes.

Daddy Tells a Story
by Sidney A. Stutz

The bedroom windows were dark as I pulled into the driveway, but I could see a small figure peeking out from behind the curtains.

"Daddy," called three-year-old Michael as I opened the front door, "I've been waiting for you to tell me a story!"

Fathers have been telling their children stories of one kind or another since the beginning of civilization. It's easy to see why. Storytelling can stimulate, educate, entertain, and reassure children. And it's a pleasant, relaxed way for busy fathers to get to know their children.

Most fathers today can spend very little time with their children during the work week. But even if they arrive home just as the children are being tucked in for the night, there's time for a quick bedtime story. Such mini-tales may hardly seem worth the effort to an adult, but they may mean a great deal to children. The stories don't need to be either long or elaborate; what really matters is that at least once during the busy day the youngsters can claim their father's undivided attention.

I discovered the importance of bedtime stories when our first child was very young. When she began to resent being put in her crib for the night, I found that I could calm her with a simple tale geared to her short span of attention.

The story might begin, "Once upon a time there was a little rabbit who decided to go for a walk in the woods because it was such a lovely day. No sooner had he started out than Mr. Squirrel scampered down a tree and said, 'May I come along, too?' Well, Mr. Rabbit and Mr. Squirrel soon met Mr. Raccoon, who said, 'Maybe there'll be good things to eat along the way; may I come along?' "

As the child's eyelids began to droop, I would tie up the threads of my simple plot and finish the story by saying good-bye to all the animals.

Admittedly, this sort of tale isn't much, but my success with such stories has taught me that what matters most to my children is not the quality of the stories I tell but my willingness to spend a few extra minutes with them each night.

As the children got a little older, my stories became more involved and began to revolve around the actions of one central character. The youngsters themselves seemed to know when they were ready for more sophisticated stories. One night I told a story about a wily hog that outsmarted a farmer. The next night, when I asked for story suggestions the chil-

dren shouted enthusiastically, "The wily hog!" Since then the wily hog has figured in dozens of stories suggested by the children — "The Wily Hog Who Drove a Tractor Through the Lettuce," "The Wily Hog Who Had Green Teeth Because He Wouldn't Brush Them," "The Wily Hog Who Beat the Chicken at Cards."

Most children enjoy stories for which they can supply the sound effects. When I tell about Grandfather's barnyard, the youngsters accompany me with assorted moos, oinks, and cackles. Ghost stories give them a chance to moan, shriek, and imitate creaking floorboards very convincingly. My daughter, who always has at least one pet cat, furnishes the sound effects for stories about a feline named Powder Puff. During any one story, she may be called on to purr contentedly, to meow politely, or even to hiss angrily or excitedly.

Many fathers realize how much stories mean to children but they don't feel confident enough to make up their own plots. Actually, once you conquer your initial self-consciousness, the plots will begin to come naturally. For example, you'll find that your

youngsters love to hear stories about their playthings. Each of my children was always eager to hear about the escapades of Ginger, the family's favorite teddy bear. They listened attentively to stories about the difficulties Ginger's mother had in civilizing her naughty cub who loved to eat soap, drink the bath water and who refused ever to use silverware.

Another kind of story children always enjoy is a tale about "the olden days" (meaning any time before they were born). Most adults have fond memories of tales told by their parents and grandparents. I can vividly recall my grandfather's story about being followed to school by a bobcat in the dark Tennessee woods and his description of pioneer weddings in Illinois. When my older children were about to start first grade, they wanted to hear what school was like when I was a boy wearing overalls and carrying a lunch pail. They enjoyed hearing about the time my cousin egged me on to drop down the clothes chute and snitch some cookies stored in my grandmother's cellar.

I'm glad my children want to hear stories about the past. They never saw the great-grandmother who kept her cookies in the cellar, but such tales have made her real to them.

The child who hears stories made to order soon learns to add details and will eventually make up stories entirely on his own. Now that Lucy is ten and Alan seven, they are providing me with more assistance. Occasionally I will start a tale and one of them will continue or request time the following night to make up another story about the same character. The fact that I am there to appreciate their efforts seems to provide an added incentive for them to make their tales at least as engaging as the ones I tell. In fact, some of their stories have been a lot more imaginative and suspenseful than my own. We all look forward to these sessions as eagerly as three-year-old Mike, possibly more.

I tell stories primarily because it's fun for me and my children, but we get far more from our story time than just entertainment. The tales have helped me to appreciate my children for their individual qualities. Lucy likes stories with the ring of truth and a touch of romance now and then, whereas Alan is more fanciful and delights in tales of ogres and demons. Michael, though only a toddler, shows a decided preference for the practical; he enjoys learning about all kinds of useful machines, from trucks to spaceships.

Stories have helped me learn more about my children's world — what makes them laugh and what frightens them. At the same time, stories have encouraged my youngsters to use their imaginations and develop the kinds of creative thinking that will be valuable to them in later life. And certainly one of the most rewarding moments for any storytelling father comes when his child says proudly one evening, "Let me tell you a story this time, Daddy."

Sure-Fire Stories for Telling and Reading Aloud
by Gusty Scattergood

Last night, Ivy, age five, and Kate, who is three, entertained us with a puppet show. They draped an orange towel over a table for the theater. Next came the puppets — all the stuffed animals in their collections plus finger puppets, hand puppets, and a few homemade sock puppets. We had made those together from Daddy's leftover socks and decorated them with eyes, noses and mouths from my scrap basket. Their heads were topped off with curled-ribbon hair. If the plot sounded vaguely reminiscent of *The Three Bears* or *Hansel and Gretel*, maybe it's because we've read a lot of folktales to them.

Books for young children should have a brisk, lively dialogue. The characters should be created mostly by action rather than long descriptive passages. The story should be simple and literal. (Young children seldom appreciate sarcasm or adult forms of humor.) When I think of bedtime, I think of quiet stories and books with magical endings. Artistically creative picture books are especially pleasing to both children and adults. Ask your child to tell you about the pictures in the book, but rather than asking, "Did you like the story?" which requires a simple "yes" or "no" response, ask "Would you rather be a real mouse or a wind-up one?", which will encourage a more imaginative response.

In choosing a book, choose one that *you*, the reader, like. For all you know, the story that you read once may become your child's favorite, which means you will be reading and re-reading it again and again. New books by favorite authors make excellent birthday presents, Christmas presents, and presents from the tooth fairy. On pages 42–44 I list favorite books gleaned from my experience as a mother and children's librarian. Seek out other books by the same authors.

Recently I heard Augusta Baker tell of her childhood and of the tremendous influence her grandmother's reading and storytelling had on her life. Then she told us an African folktale as though we were all children again. We were captivated! No child should miss the experience of hearing stories told well — slowly, with expression and enthusiasm. Many folktales and stories are so good for retelling that they're easy to memorize. Think about how you could use these stories for long car trips.

Perhaps you can make up a story about an animal with the same name as your young child — the more preposterous the better — or you can create a character and build a continuing saga about him. If you read to your children and share stories with them, they're bound to develop a love for reading and books that will stay with them through the years.

STORYBOOKS

These books have good, strong story lines. They're sometimes based on folk and fairy tales. Good for imaginative play, puppetry and retelling.

Caps for Sale
Esphyr Slobodkina
Scholastic Book Services, 904 Sylvan Avenue, Englewood Cliffs, NJ 07632 (85¢, paperback)
"A tale of a peddlar, some monkeys, and their monkey business."

Nibble Nibble Mousekin
Joan Walsh Anglund
Harcourt Brace Jovanovich, Inc., 757 Third Avenue, New York, NY 10017 ($5.95)
The classic story of Hansel and Gretel with large, interesting illustrations.

The following three books are by Ezra Jack Keats (no child should miss Keats's illustrations!).

Whistle for Willie
Viking Press, Inc., 625 Madison Avenue, New York, NY 10022 (95¢, paperback)
Peter learns to whistle and is he proud!

Snowy Day
(also Viking Press) (95¢, paperback)
Peter's adventures in the snow.

John Henry, an American Legend
Pantheon Books, Div. of Random House, Inc., 457 Hahn Road, Westminster, MD 21157 ($4.50)
Story of John Henry's race against the steam drill. Fathers particularly seem to enjoy reading it.

Where the Wild Things Are
Maurice Sendak
Scholastic Book Services, 904 Sylvan Avenue, Englewood Cliffs, NJ 07632 ($1.25, paperback)
Max is sent to bed without any supper and sails to where the wild things are. Not to be missed.

Curious George
H. A. Rey
Scholastic Book Services, 904 Sylvan Avenue, Englewood Cliffs, NJ 07632 (95¢, paperback)
George is an appealing, mischievous fellow. A monkey kids can identify with. There are five more Curious George books besides this one.

Three Billy Goats Gruff
Marcia Brown, Illustrator
Harcourt Brace Jovanovich, Inc., 757 Third Avenue, New York, NY 10017 ($2.25, paperback)
or
Susan Blair, Illustrator
Scholastic Book Services, 904 Sylvan Avenue, Englewood Cliffs, NJ 07632 (75¢)

An excellent story for play-acting. Children never grow tired of hearing this story, especially by a dad who can make his troll louder, meaner, and scarier than anyone else's.

Millions of Cats
Wanda G'ag
Coward, McCann & Geoghegan, Inc., 200 Madison Avenue, New York, NY 10016 ($4.95)
Children like the preposterousness of the story as well as the repetitive verse that goes throughout.

The Little Bear Series
Else H. Minarik, Illustrated by Maurice Sendak
Our family likes *Little Bear's Friend* (Harper & Row, Pubs., Inc., Scranton, PA 18512. $3.95). We particularly like Lucy, the doll, and Little Bear's letter at the end of the book.
A good one for grandparents is *Little Bear's Visit* (also Harper & Row. $3.95). Both books are I CAN READ books for new readers.

Tale of Peter Rabbit
Beatrix Potter
Franklin Watts, Inc., Subs. of Grolier, Inc., 845 Third Avenue, New York, NY 10022 (95¢, paperback)
Young readers love to read this book to their younger brothers and sisters. Fathers seem to be fond of this book, too.

Story of Ferdinand
Munro Leaf
Viking Press, Inc., 625 Madison Avenue, New York, NY 10022 (95¢, paperback)
Ferdinand is a bull who likes to smell flowers but doesn't like banderilleros, picadores, or matadors.

Richard Scarry's Animal Nursery Tales
Golden Press/Western Publishing Co., Inc., 1220 Mound Avenue, Racine, WI 53404 ($4.95)
A good selection of eleven favorite folktales with Scarry's animal characters as Little Red Riding Hood, Goldilocks, the Bremen Musicians, and others.

The Tall Book of Nursery Tales
Feodor Rojankovsky
Harper & Row, Pubs., Inc., Keystone Industrial Park, Scranton, PA 18512 ($2.95)
All the classic folk and fairy tales with lots of illustrations.

The Juniper Tree and Other Tales from Grimm
Selected by Lore Segal and Maurice Sendak
Farrar, Straus & Giroux, Inc., 19 Union Square W., New York, NY 10003 ($4.95)
These stories are translated from the German and may not be the most familiar versions. I think it is important for older children, five and up, to know the original version of their favorite fairy tales. (I read three of them to two five-year-olds one afternoon and they begged for more!)

QUIET BEDTIME STORIES AND BEAUTIFULLY ILLUSTRATED PICTURE BOOKS

Goodnight Moon
Margaret Wise Brown
Harper & Row Pubs., Inc., Keystone Industrial
Park, Scranton, PA 18512 ($3.95)
A quiet sharing book about a bunny settling down
for a night's sleep. Watch the little mouse creep
across the pages!

Mr. Rabbit and the Lovely Present
Charlotte Zolotow
Harper & Row Pubs., Inc., Keystone Industrial
Park, Scranton, PA 18512 ($3.95)
Mr. Rabbit helps the little girl pick a present for her
mother. Beautiful soft, dreamy pictures by Maurice
Sendak.

The following two books are by Leo Lionni, an
illustrator too good to miss!

Alexander and the Wind-up Mouse
Pantheon Books, Div. of Random House, Inc., 457
Hahn Road, Westminster, MD 21157 (95¢,
paperback)
A magic story of Willie and Alexander, two mice
who become fast friends.

Inch by Inch
Astor-Honor, Inc., 270 Madison Avenue, New York,
NY 10016 ($4.95)
Clever inchworm outwits the nightingale. Children
will enjoy finding the little green worm on each
page.

Bedtime for Frances
Russell Hoban
Harper & Row Pubs., Inc., Keystone Industrial
Park, Scranton, PA 18512 ($1.95, paperback)
Garth Williams's illustrations of this delightful
badger family make this book one of our favorites.
Children love learning that they aren't the only ones
who think there are tigers under the bed. Frances
and her family appear in several other books in this
series.

RHYMING STORIES, POETRY BOOKS

Drummer Hoff
Barbara Emberly and Ed Emberly
Prentice-Hall, Inc., Englewood Cliffs, NJ 07632
($1.25, paperback)
A good story for children to read in to a tape
recorder, especially the loud ''KAHBAHBLOOM'' at
the end. A good ''Read to me, Daddy'' book.

Madeline
Ludwig Bemelmans
Viking Press, Inc., 625 Madison Avenue, New York,
NY 10022 ($1.25, paperback)
Most children seem to relate to this madcap heroine
and will enjoy Madeline's other adventures, too.

Mother, Mother I Feel Sick
Remy Charlip
Parents' Magazine Press, 52 Vanderbilt Avenue,
New York, NY 10017 ($5.50)
A great book for acting out. Children will delight in
seeing all of the things that pop out of one little boy.

Dr. Seuss Books

This author is so prolific you are sure to find a book
you enjoy reading. My favorite is *Green Eggs and
Ham* (Beginner Books, Div. of Random House, Inc.,
457 Hahn Road, Westminster, MD 21157. $2.95). If
you read it with lots of expression, you'll find
yourself chanting it out loud all day long.

Another popular character is *Cat in the Hat*
(Beginner. $2.95). Every child should meet a cat like
this one. Fathers seem to like Dr. Seuss books and
dramatize them well.

A Child's Garden of Verses
Robert Louis Stevenson
Franklin Watts, Inc., Subs. of Grolier, Inc., 845
Third Avenue, New York, NY 10022 (95¢,
paperback)
Children still love these old-fashioned poems. A
good book for bedtime reading and sharing.

When We Were Very Young
A. A. Milne
Dell Publishing Company, Inc., 1 Dag
Hammarskjold Plaza, 245 E. 47th Street, New York,
NY 10017 (95¢, paperback)
The author of *Winnie-the-Pooh* writes irresistible
poems.

Illustrated Poems for Children
Illustrations by Krystyna Orska
Rand McNally & Co., P.O. Box 7600, Chicago, IL
60680 ($7.95)
An anthology that contains a wide variety of poets,
from Ogden Nash to Theodore Roethke, James
Joyce, and Langston Hughes. The illustrations are
bright and cheerful and the selections demonstrate
that many poems not written especially for children
can be very appealing to them.

Where the Sidewalk Ends
Shel Silverstein
Harper & Row Pubs., Inc., Keystone Industrial
Park, Scranton, PA 18512 ($7.95)
Some of the poems are funny, some thoughtful, all
are cleverly illustrated and very readable. Your child
will think some of the poems are written especially
for him, such as, ''I'm being eaten by a boa
constrictor,'' or ''I'm Reginald Clark, I'm afraid of
the dark.''

BOOKS FOR CHAPTER-BY-CHAPTER READING

These titles are better for older children. Generally, I've found that four or five years old is the youngest age at which a child can listen for a long time without pictures.

Charlotte's Web
E. B. White
Harper & Row, Pubs., Inc., Keystone Industrial Park, Scranton, PA 18512 ($1.25, paperback)
Charlotte thinks Wilbur is ''some pig'' and so will the children who listen to this story.

Winnie-the-Pooh
A. A. Milne
Dell Publishing Co., Inc., 1 Dag Hammarskjold Plaza, 245 E. 47th St., New York, NY 10017 (95¢, paperback)
I like the original version, illustrated by Ernest Shephard, better than the more recent ''cartoony'' versions. Delightful tales about Pooh and his friends.

Gusty Scattergood is a children's librarian and has her Master's Degree in Library Science from Simmons College. She is a librarian at Bryn Mawr. She and her husband, Jay, are the parents of Ivy, five, and Kate, three.

Homemade Books
by Ellen Galinsky

The top shelf of my children's bookcase has the most popular books in our house on it. It contains a book titled *The Big Monster;* another one called *Witches.* It also has *The Space Book* and *Everybody.* It would be impossible to find these books in a bookstore or library or anywhere else but our bookshelf. They are each one-of-a-kind originals, made by my son, Philip.

It all started several years ago when Philip was almost three. We had taken him to a Fourth of July fireworks display. He was so overwhelmed by the bright colors splaying across the black sky, by the loud crackling noises, and by the clown-costumed people selling cotton candy that he came home and drew and drew. When he had finished, I said to him, ''You really have done a book about fireworks. Would you like me to staple the pictures together?''

He was impressed by the fact that he had made a book, and several weeks later, he asked to make a book about clowns.

His earliest books had no words. Sometimes they had no meaning in adult terms. They were collections of drawings. And they were his — I didn't try to criticize or change them in any way. If I did introduce an idea, I did so by example, by doing a book myself. In that way, I showed him how to use words with pictures. I first photographed him at his favorite activity — hiding. I then took the photographs and put them in sequence in a small photo album. A picture of Philip hiding behind the shower curtain was captioned, ''Peek.'' Philip bursting out from behind the shower curtain said, ''A-boo, I see you!'' We did many series like that — Philip hiding under the bed, behind a chair, in a closet, even behind a large piece of rye bread toast.

Philip also loved the idea of using photographs for a book. He had the idea (perhaps taken from a Lois Lenski book called *Davey's Day*) of making a book called *Philip's Day.* He told me what pictures to take and then dictated what he wanted to say about each activity.

Philip then began to ask me to write down stories to go with his drawings. Sometimes his stories were seemingly random ideas, the connection being somewhere in his own thoughts. A story about an elephant would, by the turn of a page, become a story about a gorilla. Other times his stories had a visible sense of plot development. Here is one he wrote when he was four.

The Big Monster
Once upon a time there lived a seed.
And the seed got bigger.
And it got to be a monster.
And it got bigger than the whole city.
It was a bad monster.
It died.

The End

Philip's stories are, in a way, almost a tool that he uses to clarify his ideas. When he first heard about witches, he made numerous books about them, and in the books he examined every facet of knowledge about witches: where they lived, what they wore, what kind of magic they did, and most important, if they were real or not. His explorations were not just about the imaginary world of clowns, witches, and monsters. At four he did a book about what different animals like to eat. At five he did a book about how various species of animals protect themselves. At six, in his own handwriting, he made a book about space, It began: "The sun and the moon are in space." Then he went on, "The sun is a hot ball of gas."

At seven, Philip's books are many and varied. Passing a building that looks like a castle became the impetus for a book entitled *The King's Castle*. His *Halloween Book* had puzzles and matching and guessing games in it. Some of his books are suspenseful stories. One called *Witches* begins: "Witches are very evil. They get you at night." In *Frankenstein Lives*, Philip wrote: "Once upon a time there lived a man and the man didn't know what to do. So he did know what to do. He did something. He made a monster, and his name was Frankenstein."

I have always delighted in Philip's books. And he knows that. He knows how much I enjoy looking at the pictures and reading the stories. Perhaps because Philip knows how much these stories mean, or perhaps because they have become a major way of communicating for him, his way of welcoming the birth of his sister Lara was to do a book. It was a book entitled *Lara*, filled with drawings of a newborn baby.

Ellen Galinsky works at the Bank Street College of Education in New York City, where she founded the Family Center for child care. She is coauthor of The New Extended Family *with William Hooks (Houghton Mifflin) among other books for adults and children. She is the mother of Philip, seven, and Lara, three.*

Helping Your Child Learn to Read
by Leslie Siskin

My daughter, Cory, five and a half, has just begun kindergarten. Like all the other children in her class, she is learning to get on a school bus, to cut with scissors, and to organize things and put them in sequence. In one way she's different than the other kids — she can read easily and well. This has meant that the school personnel have had to make some adjustments for Cory, and it may mean, too, that there will be times when she's bored with the ABCs and prereading activities of kindergarten. Balancing these inconveniences, there are the endless exciting moments that I've shared with her as she has begun to realize her own abilities. I've been able to share with her the joy of discovering a whole new world of words to be read — reading her favorite books to herself, reading street signs, helping select groceries, even mastering the Sunday comics for herself.

Before Cory could learn to read, she had to develop a complex framework of skills. Reading involves discriminating and identifying visual symbols, translating them mentally into the right sounds, and interpreting the symbols and sounds in a meaningful way. It sounds tremendously complicated, and it is. But none of the steps in acquiring these skills need be complicated or difficult. Many of Cory's play activities helped prepare her for learning to read — naming objects around her, identifying pictures in a book, mimicking the sounds of animals, even rolling and following a toy car across the floor — all are steps in reading readiness.

More sophisticated skills that lead directly into reading can be taught in the same atmosphere of relaxed play. "Sesame Street" provides an easy and entertaining way of introducing the alphabet. Plastic, foam rubber, and magnetic alphabets are available in toy stores and school supply stores. They will help your child become familiar with the look and shape of each letter. Introduce them a few at a time, and let your child get to know them by name. (Start with some easily distinguishable ones; *H, O, S, T,* and *V,* for example, are much easier to tell apart than a group including *D* and *O,* or *V* and *W.*)

Reading aloud to your child and exposing her to the stories as well as the pictures is invaluable. She will learn to associate illustrations and words and to view reading as a source of pleasure. If you follow along with your finger as you read, she will notice the text, and you may soon discover her reading her own books, dutifully pointing to the words as she makes up her own story.

At this point it can be very exciting for your child to learn to recognize a real word. Since children are rather self-centered, the most important word is probably their own name. I had written Cory's name in the front of her books, so we started reading at "This book belongs to Cory." I made her a name tag and a sign to put on her door. Books in which your child's name is worked into the story are also available.

The next few words that Cory learned were from her books. One page of a favorite story said nothing but "BOOM." That was a nice noisy word, and she had been shouting it at the appropriate page for a long time. I copied it onto a file card and had Cory compare the handwritten and printed versions. We also formed it out of magnetic letters on the refrigerator. Other sources of easy-to-recognize words include trademarks and food names. If you keep a variety of cereals, have your child learn to identify the names on the boxes, and have her help you locate them when you shop for groceries. She may also be able to spot her favorite restaurant signs while riding in the car.

Once your child is familiar with the alphabet, enjoys looking at books and being read to, recognizes some words and wants to learn more, you may want to begin a basic at-home reading program. There are two traditional approaches to the teaching of reading, sight or look-say (recognizing whole words from memory) and phonics (learning to sound out words and recognize patterns), as well as a number of more recently developed methods. It's a good idea to check with the school your child will attend to find out which approach they use and whether there might be any problem later from the method you use to teach your child to read.

The following is the basic structure I used for Cory, drawing on and modifying methods I had used in teaching reading at school. We worked on the concept of putting little things together to make something new and wonderful. Sounds and letters would be joined together to make names and words. Cory understood that; it was like mixing ingredients together in different ways to make cakes or cookies.

First, we went back to the alphabet to learn the sound each consonant makes. *S* is a good letter to start with — it looks like a snake, which not only starts with an *s*, it hisses with an *s* sound. We made a flash card for the letter, drawing and labeling a "slithery slimy snake" on the back. That way if Cory

couldn't remember the sound she could flip the card over for a clue. For each new sound we made up a new alliterative phrase and a new card. We even sang songs about "cute, cuddly Cory" and, for Cory's two-year-old brother, "nice, neat Nathaniel."

I found both the Berenstains's *The B Book* and Dr. Seuss's *Alphabet Book* extremely useful as my imagination waned. Children also like to fill in their own answers to Dr. Seuss's questions of what begins with each letter. Introduce new sounds slowly, and as you did with the shapes of the letters, separate those that might be easily confused (*t, d*) as well as those that look alike. The first ones I suggest are *s, r, m, f, t, c, h,* and the first letter of your child's name. (Save the soft sounds of *c* and *g,* preceding *e, i,* and *y* for a much later date. If your child's name is Cindy or George just treat that as something special.)

When you teach each sound, try to keep it as pure as possible. Be aware of the position of your mouth as you form the sound and try to maintain that position. If you continue the sound while opening your mouth, you add an "uh" sound which may make things more difficult later on.

Once your child has a fair understanding of beginning consonant sounds, it's time to introduce a vowel (*a, e, i, o, u*) and the short-vowel sound. The short-vowel sounds are the most common in beginning reading books and that's why I think they're the best of the vowel sounds to begin with. On one side of a flash card I put a vowel and asked Cory to make the sound of that letter. On the back of the flash card I put a word that begins with the short-vowel sound and a simple drawing of the word to help her figure out the sound. My clue words were: *a*pple, *E*skimo, *i*gloo, *o*ctopus, and *u*mbrella. Then I made some three-letter words illustrating the short-vowel sounds for practice (sat, rat, mat, cat, and so on).

I put the single-letter consonant flash cards on one color, the single-letter vowels on another color, and whole words on a third color of cards. At a separate sitting we added a few words to memorize without trying to sound them out, sight words: "the," "on," "and," "a," and "Cory." That way when she got through identifying the sounds and words, she could arrange the sounds into words and the words into sentences.

Then I made a booklet out of construction paper. I wrote one of the sentences we had formed on each page, and Cory drew the illustrations. After learning the sounds made by seven consonants, one vowel, and two sight words, we had an amazing number of sentences. While "The rat sat on the mat" and "The hat sat on the fat cat on the mat" may not be very gracefully worded, it gave Cory tremendous satisfaction being able to read them.

We also kept a watch for the words she knew in her other books. Cory followed my finger as I read to her, filling in the familiar words as we came to them and often figuring out new ones. We found Dr. Seuss's *There's a Wocket in My Pocket* to be particularly valuable. I read each sentence up to the last word, which Cory knew would be a real word rhyming with the nonsense word. Once she determined the sound of the first letter, she could complete the word. She would also go through the books by herself scanning each page for known words and deciphering new ones.

Introducing words and sentences so early in the process relieved the monotony of learning the sound cards and made it easy for Cory to understand the purpose of learning those sounds. Even the flash card drills themselves can be incorporated into games and made into a pleasurable activity. Because there are so many sounds to learn, and they take a long time, it's important that you make your practice sessions something that you both look forward to doing regularly. One game I've found that works well is an identification challenge. I hold up each card, and if Cory responds with the correct sound, she keeps the card for her pile. If she misses the card, I give the correct sound, have her repeat it, and then put it into my pile to be reviewed at the end of the game. If there's any chance that your child won't finish with more cards, run through the missed pile a second time, and take this as a sign not to introduce any new sounds for a few days.

Other games and activities can reinforce the flash card skills. You and your child can make up lists of words that all begin with the same sound, or learn to recite tongue twisters. We also liked the magnetic letters which we stuck on the refrigerator. I bought the lower-case letters, since those appeared more often, and Cory could practice her sounds or arrange words while I was busy in the kitchen.

As your child finishes learning the consonants and short vowels and begins trying to sound out new words, you will run into the challenging dilemma of irregular words. Most of them actually fit phonetic patterns but unless you've had a course in phonics you probably never learned the rules. You could try to teach yourself from books at the library, but most are not written to be easily understood. If you're not that ambitious, forget it. Admit your ignorance and

add the words to a new category of flash cards: your sight word collection. Keep thinking about patterns, though, and if you make a card for a word like *night*, add some words from its family on the back (*light*, *fight*, and *right*, for example).

One pattern you can learn and teach after the short-vowel words have been well covered is silent *e* words. They start out looking just like those three-letter words, but along comes the magical letter *e* that has the power of changing the whole sound of the word by making the vowel say its name. One good way of illustrating this magical change is through *The Amazing Adventures of Silent E Man*. While pulling tabs and turning wheels, the child watches Silent E Man turn a tub into a tube, a cap into a cape (as the *e* moves in and out of view the illustration changes too), and many other marvelous transformations. Your child can play letterman too, by making an *e* on a small piece of flash card, and adding it to each of her short-vowel cards. Even if the results are unfamiliar or nonsense words go ahead and sound them out. That way you practice the pattern, and your child may learn some new vocabulary words.

Another pattern that may need explaining is what happens to words when you add *-ing*. It's a very simple rule; short-vowel words get another consonant (hop, hopping), while silent *e* words lose the final *e* (hope, hoping). An easy rule, but the distinction is very hard to remember while reading. Don't expect your child to get them right consistently; eventually, children use the sense of the sentence to tell them apart.

I hope that my suggestions will prove useful to you in teaching your child to read, but I want to add a few words of caution. The biggest danger in beginning a reading program is pushing your child to do what she's not ready to do. My son, Nathaniel, doesn't show the same interest and determination about words and reading as Cory. He probably won't be ready for reading instruction until school age, which is perfectly acceptable for me. Each child has a rate of learning that should be respected. If you are met with resistance, squirming, or fussing, back away and wait awhile. Learning to read should be fun for both of you, not frustrating!

Concentrate on the activities that give your child the most success. Some children learn sight words easily, but have trouble with sounds. Others have difficulty remembering a word by sight and need to sound out almost every word. Also, be alert for signs of vision and hearing difficulty. If your child finds it hard to tell the letters apart, leans her head close to the page in her attempts to decipher words, or has trouble repeating sounds and words or following your verbal directions, check with your pediatrician before continuing your reading program.

The Amazing Adventures of Silent E Man
The Electric Company Pop-up Series
Random House, Inc., 457 Hahn Road, Westminster, MD 21157 ($3.50)

The B Book
Stanley Berenstain and Janice Berenstain
Bright and Early Book Series
Random House, Inc., 457 Hahn Road, Westminster, MD 21157 ($2.95)

Dr. Seuss's ABC
Beginner Books
Random House, Inc., 457 Hahn Road, Westminster, MD 21157 ($2.95)

There's a Wocket in My Pocket!
Dr. Seuss
Bright and Early Book Series
Random House, Inc., 457 Hahn Road, Westminster, MD 21157 ($2.95)

Leslie Siskin is the mother of Nathaniel and Cory. She is currently doing graduate work in Learning Disabilities at the University of Virginia. She has been a teacher in a school for learning disabled children, has taught in Head Start, and has tutored children in reading as a home teacher with a school system.

REFERENCE BOOKS FOR ADULTS

Calvert School Kindergarten Course
Write:
Principal of Home Instruction, Calvert School, 105 Tuscany Road, Baltimore, MD 21210 ($80.00)
An entire year's formal kindergarten course for a child with planned lessons in "Reading Readiness," "Number Readiness," and daily programs including discussions, singing, poetry, storytelling, dramatic play, games, drawing, and other handwork. You receive a teacher's manual, water-color paints, scissors, modeling clay, large crayons, needle and yarn, and a variety of other materials. Special tuition rates are available when ordering more than one course at a time. (Total courses of instruction are offered by Calvert all the way through the eighth grade. A parent can choose to have additional advisory teaching service for grades one through eight, enabling the child to receive a certificate upon the completion of each grade. It is recognized as valid by many school systems.) Calvert School is a respected institution founded in 1897. It is a legitimate mail-order educational alternative often used by parents who must travel or are overseas.

Learning Time with Language Experiences for Young Children
Louise Binder Scott
McGraw-Hill Book Co., 1221 Avenue of the Americas, New York, NY 10036 ($11.10)
A magnificent collection of language activities for preschoolers. Poems, fingerplays, stories, rhymes, and riddles. Designed for teachers of young children, but an excellent ideabook for parents, too.

"Making Language Materials for Children"
Mary Salkever
Maryland Committee for the Day Care of Children, Inc., 608 Walter Street, Baltimore, MD 21202 ($1.25, mimeographed)
Simple word and letter games using magazines, cardboard, felt, and other easy-to-find materials.

Poems and Rhymes
Childcraft, vol. 1
Field Enterprises Educational Corp., Merchandise Mart Plaza, Chicago, IL 60654 (Write for more information)
Often the children's room of the library will have the fourteen-volume Childcraft set available for parents to check out volume by volume. *Poems and Rhymes* has intriguing full-color illustrations throughout and well-chosen poems that speak to the experiences of young children. You might enjoy reading "Discover Childcraft . . ." a free brochure that gives illustrated selections from Childcraft. I don't suggest buying the set, unless you've got money to throw away. For the same amount you could put together a fabulous collection of paperback books tailored to your child's interests and likes.

Teacher
Sylvia Ashton-Warner
Bantam Books, Inc., 414 E. Golf Road, Des Plaines,
IL 60016 (95¢, paperback)
"I see the mind of a five-year-old as a volcano with
two vents; destructiveness and creativeness. And I
see that to the extent that we widen the creative
channel, we atrophy the destructive one." Ms.
Ashton-Warner describes her methods of teaching
reading to young Maori children by allowing them
to supply the words from their own internal life.

Teaching Your Child to Read at Home
Wood Smethurst
McGraw-Hill Book Co., 1221 Avenue of the
Americas, New York, NY 10036 ($7.95)
A review of the most recent research on teaching
reading to preschoolers. The book is definitely in
favor of teaching reading to young children and it
gives prereading enrichment ideas as well as
suggestions for actual reading instruction. Suggests
storybooks, records, and basic materials.

Tutoring Is Caring
Aline D. Wolf
Montessori Learning Center, 2733 Sixth Avenue,
Altoona, PA 16602 ($12.50 + $1.00 shipping)
A whole reading program with homemade
materials. Can be used with older children and
adults as well. Uses baseball cards, wildlife stamps,
matching words with objects, and a variety of
innovative, easy-to-make games.

Using Literature with Young Children
Betty Coody
William C Brown Co., Pubs., 2460 Kerper
Boulevard, Dubuque, IA 52001 ($4.15, paperback)
This book is written for teachers of children from
one to eight. It also is an excellent sourcebook for
parents of young children. It suggests books for
reading aloud, gives ideas for storytelling, lists
books for children to act out, suggests recipes to
accompany stories like *The Gingerbread Man,* and
lists books for families to read together.

"Ring a Ring of Roses"
Flint Public Library
Order from:
Assistant Director's Office, Flint Public Library,
1026 E. Kearsley Street, Flint, MI 48502 (60¢, make
checks payable to Mideastern Michigan Library
Cooperative)
A superb handbook of approximately 400
fingerplays for parents and teachers. The book also
has sources for stories to tell little children. There
aren't any illustrations, but the simple directions are
easy to follow.

Scholastic Book Services
Scholastic Book Services offers an excellent
collection of children's books in inexpensive
paperback editions. The books in Scholastic's
catalog are divided by age and topic and each book
has a brief review. The catalog is marked with "you
may take a 25% educators' discount" on each page,
which makes the savings even more exciting. A
complete set of thirty-one Children's Classics,
including *Where the Wild Things Are, Caps for Sale,
Frog and Toad Are Friends, The Tale of Peter Rabbit,*
and other much-loved stories in paperback is
available for under twenty-five dollars (including
discount).
Scholastic Book Services, 904 Sylvan Avenue,
Englewood Cliffs, NJ 07632

"Sing 'n Sound"
An excellent record that teaches the beginning
concepts of phonics through a new alphabet song
for preschoolers. Also included are large cards with
capital and lower-case letters. The song is a painless
way to help your youngster learn the sounds that
letters make so that words can be deciphered easily.
A complete reading program using records is also
available, though somewhat boring to the restless
young listener. Order the record from:
Play 'n Talk International Headquarters, P.O. Box
18804, Oklahoma City, OK 73118 ($15.00)

PRODUCTS TO IMPROVE IMAGINATIVE SKILLS

Alphamat
This play-on game is designed to teach reading readiness while developing perceptual and motor skills. Children play graduated card games on the 27 x 36-inch colorful vinyl floormat. Three decks of cards provide games in visual matching, concept matching, and auditory phonic development and sound-symbol matching. When each game is completed correctly, the cards may be turned over in place to form a self-checking puzzle picture. Nasco, 901 Janesville Avenue, Fort Atkinson, WI 53538 ($17.95 + postage)

Bucilla ABC Sampler
A kit for making a marvelous felt alphabet toy. Twenty-six navy blue pockets are labeled with the large capital letters of the alphabet. Inside the pockets hide tiny stuffed felt creatures whose names begin with the corresponding letter: "A" is apple, "B" is boy, "C" is cat, and so on. The kit includes the felt for constructing the pockets, letters, and creatures — all with a pattern printed on them. Pellon is included for the lining of the hanging, and a stick and string for suspending on the wall. Yarn for making tails and manes, and embroidery thread for faces are also included.
Tucker's Yarn Shop, 950 Hamilton Street, Allentown, PA 18101 (Bucilla Design No. 1888, $11.00 postpaid)

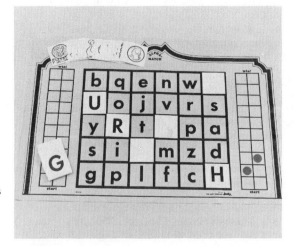

Alpha-Match
A floor game designed to reinforce initial sound and letter recognition and to increase visual and auditory discrimination. The set includes a 26½ x 17½-inch vinyl game mat, one set of picture cards, one set of alphabet cards, markers, and game instructions. Manufactured by the Judy Company. Barclay School Supplies, 29 Warren Street, New York, NY 10007 ($9.95 + a $2.00 charge for postage and handling)

Read and Play
Created by the Bank Street College of Education in New York City, Read and Play sets contain a full-color book specially designed for the beginning reader, a large laminated picture board of the story scene and sturdy playing pieces for acting out the story. "Goldilocks and the Three Bears" sets the scene for the story with the bears' house. The Momma bear, the Daddy bear and the Baby bear snap out to reinact the scene. Goldilocks is there, too, and all of the other props for the story. Other titles: "Chicken Little," and "Ancy and the Big Blue Bag." Published by I.P.S. Intelicor Products.
Order from:
The Bank Street Bookstore, 610 W. 112th Street, New York, NY 10025 ($4.99 ea. + 75¢ shipping and handling)

STORY RECORDS

The following record albums offer your child delightfully read stories for playing and listening:
Uncle Remus read by Morris Mitchell
Winnie-the-Pooh read by Maurice Evans
More Winnie-the-Pooh read by Maurice Evans
The Most of Winnie-the-Pooh read by Maurice Evans
E. B. White Reads Charlotte's Web
Order from:
Pathways of Sound, Inc., 102 Mt. Auburn Street, Cambridge, MA 02138 ($6.98 ea., except for "E. B. White Reads Charlotte's Web," $27.50)

Alphabet Bingo
A letter recognition game with each playing card square containing both the upper- and lower-case letters. Includes discs for covering the letters when they are called out. The winner is the first one to cover all of the letters on his card.
Kaplan School Supply Corp., 600 Jonestown Road, Winston-Salem, NC 27103 ($4.50 + $1.50 shipping and handling)

Wooden Telephone
This realistic-looking wooden telephone has a movable dial with numerals. It measures 5¾ inches tall. A sturdy play instrument that will encourage children to practice their telephone voices. Nasco, 901 Janesville Avenue, Fort Atkinson, WI 53538 ($7.95 + postage)

Note: Not all manufacturers and publishers will accept single orders for a product or book. Always write to them first, before sending money, to be sure that they will take your order. Make sure you've got the most recent price, including shipping and handling charges. If the company is in your state, then you may need to include state sales tax as well.

Basic Concepts

4

MONTESSORI AND PIAGET

The theories of Maria Montessori and Jean Piaget have formed the foundation for many theories about the learning of young children. For this reason, I felt that a brief introduction to them might be useful to you. You will also find a list of books detailing the practical applications of their work under General Guides for Parents about Learning Activities and Toys on page 63.

Maria Montessori, Italy's first woman physician, was the founder in the early 1900s of the Montessori Method which is now used in many preschools across the United States. Montessori believed that children have "sensitive periods" when they are especially ready to learn a particular skill. She noted that the sensitive period for language development is from birth to three years, the period for the love of order and rituals around two years of age, and the period for writing and reading sensitivity between four and a half and five and a half years old.

She developed what is called the "Prepared Environment," which is an elaborate system of manipulative materials carefully sequenced to teach concepts to a child step by step. Areas of learning in a Montessori school include practical skills such as pouring and sweeping; sensory skills such as materials to teach texture and temperature differentiation; mathematics materials to teach counting and number properties; and materials for teaching language, geography, and mathematics concepts.

Throughout Dr. Montessori's writings is a profound respect for the dignity of each child. The child is seen as an explorer; the teacher as a subtle guide, careful not to interfere with the learning processes and experimentation being done by the child. She felt that extrinsic reward and punishment systems were not necessary to the motivation of children but that materials which were carefully designed to challenge the child and allow him to teach himself were the key to motivation.

Whereas Montessori was concerned about the spirit of the child, Jean Piaget's concern is with the operation of the child's mind. Piaget calls himself a "genetic epistemologist," which in simple terms means one who studies how knowledge is acquired. A prolific theorist and writer, he has written over fifty books and monographs, mostly in French, and mostly quite difficult for the lay reader to decipher.

Piaget stresses that children are different from adults in their mode of thinking. He traces the learning of children through three phases: from birth to two years old when the child's learning is centered on the senses of touch and smell, from two to seven years old when the child develops the ability to use language and gains a better understanding of the world, and after the age of seven when he is able to deal with abstract concepts.

Piaget believes that knowledge is acquired through action and the relationships discovered between things. Concepts upon which the child works include classification, sorting, ordering of objects by their qualities, and the logic of measurement. For example, a child will be asked if the water in a tall slender container will fill a broad, flat container that actually holds the same amount of water. If the child responds "no" — believing somehow that water has been gained or lost in the transaction of pouring — then he has not mastered the concept of conservation, that the amount of liquid has remained the same regardless of changes in shape or position. The child then learns the concept through his own activity with the pitchers and the water.

Rather than picturing the young child as a miniature adult, both Montessori and Piaget have shown the child in a unique light. Children are pictured as actively seeking to learn and understand the world around them. Both put emphasis on the value of careful observation of the child rather than imposing upon them our preconceived notions about how they think and learn. Both recognize the natural, predictable stages that each child must go through in the learning process, which, if we understood them, could aid us in helping our young child to learn.

Mathematics for the Very Young
by Louise Ellison

A great many parents must be as tired as I am of the new schemes constantly being put forth to teach children academic skills at younger and younger ages — long before there are any lasting gains to be achieved by such instruction. Why, then, am I talking about math for preschoolers?

I'm not talking about learning to add or even learning to count. And I'm certainly not suggesting that busy young mothers add lesson-teaching to their already full schedules. What I am talking about is the special kind of teaching parents do all the time.

All during a preschooler's at-home years, you are actually teaching him dozens of mathematical concepts which will help him master arithmetical studies later on. Some of the first concepts a child masters are what we call "blob" concepts, vague notions about something. A few concepts are more precise — an understanding of sets; for example, classifications of foods, cars, animals. And in your youngster's everyday life many things happen to give him a most valuable mathematical idea — an awareness of precision. When you teach your child to say taller, when appropriate, rather than bigger, or shorter rather than smaller, you are training him in habits of accurate observation and precise description. Other mathematical skills — comparing, contrasting, and estimating quantities — are part of most preschoolers' everyday experiences which parents can enrich and strengthen.

One can see in parents' ordinary conversations with their younger children that they teach them a good deal about math. My neighbor Alice, mother of three-year-old Marko, is very good at this. I've noticed, for example, that instead of saying "Take some cookies if you like," she says "If you like, you may have three cookies. Do you want round ones or square ones?" She is teaching Marko to notice number and shape, and to learn (by modeling his speech after hers) the habit of precision.

One day when I was in our neighborhood park I heard a mother responding to her young daughter's question, "Aren't I bigger than Tommy?" by saying, "Let's find out. Are you taller than Tommy? Are you fatter?" And the children looked at each other, then stood back-to-back to be measured.

Learning math or learning anything isn't merely or mainly a matter of getting the correct answers. It's a matter of sensible and appropriate thinking, thinking that's in line with the facts. In that instance at my neighbor's house, Marko selected square cookies, five of them. "That's five," his mother said. "You may have only three." Marko looked earnestly at the cookies and put one back. Instead of correcting his second "wrong" move, his mother picked out what was right about it and praised that. "You knew you had to put something back, didn't you? That's good thinking. You have to take something away from five to make it three, don't you?" Then she added helpfully (to this little boy who couldn't yet count, but who had learned from hearing her use numbers in her ordinary talk that five was more than three), "Put one more back, and then you will have three." Marko's mother knew that accurate counting and accurate subtraction weren't the most important things at his age. What was important was that he had gained an understanding of the process necessary to solve his problem.

We tend to forget that math isn't the study of numbers, but the study of relations between different quantities of things, different sizes, different shapes. To be sure, numbers make up the bulk of mathematical language, and it's important for children to learn them. But math language also includes words that describe shapes, sizes, volumes, and patterns. Your child will learn math language as he learns any language — by hearing you use it and by using it himself.

There are learning possibilities for children in a multitude of their everyday activities. A child says, "Look, Mommy," pointing to two triangular blocks that he has placed together along their long sides. "I made a square!" "Wonderful," his mother says. "Two triangles that look like that make a square when you put them together, don't they?"

It doesn't matter whether or not you remember or want to use the term isosceles right triangle (in fact, it's better not to burden a young child with such a technical definition); the important thing is to call the child's attention to the particular shape of this kind of triangle.

The earliest evidence of the development of a mathematical concept that investigators have noted comes when a baby is about nine or ten months old. If you have a baby of this age, you might try confirming this for yourself. Put the baby in the middle of the floor and give him a container and three small objects to play with — say a bowl and three large spools. Let him play with them a while, picking the spools up, dropping them in the bowl, dumping them out, scattering, and retrieving them. Now stealthily remove one spool. He will probably pick up one spool, drop it in the bowl, pick up the second one and drop it in the bowl, and then he'll look around for the missing third spool. He may not look very long or even very obviously, but if you catch him turning his head or darting his eyes or hands about, you'll know that your baby realizes that he had more than two spools to play with. He has, in a sense, "counted" his spools and he knows something is missing.

Many three-year-old youngsters can't count meaningfully beyond three or four. That is, if you set one object before them and ask them how many there are, they can all say one correctly; they can also correctly name two, and usually three and four. But if you then set out five objects, some children will say "I don't know" and some will say "more."

Some may try to count the objects by touching each one and saying the numbers, but they'll usually demonstrate that they don't grasp the meaning of counting by touching some objects more than once and upping the total to six or seven, or by continuing to answer the question "How many are there," by a repetition of the count over and over again.

That's all right. A child of three needn't be able to count correctly. This isn't important; he'll learn soon enough. It's more important that he be well prepared for learning to count by comprehending the idea of different sizes, quantities, shapes.

Children learn a great deal of this all by themselves in their constant fooling around with things: their toying with quantities of spoons, pot covers, boxes, blocks; their manipulation of masses of sand, mud, water, clay; their fingering of the form of everything they touch, from the corners of a box to the hole in a doughnut.

Children seldom just look at things, as you know; they touch everything they can get hold of with their hands and their mouths — for the pleasure of the feeling, of course, and also because they have an innate desire to understand relationships. They can learn a good deal that way on their own, but they also need your help in verbalizing their learning and in correcting any misconceptions.

Let me give an example. Among a child's first words are "all gone" and "more," so we know that he has some blob concepts of "some," "none," and "all." I watched a two-year-old named Peter explore and refine these concepts in his kitchen one day. His mother had drawn a chair up to the sink and provided him with a pitcher and some spoons and cups

for water play, and he stood on the chair for a half hour enjoying himself. His mother's purpose had been only to let him release some energy in harmless splashing. She had tied a plastic apron around him and had a mop handy. But Peter managed to learn a great deal from his water play. Besides studying gravity and the principle of floating and sinking, Peter gave considerable attention to the ideas of "some," "all," "none," "more," "too-much," and "enough." For instance, he tried out "too much" by trying to pour a pitcherful of water into a cup, and he worked with "enough" by dipping seemingly endless spoonfuls of water into a cup, and cupfuls into the pitcher until each was full. When he tried out "all gone" by attempting to empty the sink cupful by cupful onto the floor, his mother introduced him to the principle of the drain, and cleaned him up for lunch.

Children work for years to distinguish bigger from taller, wider, higher, longer, thicker, broader, deeper, and even heavier and older. It's a long process, involving hundreds of physical operations and trials of words. A helpful adult can often offer assistance in the form of concrete examples. "The lizard is bigger than the turtle," Marko once said of his two pets. "He's longer," his mother agreed, "but which one is wider?"

A child sometimes needs help in understanding such near synonyms as he understands two-ness. As his eye and brain develop their discriminatory powers, he learns to recognize and reproduce three-ness, four-ness, and five-ness in the same way.

For some reason, adults get more excited by a child's use of number words than by his use of other mathematical terms such as "straight." They tend to think that only then has he started learning math. And that's when many youngsters are unnecessarily given a good deal of drill and "right-and-wrong" teaching. Such drill can be unfortunate if it bores and fatigues the child or if it makes him tense, and dampens his interest.

A four-year-old may be able to count up to a hundred, but the chances are that he would be hard put to count out a dollar's worth of pennies, or to tell you whether 63 is more or less than 41. In other words, rote-counting involves very little, if any, comprehension of what the symbols stand for.

There is, however, a simple, casual way to help a child learn numbers — a way which will help him learn the meaning of these symbols as well as their sounds. Let him hear and use these number-names as descriptive of qualities of groups, just as you helped him learn "straight" as the quality of a form, or "red" as the quality of a color. For example, say to him, "Here are five crayons," in the same way that you say, "Here is a blue crayon."

When he makes a mistake in naming or reproducing a requested number, correct it as you'd correct a color mistake. Don't say "No, that's not five; count them." Simply say, "That's four, not five," just as you'd say, "That's gray, not brown."

When your child learns numbers in the sense of recognizing small groups, he knows that five looks like more than four; and soon he will be able to grasp that 15 is more than eight because it looks like more. It's still the same principle of comparison rather than measurement; that's what is important for the child to understand.

There's no need for a preschooler to be able to count beyond ten or 20 unless, of course, he can invest higher numbers with real meaning. Can he tell that 11 sandwiches aren't enough for 15 people coming to a picnic? Does he know that 20 will be enough for each person to have one and that there will be some left over? If so, he's ready to learn higher numbers.

But all that he really needs before starting the formal study of math is an understanding of some of the concepts and terms which define quantities, magnitudes, and forms. He needs to recognize small quantities and be able to identify them, using the proper number terms. Such simple but important skills, plus an eager attitude toward learning, are the best preparation a child can have for formal math teaching in school.

COLORS

In the course of the day there are many opportunities for reinforcing color concepts. The best are those that involve eating and doing. The joy of a big orange, a red apple, a yellow banana, choosing crayons and paper to paint or draw. The love of color, which is probably the root of later artistic enjoyment, can be shared during walks in flower gardens, or while walking through the arches of trees on back roads in the spring and fall.

A more sophisticated project involves sorting shades of the same color. Paint samples from a hardware store can be mounted on a piece of poster board, for swatches on cards to be matched with those on the board.

SHAPES

The basic shapes that a preschool child can master are: circle, triangle, star, square, diamond, and if you want to add playing-card shapes — the club, heart, diamond, and spade.
● Cut out two of each shape from a grocery bag or construction paper, and have your child match one shape to the other as you tell him the names.
● Make a shape mobile from cardboard shapes covered with aluminum foil, fabric remnants, contact paper, or other bright materials.
● Make a shape felt board by gluing felt to a large piece of corrugated cardboard and cutting out felt shapes that will cling to the board. A cigar box with felt glued inside the lid makes an excellent individual felt board. The shapes can be kept inside the box.
● Make a playhouse out of a large appliance box (furniture and office equipment stores often throw away giant boxes). Cut out windows in different shapes — a circle, a triangle, and so forth.
● Buy a sorting toy. Some are square and have lids such as the one made by Creative Playthings, others are in interesting shapes, such as the Tupperware Shape-O and the mailbox by Playskool. Each toy challenges the child to place different shapes into appropriate holes.
● Make or buy a geoboard, a board with nail heads sticking up all over it with one-inch or half-inch distances between each nail. Your child then can use rubber bands to construct a triangle, a square, and other geometric shapes.
● A pegboard can also be used to demonstrate and practice shape-making. Masonite with holes in it can be bought in hardware stores. Pegs can be golf tees.

A Counting Game

Cut out the number cards and their objects. Can you match them again?

one 1		**six** 6	
two 2		**seven** 7	
three 3		**eight** 8	
four 4		**nine** 9	
five 5		**ten** 10	

Cut out the counting game on the other side.

CLASSIFICATION

Each day we're called on to sort our pennies from our dimes, to sort our dark clothes from our light ones, to choose between pepper and salt shakers. Early childhood educators are now putting emphasis on a child's learning of simple classification: sorting by shapes, sorting by colors, by sizes and, more complex, sorting by classes of things such as animals, insects, plants; or sorting into a series from largest to smallest, heaviest to lightest. There are a number of objects that are good for teaching a child sorting skills: colored beads, button collections, nuts, shells, playing cards. Boxes with compartments are easy to use, such as jewelry trays and egg cartons. You can make sorting games yourself by gluing pictures from catalogs: "things we wear," "things we cook with," "things that are red." Metal-rimmed labeling disks from office supply stores can also be made into sorters simply by giving them different colors or putting faces with different expressions on them with marking pens.

COUNTING

The first counting experience of most children is holding up fingers to the question "How old are you?" The most difficult first skill of counting is to assign a single number to each object. A child must learn to finger each object once and then to proceed to the next one. Often a child will count one object two or three times in the rush to move on. If objects are placed in a circle, he will count around and around without knowing where to stop.

Simple cards can be made up that have, say, one item, such as a dried bean, or a penny, with the large numeral one. A sorting game is interesting with the number two on one card and two beans on a card to match. Young children with perceptual problems benefit from being able to actually feel the numbers. Trace numbers with glue on heavy cardboard, pow-

der them with sand, and shake the extra sand off. Presto! sandpaper numbers to trace with fingers.

Daily routines can help a child to gain a firm concept of numbers. "Go and get two socks." "Please set the table for four people." In the case of table setting the child is being called on to count plates, knives, glasses, and so on, over and over again. Walnuts, dried beans, poker chips, crayons, any small objects can provide an opportunity for simple counting games, such as "I put down four . . . now you put down four." In the grocery store, you can ask your child to get you five apples, or two cans of soup, or give other simple counting responsibilities.

The concepts of first, second, third, and so forth, are more difficult for children to master. An easy way is to play a game: "I'm going up the stairs first, and you go second." Children can learn ranking by placing objects one in front of the other. "Which soldier is first in line? Which one is third?" Each opportunity that you take to reinforce the concept helps your child: "Your shirts are in the third drawer." "Let's read the third book together."

Simple card games are good for helping a child with number recognition, although the best route to clear number memory is using hands to draw numbers — in damp sand, with sticks in dirt, with large crayons, with marking pens, with chalk on a board, or on the sidewalk for hopscotch. A demonstration card showing the numbers one to ten is handy.

WEIGHTS

A child's first familiarity with weight is his own. It's fun to use the family scale, and to step on the penny scales that tell fortunes. A balance scale is an excellent tool for helping your child make comparisons between the weights of objects. "Which is heavier?" "Which is lighter?" A child can also help you make weighing decisions when you're grocery shopping. Talk to your child as you weigh produce: "This weighs three pounds. See the dial? It's pointing to three." Our preschoolers will soon be learning the metric system, and things will weigh milligrams, grams, and kilograms. If you're not familiar with metrics, your library can help you find some basic books to help you in making the transition to the newly emerging system of weights and measurements.

You can make a simple balancing scale from a wooden coat hanger equipped with paper cups on either side and suspended from a string. Another simple weighing device is a fulcrum made of a triangular wooden block and a wooden board. Aluminum pie pans or the bottom halves of plastic milk jugs can be fastened to each end of the board to keep objects from falling off while being balanced. Blocks, stones, and small toys are good to use in weighing experiments.

Water is a good substance for weighing because it's so heavy. Jugs can be filled to different levels. Your child can weigh them on your bathroom scales, or you can simply help him differentiate between "light," "lighter," "lightest"; "heavy," "heavier," "heaviest." "If we pour water out, will the jug be lighter or heavier?"

MEASURES

"How long was I when I was born?" Marcie asks. I pull out a measuring tape and demonstrate for her. She then measures everything in the room: shoes, books, her doll Lucina. She seems to feel very official in her measuring tasks.

Some measuring instruments: a fabric tape measure, a yardstick, a ruler, a collapsible wooden carpenter's measure, a small ruler with a sliding place keeper (available from notions departments in stores), thermometers, measuring cups and spoons. Whenever possible, try to get measures that have the metric equivalents

as well since children now will be dealing with both systems.

Behind a door you should begin keeping growth records, measuring off how tall your child has grown and noting height and the date in pencil. The measuring wall has a lot of meaning to young children. Daily measurement of the temperature outdoors in both Celsius and Fahrenheit can form the foundation for temperature concepts.

TIME OF DAY

All the other kids in my third-grade class could tell time. I was certainly embarrassed when the teacher singled me out for the privilege of telling her what time it was. Telling time is a skill you can start teaching your child early on.

Rudimentary time-telling begins with bedtime and mealtimes. If your child is to go to bed at eight o'clock, draw what eight o'clock looks like on a paper plate. Make a clock with a small hand and a large hand fastened with a brad from the dime store. Draw or paste on the numbers. Help your child learn important times by scheduling out the day on the paper clock. "This is the time that we eat lunch, twelve o'clock." "This is the time I come and pick you up at nursery school, eleven o'clock." "This is the time Daddy (or Mommy) comes home, six o'clock." Little children can't learn to recognize more than the hour and half-hour, but they're very proud when they can tell that it's five o'clock and time for dinner, or when they're able to determine bedtime ("Just five more minutes, Mommy!").

Old pocket watches, discarded wrist watches or broken digital clocks are good toys and familiarize children with time concepts. I remember the grandfather clock at my house as a child and its *dong-dong* ringing out the passing of time. Cuckoo clocks are a joy to little children, too. Why don't they ever work?

DAYS OF THE WEEK

To a child, each day is a year. That's what makes waiting for Dad or Mom to come back from a trip so difficult. If you know that your child is going to have to wait for something — a visit, a trip, or a holiday — a simple, large one-week calendar taped at child's eye level on the wall can help him visualize the passage of days. (It's not until much later that a child can conceive of weeks, months, and years.) Each evening, your child can cross off the day that has just passed. It's helpful, too, to explain that "Today is Monday, it's the day we go grocery shopping," or "Today is Saturday, we all stay home." *Yesterday* is a very difficult concept. Children use it interchangeably with *tomorrow* and sometimes invent words like *yestermorrow* for that peripheral, hard-to-imagine future or past. Here again, a parent can help a child learn the concept of *yesterday* by recalling a special event or a mild accident, such as falling down, to set the day apart.

MONEY

Children learn very quickly that they are living in a world in which money is important. A penny makes tiny toys come out of a machine. A quarter runs the horse in front of the store. Parents can begin early to teach their child how money works.

• Money can be exchanged for goods.

• Coins have different names and values.

• Although people would like to, they can't always buy the things that they see and want — the concept of "too expensive."

• Develop a child's "consumer" sense — learning to decide between small items that are nearly the same price.

• Money can be saved in an old-fashioned piggy bank.

• Counting skills are enhanced by playing with pennies or nickels (not in the mouth, please!).

Concepts like "more than," "less than," "too much," "too little" come from buying experiences.

• Money can be earned. Talk about why Mommy and Daddy go to work. What money is used for, how it provides a place to live and food to eat.

• Children can develop beginning concepts of sharing — buying something for others to use, too.

The best way to teach children about money is to give them the opportunity to play with it and deal with it. A toy cash register stimulates playing store. The concept of getting change back from a purchase is difficult for a young child to understand. Four-year-old Marcie, for instance, thought that people in stores gave money away, since they were always holding out their hands filled with change from the cash register.

Actual purchasing experiences are good. Your child can help you find the price on an item, take the money to the cashier, and receive the change, the receipt, and the item in a bag. If you ask a child whether he would like to have a nickel or a dime, he will choose the nickel, assuming that because it is bigger it is worth more. Simple homemade cards with actual coins glued or taped on them can help teach your child coin equivalents.

Are you an impulsive buyer? Are you very careful about money? Do you like to buy certain items and not others? Is money a cause of anxiety in your family? Your child will learn about money through your attitudes toward it. We can help our children gain wisdom in the use and saving of money by our own recycling and sharing of clothing and our care in keeping our lives simple and free from the burden of too many toys and too many objects. We can teach our children to share money by dropping coins into the Salvation Army buckets at Christmastime or making other donations. (The Salvation Army gives shoes to kids when no other agency will, so it's a particular favorite of mine!)

PICTURE BOOKS TO REINFORCE BASIC CONCEPTS

COLOR
The Adventures of the Three Colors
Talus Taylor and Annette Tison
William Collins & World Publishing Co., Inc., 2080 W. 117th Street, Cleveland, OH 44111 ($4.76)
Impressive translucent pages of color placed over text pages to show how many beautiful shades can be made from using only pink, blue, and yellow, Excellent for stimulating an interest in color.

Color Seems
Ilma Haskins
Vanguard Press, Inc., 424 Madison Avenue, New York, NY 10017 ($5.95)
A beautiful book to be enjoyed by all ages. Uses abstractions rather than pictures to demonstrate aspects of color, such as warmth and cold.

Green Says Go
Ed Emberley
Little, Brown and Co., 200 West Street, Waltham, MA 02154 ($4.95)
Excellent book for reviewing colors. Discusses what the colors represent.

Red Is for Apples
Beth Hoffman
Random House, Inc., 457 Hahn Road, Westminster, MD 21157 ($4.99)
Water-color illustrations and verse introduce colors and new vocabulary for young children. The book describes the colors in a young baby's environment.

What Is Color?
Alice Provenson and Martin Provenson
Golden Press, Western Publishing Co., Inc., 1220 Mound Avenue, Racine, WI 53404 ($4.95)
Excellent examples of each color with clever illustrations.

COUNTING
Circus Numbers
Rodney Peppe
Delacorte Press
Distributed by:
Dial Press, 1 Dag Hammarskjold Plaza, 245 E. 47th Street, New York, NY 10017 ($5.95)
The numbers one to ten, twenty, and one hundred are colorfully illustrated by presenting people, animals, and things found in the circus.

Counting Carnival
Feenie Ziner and Paul Galdone,
Coward, McCann & Geoghegan, Inc., 200 Madison Avenue, New York, NY 10016 ($4.29)
Numbers one to twelve are introduced through counting children. Differences between being alone and with others.

Numbers of Things
Helen Oxenbury
Franklin Watts, Inc., Subs. of Grolier, Inc., 845 Third Avenue, New York, NY 10022 ($4.90)
Beautiful illustrations. Left page clearly shows numerals and their names written out. The right page shows the correct number of objects.

1 is One
Tasha Tudor
Random House, Inc., 457 Hahn Road, Westminster, MD 21157 ($1.95, paperback)
Counting is illustrated through a variety of paintings of numbers and animals.

1, 2, 3 to the Zoo
Eric Carle
William Collins & World Publishing Co., Inc., 2080 W. 117th Street, Cleveland, OH 44111 ($5.95)
Presents the numbers one to ten by showing the number on the left-hand corner of the page and by bright illustrations of the corresponding number of objects.

Teddy Bears 1 to 10
Suzanna Gretz
Follett Publishing Company, 1010 W. Washington Boulevard, Chicago, IL 60607 ($5.95)
Imaginative counting book with a story. Illustrations are enchanting.

SHAPES
Are You Square?
Ethel Kessler and Leonard Kessler
Doubleday & Co., Inc., 501 Franklin Avenue, Garden City, NY 11530 ($3.95)
A good book for helping children think about shapes in general. Questions help to stimulate a child's thinking.

Shapes
John J. Reiss
Bradbury Press, Inc., 2 Overhill Road., Scarsdale, NY 10583 ($6.95)
Colorful illustrations emphasize the awareness of different shapes and how they appear in the environment rather than naming them.

Shapes and Things
Tana Hoban
Macmillan Publishing Co., Inc., Riverside, NJ 08075 ($5.95)
This book is excellent for representing a common object shown only as a shape. Letters are also shown as shapes on the endpapers of the book.

Things Are Alike and Different
Illa Podendorf
Children's Press, Inc., 1224 W. Van Buren Street, Chicago, IL 60607 ($5.25)
Adult guidance is needed, but a good supplement for talking about shapes, colors, sizes, and textures.

The Wing on a Flea: a Book about Shapes
Ed Emberley
Little, Brown and Co., 200 West Street, Waltham, MA 02154 ($5.50)
Triangle, rectangle, and square are introduced and the child is helped with noticing how these shapes appear around him.

GENERAL GUIDES FOR PARENTS ABOUT LEARNING ACTIVITIES AND TOYS

"Activities for Preschool-age Children"
Order from:
Extension Office of Information, The Ohio State University, 2120 Fyffe Road, Columbus, OH 43210 ($1.70)
Day-by-day cards of home learning activities for a preschooler. Each card suggests a myriad of things to do. Explorations with food, learning about sounds, matching and counting games, activities using the sense of touch and smell.

"Guidelines for Choosing Toys for Children"
Order from:
Public Action Coalition on Toys (PACT), 38 West Ninth Street, New York, NY 10011 ($1.00)
A brochure by an organization seeking to encourage the development of safe, quality toys for children and to discourage toys that injure, exploit, or limit a child's growth or safety. Gives safety tips in choosing toys and suggests questions that a parent should ask about each toy that is bought. Gives age guidelines.

Learning Through Play
Jean Marzollo and Janice Lloyd
Harper and Row, Pubs., Inc., Keystone Industrial Park, Scranton, PA 18512 ($2.95)
An excellent collection of learning activities using homemade materials. Feel-and-Say box, ring toss, how to construct a reading corner, riddles, homemade puzzles.

Let's Play and Learn
Harriett Hartman
Human Sciences Press, 72 Fifth Avenue, New York, NY 10011 ($5.95, paperback)
A collection of learning activities for parents and children. Includes ideas for teaching the basic shapes, numbers, discriminating sounds, cooking and exploring experiences.

Making Games and Equipment for Young Children
Claudia Fuhriman and Sally Miner
Order from:
The Cooperative Extension Service, Bulletin Room, UMC 48, Utah State University, Logan, UT 84322 (35¢)
An excellent collection of activities and games for young children from materials easily found. All together there are almost a hundred practical activity suggestions such as a lacing board for increasing children's matching skills.

Montessori on a Limited Budget: A Manual for the Amateur Craftsman
Elvira Farrow and Carol Hill
American Montessori Society, 150 Fifth Avenue, New York, NY 10011 ($8.00)
An excellent source for ideas on making your own learning materials. Includes a dressing frame, sorting materials, sewing frames, counters, cylinders, sandpaper letters and other Montessori materials. Stencils in the back of the book are for tracing numbers, letters, and basic shapes.

A Teacher's Guide to Cognitive Tasks for Preschool
Owen W. Cahoon
Brigham Young University Press, 205 University Press Building, Provo, UT 84602 ($2.95, paperback)
A series of simple tasks using household materials for teaching young children basic concepts such as weight, length, seriation, and sorting. Primarily written for teachers from a Piagetian point of view, but interesting for use by parents in exploring their children's concepts.

"Tell and Do for Children and Parents"
Columbus Public Schools
Order from:
Eileen Young, Ohio State Department of Education, 933 High Street, Worthington, OH 43085 (Free)
A book of cutout games that teach classification skills, size relationships, and word concepts for parents to use with their children. Along with each game are suggestions for further activities.

Thinking Is Child's Play
Evelyn Sharp
Avon Books, 959 Eighth Avenue, New York, NY 10019 ($1.75, paperback)
This book presents a simplified explanation of Piaget's basic concepts relating to quantity, classification, seriation, and conservation of number. Forty games are suggested using ordinary materials such as paper plates, napkins, spools, and playing cards. The games can be helpful in giving you the insight into the way children think as well as giving you activities to share together.

Workjobs for Parents: Activity Centered Learning in the Home
Mary Baratta-Lorton
Addison-Wesley Publishing Co., Inc., Jacob Way, Reading, MA 01867 ($3.95, paperback)
A superb collection of at-home activities to teach counting, sorting, color recognition, simple number concepts.

"Totline: The Activity Newsletter for Home or School"
Warren Publishing, P.O. Box 2253, Aderwood Manor, WA 98036 (six issues per year, $5.00)
A mimeographed eight-page idea newsletter that is filled with creative and challenging activities for young children. The October/November 1978 issue, for example, included sections on creative movements, coordination skills, holiday crafts, and recipes for nutritious snacks — over fifty innovative things to do with your youngster!

SCIENCE

"Science Equipment in the Elementary School"
A Cornell Science Leaflet
Order from:
Mailing Room, Building 7, Research Park, Cornell University, Ithaca, NY 14853 (25¢)
How to make science experiments, using straws, paper clips, cardboard tubes, and other simple objects.

Science Experiences for Elementary Schools
Charles K. Arey
Teachers College Press, Columbia University, 1234 Amsterdam Avenue, New York, NY 10027 ($1.95)
A whole series of simple experiments to explain scientific principles, such as magnetizing a bobby pin or making a paper snake to demonstrate rising heat.

Simple Science Experiments
Mary Yates Hall
Instructor Curriculum Materials, Instructor Park, Dansville, NY 14437 ($1.95)
A collection of experiences for young children accompanied by questions to stimulate their thinking.

The True Book of Metric Measurement
June Behrens
Children's Press, 1224 W. Van Buren Street, Chicago, IL 60607 ($6.60)
A clearly written book for young children explaining the reason for standard measurement. The concepts of meter and other metric measures are explained using objects in the child's surroundings.

Weighing and Balancing
Jane Jonas Srivastava
Thomas Y. Crowell Co., 666 Fifth Avenue, New York, NY 10003 ($1.45)
A picture book for kids that discusses balancing. How to make balances from a dowel and paper plates, coat hangers, and an egg carton. Talks about the value of weighing devices in everyday life such as in the doctor's office and the grocery store.

GUIDES TO CHILDREN'S MATHEMATICS AND COGNITIVE CONCEPTS

Creative Ideas for Teaching Exceptional Children
Avaril Wedemeyer and Joyce Cejka
Love Publishing Co., 6635 East Villanova Place, Denver, CO 80222 ($4.95, paperback)
The fact that the book has been written for children with learning problems makes it well suited to the learning activities of the normal young child. The emphasis is on providing the child sensory experiences to aid in his learning of concepts. The book is divided into number concepts, language activities, sensory motor activities.

Let's Play Math
Michael Holt and Zoltan Dienes
Walker and Co., 720 Fifth Avenue, New York, NY 10019 ($6.95)
A marvelous collection of sorting and counting games for preschoolers and early school-age children. Each activity is labeled by age. All of the games are make-it-yourself and use the child's own toys. The book has games to teach concepts such as sets, shapes, simple geometric problems, ordering, and time concepts.

"Logical-Mathematical Thinking and the Preschool Classroom"
Jeanne Walton
The Head Start Regional Resource and Training Center, 4321 Hartwick Road, Room L-220, College Park, MD 20740 (60¢)
Twelve activities for teaching young children to think in logical patterns. One activity suggested: letting the child match pairs and objects such as plastic cowboys and plastic horses, keys and key chains, cars and little boxes for garages. The child should be given more horses than cowboys, for example, to help him try to solve the problem of how many more will be needed.

TOYS TO TEACH CONCEPTS

MONEY AND COUNTING

Money Dominoes
Twenty-eight sturdy cards, each containing a picture of a coin as well as a money value. Money values and coins are to be matched. Younger children can try to match money picture to money picture.
Developmental Learning Materials, 7440 Natchez Avenue, Niles, IL 60648 ($3.00)

Photo Number Cards
The set consists of 3 x 4-inch cards with colorful photographs printed on heavy stock. Ten master cards depict the numerals one through ten. The remaining fifty cards show objects in different number groupings. Pictured are toy cars, boxes, balls, paper cups, and light bulbs. Helps children improve their counting and number recognition skills.
Developmental Learning Materials (DLM), 7440 Natchez Avenue, Niles, IL 60648 ($3.25)

Cash Register
A body constructed of steel and chrome with a plastic cash drawer that opens with a "ding" when the open bar is pressed. Eight keys to press showing different money values, each one raises a plastic flag in the window. Small supply of play money is included. Available in many toy stores.
abc School Supply, Box 13086, Atlanta, GA 30324 ($6.50 + $2.00 handling charge)

Art Darts
A safe dart game that utilizes Velcro (a unique cloth coupling device), enabling the darts to stick to the board on contact. No points or magnets. Set includes a 12-inch diameter brightly colored rigid dart board to reinforce number concepts and three colorful darts.
Kaplan School Supply Corp., 600 Jonestown Road, Winston-Salem, NC 27103 ($8.95 + $1.50 shipping and handling. Three extra dart balls, $2.50)

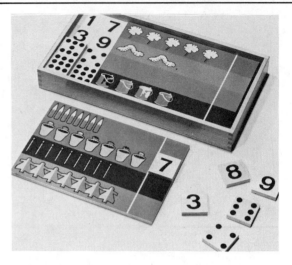

Counting Songs
Three 7-inch records, 33 rpm, with sing-along counting songs. The Merrill Staton Children's Voices sing favorites like "Nick-Nack Paddy Whack," "Over the Meadow," and "Green Bottles." Six songs in all. A guidebook is included that gives the words to the songs, the historical background, and suggests activities related to each song. Manufactured by the Judy Company.
Barclay School Supplies, 26 Warren Street, New York, NY 10007 ($6.95 + $2.00 postage and handling charge)

Counting Lotto
Imported from Holland, this beautifully painted wooden lotto set has four large working boards with numbers of objects beginning with one teacup and going up to nine matchsticks. Your child places a matching wooden tablet, with numbers on one side and with dots on the other, on the working board, to correspond to the objects.
Nienhuis Montessori U.S.A., 320 Pioneer Avenue, Mountain View, CA 94041 ($30.50)

Number Cubes
Twelve 3-inch cubes have dots like dice for playing counting games. Each number has its own color. You and your child can devise your own games using the cubes. Packed in a plastic carrying case. Dick Blick, P.O. Box 1261, Galesburg, IL 61401 (Twelve cubes for $7.80 + postage)

Giant Numbered Dice
A pair of bright yellow dice with indented numbers. The dice measure 3¾ inches in diameter. You can use them to practice recognizing numbers and later for adding numbers together.
Lakeshore Curriculum Materials, 8888 Venice Boulevard, Los Angeles, CA 90034 ($4.25 a pair + 15% shipping and handling. CA residents add 6 or 6½% sales tax)

Number Bingo
A number recognition game with large print numbers (one through twenty). Comes with tabs to place over the number when it's called. The leader draws a card with a large number printed on it and calls it out for the other players. The "winner" is the first one to cover all of the numbers on the card.

and can be fitted back into the base. Helps with beginning time concepts, number recognition, and shape recognition. From the catalog of an English mail-order firm now opening stores in the United States.
Mothercare-by-Mail, P.O. Box 228, Parsippany, NJ 07054 ($5.00)

Kaplan School Supply Corp., 600 Jonestown Road., Winston-Salem, NC 27103 ($4.50 + $1.50 shipping and handling)

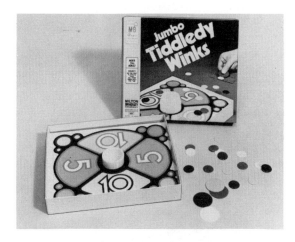

See Thru Clock
An old-fashioned alarm clock with an open face so that your child can watch the brightly colored movement wheels working. Can be used as a toy for moving the hands and listening to the alarm, or can be used as a real timekeeper.
Kaplan School Supply, 600 Jonestown Road, Winston-Salem, NC 27103 ($8.95 + $1.50 postage and handling)

Jumbo Tiddlywinks
A game for the whole family to play! The game includes brightly colored winks, four giant-sized and sixteen smaller-sized, four pieces of felt for cushioning, a scoring target with large, colored numbers to help with number concepts, and a glass cup. Suitable for ages five and up.
Kaplan School Supply, 600 Jonestown Road, Winston-Salem, NC 27103 ($1.80 + $1.50 shipping and handling)

Big Timer
Times from one to sixty minutes. Large numbers at five-minute intervals with one-minute markers. Easily read from across the room. Sits on a desk or counter or can be mounted on the wall. White plastic with a long-ringing bell. Measures 7 inches in diameter. A good way to learn time concepts.
Novo Educational Toy and Equipment Corp., 11 Park Place, New York, NY 10007 ($10.95. Minimum order $20.00)

MEASURING AND TELLING TIME

Fit-a-Block Clock
The minute and hour hands are synchronized to move like a real clock. Each number is removable

Compass

An inexpensive compass with a beveled glass top
and a highly polished brass case. Measures 45
millimeters in diameter. If you haven't seen an
Edmund catalog (free) you've missed an intriguing
collection of scientific and pseudo-scientific devices.
Edmund Scientific Co., 300 Edscorp Building,
Barrington, NJ 08007 (Cat. No. 40,470, $1.75)

Inexpensive Stopwatch

Has features for easy understanding by a child: red
sweep hand points out each second and quarter-
second on the dials, the black hand moves gradually
to the next minute in proportion to the second
hand. The watch sets to zero by turning the crown.
A lanyard for wearing around the neck is included.
Packed in an attractive, see-through plastic storage
case.
Selective Educational Equipment (see), Inc., 3
Bridge Street, Newton, MA 02195 ($10.50 + $1.25
postage and insurance)

Jumbo Dial Thermometer

A large thermometer with bold ¾-inch numerals
that make it easy to read. Measures 12 inches in
diameter. Gives the temperature from −30° to 120°
Fahrenheit with corresponding Celsius range.
Edmund Scientific Co., 300 Edscorp Building,
Barrington, NJ 08007 ($9.95)

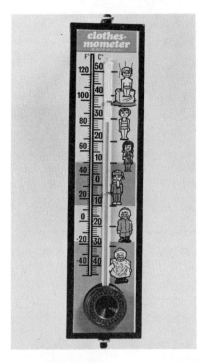

Clothes Mometer

Now preschoolers can tell what to wear in the
morning! The Clothes Mometer is color coded from
cold blue to warm yellow. It has both Fahrenheit
and Celsius readings and shows the appropriate
clothing for each temperature area.
Skillbuilder Playthings, Ltd., 1725 DeSales St.,
N.W., Suite 312, Washington, DC 20036 ($3.50)

LENSES

Investigating Optics Kit

One of several "Science in a Shoebox" kits mentioned in this book, this kit includes a convex lens, a concave lens, and cardboard holders that enable children to make a telescope, a camera, or other lens combinations. Instructions are included. From a catalog of educational science equipment. Eduquip-McAllister Corp., 1085 Commonwealth Avenue, Brighton, MA 02215 ($6.95 + 20% postage and handling)

Telescope

A portable telescope that magnifies from fifteen to forty times the normal image size. The telescope is constructed with quality coated optics and has three polished chrome draw tubes that telescope into a fourth section with a black leatherette finish. Length, 6¾ inches closed, 10¾ inches extended. Pigskin leather case. From a giant catalog of scientific educational equipment. Central Scientific Co., Inc., 2600 S. Kostner Avenue, Chicago, IL 60623 ($27.00 plus postage)

Elementary Microscope

Rugged, all-plastic microscope. It's only 5 x 5 x 7.5 centimeters high, but it has a 50-power compound lens and accepts standard slides. The lens and stage, as one piece, slide up and off the arm and this one small piece can be used as a field microscope or a microprojector when held in front of a pocket flashlight or any projected light source. Selective Educational Equipment (see), Inc., 3 Bridge Street, Newton, MA 02195 ($4.00 + $1.25 postage and insurance)

Plastic Fresnel Lens

A flexible wide-angle lens that mounts with a clear adhesive on a window or mirror. Can be used to play optical tricks by bending the lens. It will turn any limited view into a wide-angle panoramic scene. Brochure, "Fun with Fresnel Lenses," included. Edmund Scientific Co., 300 Edscorp Building, Barrington, NJ 08007 (Cat. No. 71,542, $5.50 + $1.00 postage and handling)

CONCEPTS OF PHYSICAL SCIENCE

Giant Gyroscope
Did you have one when you were a child? This giant, all-metal gyroscope performs tricks of motion on strings or on the point of a pencil. Comes with instructions. Measurements: 4⅝ inches in diameter, 7½ inches high.
Nasco, 901 Janesville Avenue, Fort Atkinson, WI 53538 ($3.55 + postage)

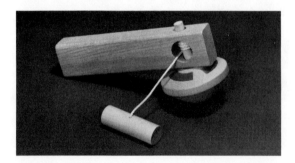

Spindle Top
Designed for Creative Playthings, this top has a timeless, classical design that makes it almost foolproof. The handle and cord give a sure, fast, long-lasting spin. Excellent for improving coordination, it's fascinating time after time. Made of natural wood with a 5½-inch handle.
abc School Supply, Inc., P.O. Box 13086, Atlanta, GA 30324 ($1.95 + $2.00 handling and service charge for orders under $15.00)

Cosmobile
Here is the entire solar system in the form of a colorful, decorative mobile that teaches basic astronomy as it adds life, color, and motion to a child's room. The planets rotate in their orbits around the sun and seemingly float in space. Sun and planets have their respective colors and markings and are all appropriately scaled, not only in size but also in distance. Planetary supports are copper-plated steel rods only ⅟₁₆-inch thick, the longest extending 3 feet.
Central Scientific Co., Inc., 2600 South Kostner Avenue, Chicago, IL 60623 ($27.00)

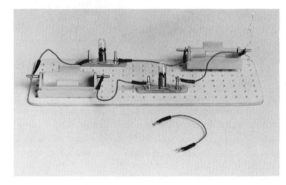

Circuit Kit
Youngsters will enjoy connecting batteries, wires, and bulbs in various combinations to try to make bulbs light up. Almost like a puzzle, the batteries and bulbs and wires can be connected in a multitude of different ways. Some arrangements work and some don't — which leads to a discovery of basic principles. Real batteries, wires, and bulbs are supplied. A "Science in a Shoebox" kit.
Eduquip-McAllister Corp., 1085 Commonwealth Avenue, Brighton, MA 02215 ($7.50 + 20% postage and handling)

WEIGHTS

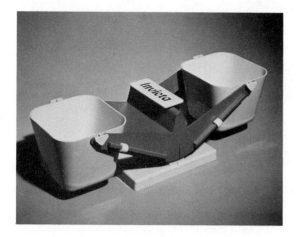

Rocker Scale
Tubs are designed to adjust themselves as they swing on independent pivots. The pivots insure that the mass being studied has its center of gravity directly below the pivot point to give a true reading. Tubs can be removed from the arms. Four compensators can rectify the initial imbalance. Plastic. Measurements: 6 inches wide x 12¾ inches long x 4½ inches tall. Catalog of educational games and toys ($1.00).
Novo Educational Toy and Equipment Corp., 11 Park Place, New York, NY 10007 ($10.45 + postage. $20.00 minimum order required)

Seesaw Balance Beam and Weights
Five different colored weights are provided. Each is the same size, and differs only in weight. Only after experimentation can equal weights be discovered. Plastic beam and stand are included along with vials of beads that are the same size but different weights. A "Science in a Shoebox" kit.
Eduquip-McAllister Corp., 1085 Commonwealth Avenue, Brighton, MA 02215 ($5.50 + 20% postage and handling)

SORTING AND MATHEMATICAL CONCEPTS

Plastic Scales and Weights
A simple plastic scale for weighing and balancing experiments. The stackable plastic weights come in a set of forty with twenty each of 5 gram and 10 gram weights.
School Days Equipment Co., 973 N. Main Street, Los Angeles, CA 90012 (Scales, Cat. No. IA 272, $10.50; Weights, Cat. No. IA 1271, $4.50 + postage. $10.00 minimum order required)

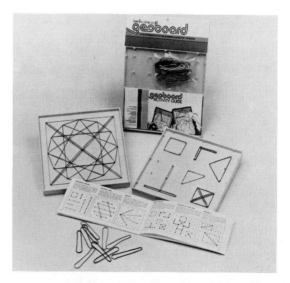

Geoboard Kit
With this simple, dynamic play tool and a few colored rubber bands any child and parent can have fun exploring geometry! The Geoboard — a 7¼-inch-square plastic board with pegs — has two faces: one with a twenty-five-peg square lattice, the other with a seventeen-peg circular lattice. By

stretching the rubber bands that come with the kit anyone can create hundreds of fascinating shapes and designs. A thirty-two-page illustrated booklet, the "Geoboard Activity Guide," is included. Order from:
Learning Games, Inc., 34 South Broadway, White Plains, NY 10601 ($3.00 + 41¢ postage and handling)

Geometric Template

A template of geometric forms for tracing made from unbreakable, transparent Lexan plastic with the five basic shapes cut out. The template measures 11¾ x 7¾ inches and is packaged in a poly bag. The transparency of the template provides a see-through quality so that a child can create more complex formations by combining one shape with another. From a small brochure of learning materials also includes hand puppets and a wooden domino set.
Pumpkinseed, Coldwater Tavern Road, Nassau, NY 12123 ($2.50 + $1.00 shipping and handling)

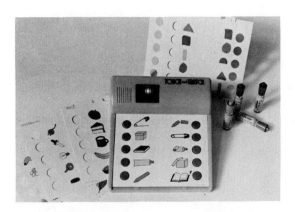

Touch and Match

An ingenious yet simple teaching machine for preschoolers. Children are intrigued by the buttons you press to match colors, shapes, or sizes. Match them correctly and the light flashes, the buzzer sounds. Comes with eight different programs plus two blank cards to create additional exercises. Operates on two C batteries (not included). From the "Toys that Teach" catalog. Prices subject to change.
Childcraft Education Corp., 20 Kilmer Road, Edison, NJ 08817 ($7.99 + $1.95 shipping and handling)

Classification Play Tray

A classification game to encourage concepts of matching, naming, and labeling, this set has color photographs of children's everyday clothes for a variety of classification possibilities: shoes, gloves, dresses. Dress-up clothes versus rainy day clothes. Cards come packaged with one plastic tray and a parent's guide. Similar trays also available with currency and foods. Manufactured by the Judy Company.
Barclay School Supplies, 26 Warren Street, New York, NY 10007 ($14.95 + a $2.00 charge for postage and handling for orders under $15.00)

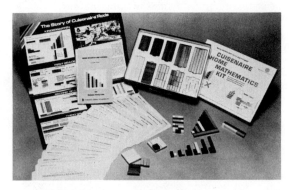

Cuisenaire Home Mathematics Kit

An excellent set of small colored rods for teaching young children mathematical relationships. The kit includes 155 Cuisenaire colored rods — the white rod is the unit, and all other colors are multiples of that unit — as well as a guidebook for parents. Fifty activity cards include a section for preschoolers. Because of the carefully planned relationship of the rods to one another, children learn simply from manipulating the rods. For the kit to be truly educational, parents are urged to act as active participants, interpreters, and programmers for setting up problems for the child to tackle while play with the rods is in progress. Age range: three to fourteen years.
Learning Games, Inc., 34 S. Broadway, White Plains, NY 10601 ($15.95 + $1.71 shipping charge)

Unifix Cubes

Unifix interlocking cubes come in ten assorted colors. Each cube is ½ inch. There are a number of accessories to go with the cubes to make them a valuable aid in learning number and sorting concepts. Write for the Hammett Catalog of educational equipment and supplies for more information.

J. L. Hammett Co., 2393 Vaux Hall Road, Union, NJ 07083 (One hundred cubes, $5.75; One to Ten Stair, $2.75; Number Indicators, $5.60; Underlay Cards, $4.55; Operational Grid, $2.90. Processing and delivery fee of $2.00 for orders under $25.00)

Sorting and Order Kit
A jumbo assortment of items to sort by shape, by color, by size. The set includes: two hundred plastic beads, two hundred pegs, one hundred unit tablets, one hundred one-half unit tablets, two hundred and fifty ⅝-inch round plastic counters, two hundred and fifty ⅞-inch round plastic counters, seventy-two grouping and setting shapes, three counting and sorting trays for use with the items.
School Days, 973 N. Main Street, Los Angeles, CA 90012 ($30.75 plus shipping)

Stringing Beads
The bead set has eighty wooden beads — forty are round and forty are cubes in red, blue, green, and yellow. They come in a drawstring bag with six stringing laces and a teacher's guide. Manufactured by the Judy Company.
Barclay School Supplies, 26 Warren Street, New York, NY 10007 (Stringing beads, $9.95 per set. Postage and handing $2.00 for orders under $15.00, or 15% of orders over $15.00)

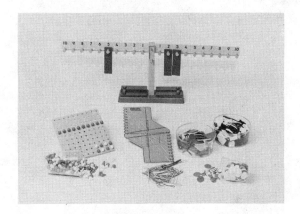

Integers Kit
This comprehensive kit has many uses in helping children discover basic mathematical concepts. Contents: Math balance with twenty weights, an integers board with twenty work cards, a plastic pegboard with one hundred holes and one hundred plastic red and white pegs, two hundred and fifty round plastic counters in assorted colors, one hundred tiles in five colors, one hundred and twenty-five half-sized tiles in five colors, and a basic shapes set. There are one hundred and ninety-two pieces in all. Manual included.
School Days, 973 N. Main Street, Los Angeles, CA 90012 ($35.45)

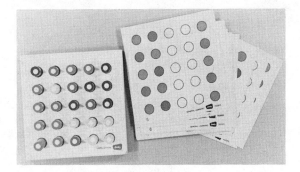

Mini Peg Board and Patterns
The Mini Peg Board has 25 holes for pegs. It measures 7¾ inches square and has wooden pegs in red, yellow, blue, and green. A guidebook is included. Helps children learn color discrimination and placement. Manufactured by the Judy Company.
Barclay School Supplies, 26 Warren Street, New York, NY 10007 (Board, $10.90, see ordering instructions above)

Note: Not all manufacturers and publishers will accept single orders for a product or book. Always write to them first, before sending money, to be sure that they will take your order. Make sure you've got the most recent price, including shipping and handling charges. If the company is in your state, then you may need to include state sales tax as well.

Cooking and Nutrition

5

A young child's attitudes toward food are shaped during the preschool years by her parents and family. All of us have a storehouse of memories — like my memory of my grandfather giving me a giant stalk of fragrant sugar cane to chew on, or discovering honeycomb chewing gum, making snow cream for the first time, or walking into our kitchen and smelling the exquisite aroma of something cooking on the stove. I was a "picky" eater and so I also have bad memories of battles at the dinner table about what I would or wouldn't eat.

It's so tempting to try to cajole a child into eating, especially if you've put a lot of time into fixing a meal. I think it's best in the long run not to pay too much attention to a child's eating — "You didn't eat carrots!" "You can't have any of this until you finish that." Accept the child's word that he is hungry or not hungry. In the meantime, try to have only nutritious foods as between-meal snacks so that whenever or whatever the child eats will be to her body's best advantage.

NUTRITIOUS SNACKS

Broccoli florets
Cabbage wedges
Carrot sticks
Cauliflower florets
Celery sticks, plain or spread with peanut butter, cream cheese (with a line of raisins makes "ants on a log"), or grated sharp cheese moistened with mayonnaise
Cucumber slices
Green pepper rings or strips
Raw sweet-potato sticks
Whole cherry tomatoes
Hard-boiled eggs
Tuna chunks
Apples, cut in wedges or cored and stuffed with peanut butter
Tangerines, oranges
Bananas
Berries and cherries
Peaches
Fresh pineapple chunks
Pieces of fresh coconut
Nuts
Raisins (in small boxes are a special treat)
Fruit juices, 100 percent fruit juices rather than "drinks," "nectars," or "punches." Examples: apple juice, grape juice, orange juice, pineapple juice, tomato juice, V-8 juice. An acceptable cola substitute can be made from prune juice and soda water.
Junket custard
Meat cubes
Strips of luncheon meat
Sardines
Liverwurst
Whole-grain bread with butter
Crackers with cheese or peanut butter
Toast, plain or with peanut butter
Cheese wedges
Slices of apples and cheese together

Show respect and love for your child when you are cooking and serving foods.

• Let her help you do the grocery shopping and push the cart sometimes. Help her to learn about fruits and vegetables and to read the labels on cans and boxes.

• Let her help you put foods away. Give her a chance to help you fix meals — to spread her own sandwiches, to pour her own juice.

• Try not to resent a child's dependency but help the child to become independent as quickly as she can.

• Be gentle with a child who breaks a glass or spills things. After all, everyone does sometimes.

• Teach your child to like and eat fresh fruits, vegetables, and healthful things by providing them as snacks instead of candy, soda pop, or junk foods.

- Make mealtimes quiet and relaxing — don't fight, yell, or hold tense adult discussions. Make eating enjoyable.
- Help your child learn to thank the cook as a way of recognizing that someone has done something for her.
- Give your child jobs to do like setting and clearing the table so she feels like a responsible member of the family.

LEARNING IN THE KITCHEN

The kitchen is the best learning laboratory in your house! Where else can you and your child practice science, math, language, and art right from the equipment and materials provided there?

- Counting: nuts, dried beans, rice grains, plates, forks, glasses, and other implements for setting the table.
- Ordering: largest boxes and cans to smallest. Which is the tallest? Which is the shortest? Which holds the most, the least?
- Science: What is a liquid? What is a solid? Make Jell-O to experience a liquid turning into a solid. Make ice sticks from fruit juices, melt ice cubes. Pour liquid from one measuring cup into another.
- Vocabulary: Learn the meaning of words like: boil, chop, grind, tear, mash, stir, sift, mix, shake, measure, slice, bake, fry.
- Following directions: "the drawer on the left," "stir until smooth," "wait to put this in until I tell you."
- Aesthetics: Appreciate the exquisite coloring of fruits and vegetables — the inside of a pumpkin, the deep purple of eggplant. Mix colors in the baking process. Learn to appreciate textures and shapes.

BEGINNING DISHWASHING

Dishwashing is a learned skill. Many of the exasperating mistakes that young children make — like dropping a glass into the sink so that it breaks, or putting clean dishes back into soapy water — can be easily corrected with careful directions. One good way to start is to cover an area of the kitchen floor with towels and allow the child to work on the floor where she doesn't have to contend with balancing on a chair. Two dishpans can be used, one with warm soapy water and one with warm, rinse water. Rather than expecting your child to do all the dishes at once, it's better to give her a single task, such as washing the silverware. Demonstrate exactly what you want her to do and then leave her to complete the task.

There has to be some appreciation for the meandering quality of a child's work — that she may become distracted or bored along the way. If so, then perhaps it's too early in her maturity to expect this task from her, or perhaps a gentle redirecting will help her get started again. On another evening, offer the same setting, but this time let her do the glasses — explaining that you want her to clean both the outside and the inside. In our house it's a game with us to call "quality control" on someone's dish. The dish has to be recycled, but no one is accused or belittled because of a food spot. You should offer ample praise for the work that's done. Comment on the articles themselves: "My, that's a really clean glass. It sparkles!" Tell someone else about what your child is doing in her presence: "Jenny is helping me wash the forks tonight." In time, your child can build up to doing more of the work using the regular sink.

One note of importance: It's best to take a "how'd you like to help me with *my* project?" attitude in sharing chores with your small child. That way, she can gracefully slip out if it becomes too difficult, tiring, or boring without your feeling that she is being irresponsible. To avoid great frustration explain carefully that you want her to do just as you tell her, and to wait until you give the go-ahead before beginning. Have all the needed materials or ingredients gathered together before starting so that you can keep a close eye on the proceedings.

USING THE STOVE

Some safety points. The most dangerous times for a child to be around the stove are:

● When you are deep-frying with hot grease or boiling water. You should wear close fitting clothing so that your sleeves won't catch the handle of a pan knocking it over. Pan handles should be turned to the back of the stove. Children should be warned to keep away.

● When you are sleeping late and your child tries to cook her own breakfast. Hair and pajamas are the first things to ignite and they burst into flame quickly. It's important to warn your child at the outset that she is not *ever* to use the stove without your being present.

● Another danger of using the stove is that it is at the wrong height for children. They cannot see what is being done above them (Try stooping down to your child's height and you'll see immediately why your child asks you so frequently what you are doing and if she can see.) They then must compensate by dragging over a chair to stand on — and chairs have very limited space on which to stand, so it's easy to miscalculate in a moment and to come crashing to the floor. There's no good answer at the present for helping a child to work safely at a higher level. (I picture a sturdy, flat-surfaced bench that has a railing around three sides so that a youngster is safely enclosed while working. Perhaps, if you come up with a good design you will send it to me for the next edition of this book.)

Are your heat control knobs in the front or the back of the stove? If they're in the front, as they are on gas ranges, then using the knobs and learning how to work them is the first step. It's important to demonstrate to a child exactly what part of the stove gets hot and what part doesn't. If they're in the back then it should always be an adult's responsibility to operate them, since it's not safe for a child to reach over burners.

Next, she must learn about potholders. It's good to have a dry run practicing picking up and putting down pots with a potholder, all the while explaining how potholders keep us from burning our hands on hot handles. Allow your child to have some time for imaginary play with potholders and heavy, regular pans, spatulas, and Play-Doh in order to get introduced to the real thing.

Scrambled eggs are a good first cooking lesson. Break the eggs into a large measuring cup. Let your child try doing this herself. (It's your job to fish out the extra bits of shell that get in the cup by mistake.) Then let her beat the eggs, melt the butter in the pan, pour in the eggs, and stir them slowly with a big wooden spoon until they're done. You serve the plates. If your child balks at scrambled eggs, make a sandwich of them with mayonnaise or try an egg in a hole. Crack raw eggs into the cutout centers of buttered bread in a fry pan.

It's good at this point to introduce rules about operating other kitchen appliances — no plugging and unplugging allowed, no putting knives in the toaster, no turning on the blender except when told. Perhaps these sound needlessly authoritarian, but I'm convinced that certain ground rules must be set for the maximum safety of the young child.

USING A KNIFE

When Marcie's play-school teacher allowed Arata, a five-year-old Japanese child, to cut vegetables for the stew the class was making, he chopped the vegetables neatly into small pieces and then scraped them off the chopping board into the stew pot. Obviously, Arata's mom or dad had taught him how to work with a knife.

Believe it or not, the most important rule of working with a knife is that it must be sharp. Most kitchen cutting injuries take place when a person is attempting to use too much pressure to make a knife work. There are other simple rules to knife use that need to be pointed out:

● The child must learn to differentiate the dull side of the knife from the sharp side.

• The knife must be small enough that she can balance it easily. Ideally, it should have a rounded tip, rather than a pointed one.
• The work surface should be at about the height of the child's elbows. No standing on chairs — since an impulsive jump or loss of balance could be dangerous.
• The child must learn to place her free hand either with her palm on top of the knife to press it down, or to the side of the vegetable being cut, but *never* under the blades of the knife.

The first knife skill to be learned is spreading: soft butter, peanut butter, jelly, mayonnaise, and sandwich spreads. Next comes cutting up soft foods, pressing down or using a sawing motion, whichever is more comfortable

Here is a recipe for a practicing cutter:

Cream of Mushroom Soup
1½ cups fresh mushrooms, sliced
1 onion
3 tablespoons butter
3 tablespoons flour
½ teaspoon salt
⅛ teaspoon pepper
1 quart milk
2 chicken bouillon cubes
1 tablespoon ketchup
½ teaspoon Worcestershire sauce

1. Let your child cut up the mushrooms. Stems are all right, too, unless they seem too fibrous.
2. Cut the onion into 1-inch slices and let your child cut them into smaller pieces. Have her slice off the three tablespoons of butter for you.
3. Melt the butter in a saucepan and gently cook the mushrooms and onions until the onions are transparent. (Your child can help if you feel secure about her being close to the stove. Turn the pot handle to the back and supervise constantly.)
4. Put in the flour, salt, and pepper and stir until it becomes a paste.
5. Gradually pour in the milk, while stirring, then add bouillon cubes, ketchup, and Worcestershire sauce.
6. Cook over medium heat until thick, stirring constantly with a long-handled wooden spoon. Five to ten minutes is all it takes! Serve immediately.

Kitchen Safety Rules for Preschoolers:
• Always wash your hands before preparing food.
• Always let grownups turn on the stove.
• Don't try to plug or unplug appliances.
• Never put knives or other metal objects in the toaster in order to get the toast out.
• Call a grownup when you break a glass. Do not ever touch broken glass yourself.
• Be sure no appliance cords are hanging down, since the appliances might get pulled over.
• Keep away from the stove when your mom or dad is cooking hot things.

COOKBOOKS FOR CHILDREN AND THEIR GROWNUPS

The Blue Goose Buying Guide for Fresh Fruits, Vegetables, Herbs and Nuts
Educational Department, Blue Goose, Inc., P.O. Box 46, Fullerton, CA 92632 ($2.00)
This handy book for grownups has color photographs of every imaginable fruit or vegetable in the United States (including cherimoyas, white sapotes, and things I've never heard of!). Each vegetable, fruit, or herb has a description, a lengthy discussion of its history, ways to tell whether the item is ripe and fresh, the seasons when it's available. A consumer's guide par excellence, it can be used as a sourcebook for both you and your child to learn about the foods we eat.

How to Open a Coconut
"The person who buys a coconut for the first time wants to know how to get at the meat and milk. There are three soft spots at the top of the shell. Pierce these with an ice pick, or similar sharp instrument, drain the milk; then tap all over with a hammer until the hard shell cracks and falls off. Another way to break off the shell is to heat the coconut in the oven for 30 minutes at 350 degrees F . . . Good quality coconuts are those which are heavy for their size and in which milk sloshes around. Coconuts without milk are spoiled. Nuts with moldy or "wet eyes" are unsound.

Cool Cooking for Kids, Recipes and Nutrition for Preschoolers
Pat McClenahan and Ida Jaqua
Fearon Publishers, Inc., 6 Davis Drive, Belmont, CA 94002 ($5.50)
Although the book is primarily for working with groups of children, the hints and recipes are excellent for use by parents, too, particularly those participating in day-care cooperatives. Ideas for experiments in measuring, teaching nutrition, dealing with a contrary eater. Recipes are divided by those that need a heat source and those that do not.

Aggression Cookies
1 cup flour
1 cup brown sugar
1 teaspoon baking powder
1 cup softened margarine
2 cups oatmeal
Preheat the oven to 350 degrees. Dump all ingredients into the bowl. Mix well with your hands, and form into 1-inch balls. Place on greased cookie sheet about 2 inches apart. Have each child make a fist, dip it into the flour can and "pound" his cookie to flatten it. Bake 10 to 12 minutes.

In this experience, the doing is much more important than the end result. The children may even want to personalize their cookies with faces or initials before pounding.

Creative Food Experiences for Children
Mary T. Goodwin and Gerry Pollen
Center for Science in the Public Interest, 1779 Church Street, Washington, DC 20036 ($4.00)
A most thoughtful book for teachers of young children that guides you in helping your child understand the basics of nutrition. How to make applesauce, buttermilk, butter. Foods from other countries. Delicious, simple recipes for salads, desserts, and main dishes. You'll love this book!

Let's Make Peanut Butter
Objective: The children will observe the changes that occur when peanuts are ground into butter.
Materials: peanuts (roasted in shells)

corn oil	spoon
salt, bread or celery	spreader
blender	small plate
bowl	

Procedure:
1. Discuss favorite ways of eating peanut butter.
2. Have the children remove the peanuts from the shells; remove the brown skins. Observe shell size, shape and texture. Compare the shell with the peanut. What part of the plant is the peanut?
3. Put about 1–1½ tablespoons of oil in the blender. Gradually add about one cup of peanuts and sprinkle lightly with salt. Observe changes as the peanuts are crushed and blended into a smooth texture.
4. Serve on bread or stuff the peanut butter into celery ribs.
5. If a blender is not available, you may use a food grinder. The texture of the peanut butter will be coarse and crunchy.

Feed Me I'm Yours
Vicki Lansky
Bantam Books, Inc., 414 E. Golf Road, Des Plaines, IL 60016 ($1.95 + 35¢ postage and handling)
A cookbook for parents of babies and preschoolers with sandwich-filler ideas, simple dinner recipes that are appealing to little ones, nutritious cookie recipes, and ideas for play in the kitchen. My favorite part of the book is the birthday party suggestions carefully selected by age.

Cereal Balls
1 cup ground-in-a-blender cereal (shredded wheat, granola, wheat germ, etc.)
1 tablespoon honey
1 tablespoon peanut butter (optional)
milk — as much as needed
After grinding cereal, add honey, peanut butter, and blend. Add as much milk as necessary so that mixture can be rolled into balls. Refrigerate in a covered container.
Additional variations:
1. Roll into logs and roll these in coconut or wheat germ.
2. When traveling, add powdered milk and brown sugar (eliminating the peanut butter) instead of the liquid milk and the honey, and store in a plastic bag. When needed, just add water for preparation as a breakfast food or snack.

The Good for Me Cookbook

Karen B. Croft
R & E Research Associates, Pubs., 4843 Mission
Street, San Francisco, CA 94112 ($1.95, paperback)
An excellent cookbook for young children using
healthful ingredients. Includes foods from other
countries: spaetzle noodles, Japanese shusi, German
muelsi cereal as well as American gingerbread,
meatloaf, and vegetable soup.

Energy Chews

Melt ½ cup butter. Add 1½ cups honey, 4 tablespoons carob powder, 1 cup peeled, grated apple, ¼
teaspoon salt, and ½ teaspoon cinnamon. Boil for
one minute. Remove from heat and add 3 cups rolled
oats, 1 cup chopped nuts or grated coconut, and 1
teaspoon vanilla. Blend well. Drop onto an oiled
cookie sheet, or waxed paper. Let cool and serve.

Kids Are Natural Cooks

Parent's Nursery School
Houghton Mifflin Company, Two Park Street,
Boston, MA 02107 ($6.95)
A superb sourcebook for guiding your child's
cooking experiences. The recipes are simple and use
only nutritious ingredients, including whole wheat
flour, honey, and yoghurt. How to cook a pumpkin,
make pumpkin pie, roast the seeds and make
pumpkin bread. Recipes for granola, butter,
yoghurt, ice cream, and fruit leather, to name only a
few.

Gingerbread People

You don't need a cookie cutter to make these gingerbread boys or girls. You just shape them with your
hands — as big or as small as you like. This recipe
will make a dozen fairly large people (about 8 inches
tall) or more smaller cookies.

Preheat oven to 350°. Pour 1 cup molasses into a
small pan. Heat it on the stove till it bubbles around
the edge. Meanwhile, butter 2 or 3 cookie sheets.
Pour the hot molasses into a large mixing bowl. Cut
up into little pieces 6 tablespoons butter. Put the
butter into the hot molasses and stir it around till it's
all melted. Then add:
2 tablespoons water
½ cup brown sugar
1 teaspoon cinnamon
½ teaspoon nutmeg
½ teaspoon cloves
1 teaspoon ginger
½ teaspoon salt
½ teaspoon baking soda
Stir until all the dry things are dissolved. Then add:
3 cups whole-wheat flour
½ cup powdered milk
Stir until it's all mixed together into a good dough.
Add a bit more flour if it's too sticky.

Now take a bowl of water. Dip your hands in the
water so the dough doesn't stick to you. Shape the
gingerbread people like this: roll a small ball for the
head and a larger ball for the body, 2 little snakes for
arms and 2 bigger snakes for legs. Put them all together on the cookie sheet to make a person, and pat

them out flat. (Of course, you can also make other
things besides people — animals, houses, cars, etc.)

Decorate your cookies with raisins. Bake them
about 5 minutes, 'til they're turning darker brown
around the edges. Let them cool a minute or two on
the cookie sheets, then take them off with a spatula
to finish cooling.

Growing Food — Growing Up — A Child's Natural Food Book

Esther Lewin and Birdina Lewin
The Ward Ritchie Press, 474 S. Arroyo Parkway,
Pasadena, CA 91105 ($2.95)
A well-illustrated cookbook and nutrition book for
young children. Very simply stated with
explanations for growing sprouts, making crunchy
granola, bran muffins, peanut butter, carob candy.

Let's Make Cottage Cheese

1 quart non-fat milk
1 teaspoon store-bought cottage cheese
1½ teaspoons sour cream
¼ teaspoon sea salt
Pour milk into a very heavy pan. Put pan on stove.
Turn heat to very, very, very low. Cook for exactly 6
minutes. Pour the milk into a bowl. Put the cottage
cheese into the milk and stir 20 times. Put a lid on
the bowl. Leave a little space open. Let it stand in
the kitchen until the next day.

Spread a big piece of clean cheesecloth inside of a
strainer. Put the strainer in a bowl that is a little bit
smaller than the strainer. Carefully pour the milk
into the cheesecloth. Fold the extra part of the
cheesecloth over the milk. The white part that stays
in the cheesecloth is called the curd. The water that
drips into the bowl is called the whey. Curds and
whey are what Miss Muffet ate. She was really eating
cottage cheese. Spill out the water that drips into the
bowl. You may have to do this 2 or 3 times. Let the
cheese drip until the next day.

Lift the cheesecloth and scrape the cheese into a
bowl. Add the sour cream and mix it up. Add the
salt and mix it up. Cover the cheese and put in the
refrigerator until you want to eat it.

The Mother-Child Cookbook

Nancy J. Ferreira
Pacific Coast Publishers, Menlo Park, CA 94025
($3.50)
An excellent guide for parents and teachers.
Includes outdoor recipes, international dishes. The
cooking projects are divided by skill and age level.
The book is the result of the experiences of the
parent helpers at the Los Gatos-Saratoga
Observation Nursery School in California.

BROCHURES

"Cookies for Children"
Marialice Cunningham, Ruth Upchurch, and Ruth E. Baldwin
Publications Office, 211 Whitten Hall, University of Missouri-Columbia, Columbia, MO 65201 (15¢)
An excellent collection of recipes for nutritious cookies and directions for a cookie mix that can be made up ahead of time and stored in a covered container up to six weeks at room temperature.

Peanut Butter Cookies
½ cup smooth peanut butter
½ cup brown sugar
¼ cup shortening
1 egg, unbeaten
½ teaspoon vanilla
½ cup raisins (optional)
2 tablespoons milk or water
1 cup flour
¼ teaspoon salt
1 teaspoon baking powder
¼ cup dry milk
Cream together peanut butter, sugar, shortening, egg and vanilla. Mix dry ingredients and add alternately with liquid. Stir in raisins, if desired. Drop from a teaspoon (if raisins are used) or form into 1½-inch balls and flatten with a fork. Use an ungreased baking sheet. Bake in moderate oven (350 degrees F) 12 to 15 minutes or until light brown in color. Yields 3 dozen 2-inch cookies.

"Food Experiences for Preschoolers: The Food Curriculum"
Marilyn Blossom, Anna Hertzler
Publications Division, 211 Whitten Hall, University of Missouri-Columbia, Columbia, MO 65201 (10¢)
A four-page leaflet (GH6077) jammed with ideas for helping your child learn from food experiences.

Following Recipes
Before a child can read words, he can read pictures. A special recipe card or poster with words and pictures is a great help. Children develop prereading skills by following pictures and they learn to recognize packages such as canned goods, powdered sugar, flour, and salt.
Gathering all the supplies and matching them to the list of ingredients is the first step. The recipe pictures should tell how full the cups should be and which measuring spoons to use. Pouring skill is required for measuring milk, oil, or water. A sponge should always be handy in case the cup turns out to be a "little short." Measuring and leveling teaspoons and tablespoons of ingredients such as baking powder, salt, and spices may require some assistance because an error here could ruin the final product. Have the child hold the measuring spoon over an empty bowl or a piece of wax paper while filling it. Show him how to smooth the spoon with a knife to make it level. If the child has not perfected the art of breaking and separating eggs, use a separate bowl so that the shells do not get into the finished product.

Note: Not all manufacturers and publishers will accept single orders for a product or book. Always write to them first, before sending money, to be sure that they will take your order. Make sure you've got the most recent price, including shipping and handling charges. If the company is in your state, then you may need to include state sales tax as well.

Gardening

6

Gardening teaches your children very basic lessons about the processes of life. We can help a child realize that every vegetable and fruit that we eat has been planted, tended, grown to maturity, and harvested in the process known as farming. Children can watch how things grow, can come to understand the plant's needs for nutrients in the soil, for water and sunshine. There is a quiet joy that comes from nurturing a living thing and with gardening the pleasures are the fragrances, the moist coolness of the soil, and the excitement of watching change. (Not to mention children's antics with water, dirt, bugs, and worms!) Successful gardening isn't a matter of luck, it's a matter of knowledge. You and your child can learn together and share the pride of success.

WINTERTIME EXPERIENCES

There's nothing better than plants for driving away the dullness of the long, gray winter months. The easiest project to undertake is sprouting. Within only a few days, a young farmer can taste her success. You need not rush out to a health food store for a twelve dollar sprouter. All you need is a container with holes in it that are small enough to keep the sprouting seeds from dropping through, such as a mason jar with a piece of pantyhose stretched across the top with the jar top or a rubber band; a coffeepot with a strainer; a colander; a strainer; a silverware drainer; or a tin can with holes punched in the bottom.

The easiest sprouts to manage are mung beans, which are the sprouts used in oriental cooking. Smaller than a pea, they can be bought dried in international grocery stores, health food stores, and some supermarkets.

SPROUTING

Succulent, fat sprouts from dried mung beans require four basic things: (1) a place to grow that is out of direct sunlight, (2) gentle handling with as few disturbances as possible, (3) the pressure of a small space so that the beans press against each other as they sprout and grow, (4) cleanliness so that decomposing bacteria are not introduced into the growing area. The simplest container is a smooth-edged can, such as a soup can, with holes punched in the bottom for drainage. Use an aluminum nail to make the holes since this will help to prevent rust. Wash the can thoroughly in hot, soapy water. Rinse ¼ cup of dried beans in fresh water. Place beans in the can. Rinse them with fresh water several times a day and drain them, being careful not to disturb them. Store them on a shelf away from the sun. You should begin to see shoots on about the third day. When this happens, wring out a wet piece of cheesecloth and push it down into the can on top of the sprouts to keep them moist. If you wish, you can put a juice glass, bottom side down into the can on top of the cheesecloth to put even more pressure on the sprouts as they grow. On the next (fourth) day water the beans and rewet the cloth. By the fifth day, your sprouts should be 1½ to 2 inches long and ready to be pulled out of the can. They should be harvested before leaves appear, which is the when they turn bitter. The shells of the beans can be rinsed off by floating the sprouts in the sink, although the shells are edible, too. Drain the sprouts and store them in an open container in the refrigerator. Sprouts will keep for several days before beginning to turn brown.

Sprouts are delicious in cheese and mayonnaise sandwiches, and sprinkled in salads. They're also good to munch on just like celery or other vegetables. You may want to experiment with other kinds of seeds: lentils, garbanzos, alfalfa, or wheat; for stronger, peppery flavors try radish, cress, mustard, dill, parsley, and celery. *Don't* use seeds from seed packets intended for planting since they are often treated with insecticides and other toxic chemicals.

Containers for Sprouting

Bowl and Wire strainer

Coffeepot with a Basket

Mason Jar with Stocking Strainer

Stacked Plastic Sprouter
(available from health food stores)

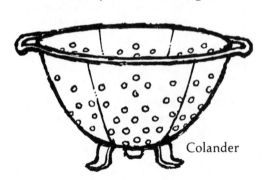

Colander

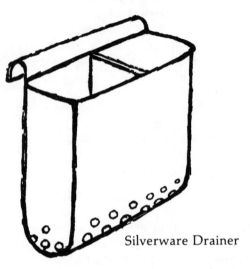

Silverware Drainer

PLANT EXPERIMENTS

Sometimes it's enjoyable to play with plants just to learn about them. Here are a few experiments that will demonstrate basic principles.

Take a celery stalk and make two long slices upward from the base, stopping before you get to the top. (The top should remain intact.) Put each end of the celery in a separate glass of water colored with food coloring. Within a matter of hours the celery will turn the color of the water it is in. Now try cutting it crosswise so that your child can see the celery's veins for taking in water. The same experiment can be done with a daffodil in ink. The entire flower will change color. Both experiments help your child understand how plants need water to live and grow.

Grass is easy to grow! Sprinkle seeds on a sponge placed on a plate, or in a paper cup filled with soil. Draw a face on it and let your child give his pretend friend a haircut with scissors.

Prop a potted plant to lie on its side for a few days. The plant will attempt to right itself by following the light and bending to grow in an upward position.

Try growing plants from the seeds of foods that you eat, such as peaches, mangoes, plums, apples, grapefruit. An avocado seed can be sprouted by suspending it with toothpicks belly button down over a glass of water. Keep it in a warm, dark place and change the water every few days. When the stem reaches six or seven inches, the plant should be cut in half to insure that it won't be a single, leggy stem. When the roots are abundant, the seed's ready to be transferred to a pot.

Temporary plants can be grown from the tops of carrots, pineapple, and sweet potatoes (if they haven't been treated by grocers to prevent sprouting). Just place them in a saucer of water in a sunny window.

TERRARIUMS

You and your child can make a small plant jungle that waters itself. The container you use should be clear glass or plastic: an empty fishbowl, an aquarium, a brandy snifter, gallon-size glass jars used for mayonnaise and pickles by restaurants. Make sure that whatever home you select for your garden is clean, preferably dishwasher sterile, and that the opening is big enough for your hand. The terrarium should have a clear cover such as a plastic top, a glass dish, a glass ashtray, or a piece of window glass that will seal off the top while letting light through. It's a good idea to get sterilized soil from a garden or variety store because it has the right airiness and is less likely to be soggy. Regular garden soil is liable to be too soggy. Shop around, too, for miniature toy animals or people and a pocket mirror, which will serve as the lake in your tiny wonderland.

You and your child can go together to a woodsy ravine or along a woodland brook to select mosses, lichens, and tiny plants. Take along a plastic bag to carry your collection. Look for several small, bushy plants to serve as trees. Small rocks, acorns, and seed pods will fit in, too. The plants that grow best in a terrarium are the kinds that grow in the shade of the forest floor.

When you get back home, you're ready to plant your garden. Put pebbles in the bottom of the container to help drainage. Slope the pebbles and then the soil in the terrarium so that it can be easily seen from one side. Put the tallest plants in the back and the smallest in the front. Avoid crowding, and don't let any plants press against the side of the container. Put the mirror in and surround it with moss. Situate the small animals and people. Now water everything with a gentle spray.

The soil should be lightly moist but not at all muddy. (Caution: don't overwater — too much water may ruin the whole project. Better too dry than too wet!) Leave the terrarium uncovered for one day so that it can dry out. Attach the top firmly on the container. Place your terrarium in a light place, but not directly in the sun. If the moisture balance is right, the terrarium will be self-maintaining and will occasionally fog up as the plants expire moisture into the air. Watch carefully for signs of decay and remove any leaves that fall off, or rotten stems. (Your nose is a good indicator!)

HOUSEPLANTS

Children can learn to enjoy the responsibility of maintaining houseplants, although they need reminding about watering them. They may also tend to overwater plants. A child's plants should be at his level, and preferably in his own room. He should have a small watering can with a long spout — since his aim may not be very good.

From a child's point of view, the ideal plant is one that blooms profusely. African violets fall into this category, but some tend to be sensitive to cold water and overwatering. Coleus plants have brightly colored leaves and are easy to grow. Marigolds and impatiens can also be grown indoors from seed.

Foolproof, sturdy plants are often on sale in dime stores. One sturdy plant is the sansevieria, or snake plant. It can tolerate almost any conditions, including draft. It has no stems — just slender, tall leaves. It can be cut into pieces, and each piece will root. Jade and ivy plants will flourish with minimum care. (Philodendron leaves are poisonous and the plant should be avoided if you have a baby in the house.)

The best pots for a child's plants should be porous to absorb the excess water. Have a deep drain dish under them and an inch or so of pebbles inside the pot to allow proper drainage.

Experiment with plants that will root themselves from leaves. Begonias, African violets, and jade plants will all cooperate. Leaves can even be sent through the mail if carefully placed between two sheets of paper! Ask friends to mail you some "slips."

FORCING BULBS AND BRANCHES

If you plan carefully, you can have daffodils, hyacinths, crocuses, and other spring flowers blooming in your home in the winter. Be prepared for a long wait, though. Paper white narcissus and Soleil d'Or ("so lay door") are the easiest to force, since they require only pebbles, or marbles, and water. They don't need a cooling period to break their dormancy.

Hyacinths, crocuses, and other spring bulbs should be planted halfway out in a pot filled with soil. These bulbs need a period of cold between 35 and 48 degrees (40 is ideal). A basement, an unheated room, or even the refrigerator will do. After about twelve weeks of cooling, during which the bulbs develop roots and top growth, they can be brought into the heated part of the house. Blossoms will appear in three to four weeks.

Branches from fruit trees, pussy willows, and forsythia can be cut in late winter and forced into bloom indoors in a vase of water.

OUTDOOR GARDENING

A garden plot doesn't have to be very large to be productive. We found a little spot 4 feet by 4 feet that wasn't planted in grass when we lived in an apartment and had a fine harvest of tomatoes and squash for ourselves. The closer to the house the better, so that you can tend it and water it without much trouble. Vegetables need full sunlight for at least five to six hours a day.

It would be best to enter the gardening proposition with your child as a cooperative venture, since there will be work that he will not be able to complete by virtue of his restlessness and quick fatigue. You'll need to loosen the ground first with a hoe, breaking up the soil into fine, pea-sized pellets so that your plants can get enough air and moisture. This is the time to add fertilizer such as 5-10-10 (5 percent nitrogen, 10 percent phosphoric acid, and 10 percent potash), working it into the ground as directed. If you prefer, manure is an excellent fertilizer, or compost can be used in the soil in place of fertilizer.

Composting provides a valuable lesson in the way in which nature breaks down decaying material so that it may be reused as a source of food for living things. Your compost pile can be made of leaf rakings, weeds, grass clippings, organic garbage, and egg shells. No meat. You need to set up a collection bucket from the kitchen, or even just a cut off milk container for plate scrapings to be taken out to the heap. Throw dirt over the materials so that they won't blow away. Some gardeners sprinkle a little agricultural lime over each addition and then work it in as a way of enriching the pile. The pile should be kept barely moist, and it should be turned over every few weeks to insure that it decays evenly. The center of the pile will get hot because of the chemical action taking place. (Let your child feel the heat caused by decomposition.) If it gets too hot it will dry out and the action will be slowed down — thus the need for being damp but not soaking wet. The ideal compost has had several years to turn into a crumbly, rich black soil, but compost can be used as quickly as in a month, even if it isn't all broken down. The beauty of composting is that it is a natural recycling of materials. It doesn't burn plants as commercial fertilizers will, and it can't be overdone — the more the better. The best time to put it into the garden is in the spring when you first begin to work the soil.

A note about your local, friendly earthworms who will be uncovered as you dig. Earthworms eat dirt, they digest it, and they condition it inside their bodies. They are nature's plow-men, burrowing into the ground making holes that air and rain can get into. Let your child hold and feel an earthworm, then watch how it burrows back into the cool, moist darkness of the soil.

Children need plants that grow quickly. Beans, lettuce, and radishes do (although most kids don't like to eat radishes because they're too hot). Tomatoes are a must — since there's nothing comparable to the sweet juiciness of the home grown variety. "Better Boy" is a good choice because of its resistance to disease. "Tiny Tim" and cherry tomatoes can be eaten in one bite right off the vine. In the mornings, summer squash (yellow, crookneck) produces beautiful lilylike blossoms under its giant leaves. Corn is nice, too, if just for the sake of watching its elegant growth.

Flowers are a necessity to complete the young child's joy in gardening. Nasturtiums produce profuse, fragrant blooms from a large, easy-to-plant seed. The petals can be eaten in salads — although it's a bit peppery for most youngsters' tastes. Don't forget sunflowers — tall, magnificent queens of the garden — that remain after everything else has died to feed the birds in winter.

Sit down with your child to decide what plants should go where. The smallest plants should be in the front and the tallest in the back so that none get overshadowed by others. If you're planting on a hillside, the rows should go across the hill not down the hill. Decide if you want to stagger your crop to avoid the vegetables all being ripe at once.

Instruct your child about planting one seed at a time. Kids assume that you make a hole and dump in all of the seeds, which can be a disaster if the seeds are tiny and difficult to retrieve. Your child can help with watering the newly planted seeds — but care must be taken that they are not washed back up to the surface by too forceful or prolonged a flooding.

GARDENING IN CONTAINERS

Container gardening is an excellent way of growing vegetables and flowers if you live in an apartment or have limited space. Almost any container is suitable — washtub, plastic garbage pail, plastic garbage bag rolled halfway down, pots of all descriptions, or a trash can. My husband, Paul, amazed me one year by growing a beautiful crop of tomatoes on our apartment balcony in plastic trash cans. Our balcony railings served as supports for our plants. When they finally wilted in winter we took the pails out to dump the dirt and discovered that the tomatoes' roots had filled every square inch of space.

It's best to buy a greenhouse soil mixture such as Pro-Mix, Redi-Earth, or Super Soil because it offers better drainage, is lightweight, and is less likely to carry fungi and disease than regular dirt. (A pail full of garden soil can weigh as much as fifty pounds!) A liquid plant or tomato fertilizer or timed release pellets makes fertilizing an easy job.

Don't plant more than one type of plant in each container. It's a good idea to stick to miniature or small varieties of vegetables. Almost any kind of flower will do well, but squash and other large plants just don't have enough growing room when confined. Herbs are ideal to grow on a porch or balcony. Sweet basil is very hardy, grows rapidly from seed, and has a delicious fragrance. It should be harvested before blooming, but we've enjoyed viewing the stalks of tiny white blooms as well. Parsley, chives, thyme, and marjoram are other herbs that can be grown in pots and put a delightful fragrance into the air.

As in plot gardening, it's important that your plants be able to get four to five hours of direct sunlight. You might consider buying a metal shelf to put them on, or making a step riser to permit all of them to get sunshine. Miniature varieties of tomatoes, cucumbers, and beans can be put in hanging baskets.

BOOKS

A Child's Garden
Public Relations Department, Chevron Chemical Co., P.O. Box 3744, San Francisco, CA 94119 (50¢)
Describes a model adventure garden for young children and gives very practical suggestions for setting one up. Lists experiments to do with plants and also lists all of the major vegetables giving their varieties and growing needs.

Gardening, How to Grow Things
McPhee Gribble Publishers, Viking Penguin, Inc., 625 Madison Avenue, New York, NY 10022 ($1.50, paperback)
Growing plants in pots, gardens, and even in the cracks in the sidewalk. Pumpkins, trees, potatoes, sunflowers, water gardens, geraniums — a great idea book for such a small price.

Growing Up Green: Parents and Children Gardening Together
Alice Skelsey and Gloria Huckaby
Workman Publishing Company, 231 E. 51st Street, New York, NY 10022 ($4.95, paperback)
A guide to help parents explore nature, plants, trees, cacti with their children. Directions for growing strawberries in a barrel, planting a garden just for birds to feast on, gardening how-to's, and things to do just for the fun of it. An excellent sourcebook with a philosophy of respect and caring for living things throughout.

The Hidden Magic of Seeds
Dorothy E. Shuttlesworth
Rodale Press, Inc., Emmaus, PA 18049 ($5.95)
A good, factual picture book with full-color illustrations that explain the growth of seeds, the parts of a flower, the seeds of fruits. Discusses how to start your own garden. Simply worded explanations of botany facts.

How to Grow Herbs and Salad Greens Indoors
Joan W. Meschter
Popular Library, Inc., 600 Third Avenue, New York, NY 10011 ($1.50, paperback)
Ah-h-h, an answer for those dreary winter blues. An indoor garden under lights with onions, tomatoes, even cucumbers. Even if your crop is minuscule, you and your child will thoroughly enjoy watching plants grow, mature, and bear fruit. A good first plant growing experience.

Indoor and Outdoor Gardening for Young People
Cynthia and Alvin Koehler
Wonder Books Division of Grosset & Dunlap, Inc., 51 Madison Avenue, New York, NY 10010 ($1.00)
I found this little spiral-bound book in an A & P grocery store. It has experiments for watching seeds grow, suggestions of activities such as how to raise tiny mustard plants for a sandwich, growing a sensitive plant, growing plants from leaves, and dozens of other plant projects.

"Minigardens for Vegetables"
Consumer Information Center, Pueblo, CO 81009
(35¢)
Instructions on soil preparation, seeds, planting,
and care for vegetables grown in containers. A great
source of ideas for the possibilities for balcony and
back-porch gardening.

SUPPLIES FOR GARDENING AND PLANT GROWING

Paddy O'Hair
Meet Mr. O'Hair, bald as can be until you plant his
pate and sideburns with grass seeds. Made of a
porous pottery, the head holds water to provide
moisture for the grass seed. Your child can practice
being a barber! Seed included.
Aldermaston, Inc., 86 Forest Avenue, Glen Cove,
NY 11542 ($4.00 + $1.00 postage and handling)

Child-sized Gardening Tools
Lightweight but sturdy enough for real digging.
The heads are of high-grade steel finished in a rich
copper bronze. The handles are made of ash.
Measurements: shovel, 36 inches long with a 6 x 8-
inch blade; rake, 37 inches long with eight tines
forged in one piece; hoe, 39 inches long with a 4½ x
3-inch blade. From a catalog of play equipment for
children preschool-age through the intermediate
grades. ($1.00)
Constructive Playthings, 1040 East 85th Street,
Kansas City, MO 64131 ($13.00 for the set plus
postage and insurance)

Mushroom Garden
Within thirty days after water is added to your
mushroom garden, "pinhead" mushrooms will
begin to push through the surface of the specially
prepared soil. After these have matured, your
garden will continue to produce mushrooms at
intervals of about a week for four or five weeks.

Darkness is not necessary, grows at room
temperature. Garden includes a 6 x 4¾-inch
marbleized green plastic pot, a watering sprinkler
and easy-to-follow instructions.
Nasco, 901 Janesville Avenue, Fort Atkinson, WI
53538 ($4.55 + postage and handling)

Indoor Greenhouse
A miniature greenhouse that will do everything a
big one will do. Bakelite vinyl top supported by
polished aluminum frame. It folds down for easy
storage. Has automatic watering with rot-proof
fiberglass wicks and a two pint reservoir.
Measurements: 24 x 24 x 18 inches. Fluorescent light
optional.
Nasco, 901 Janesville Avenue, Fort Atkinson, WI
53538 ($27.95 + shipping and handling. Fluorescent
light, double tube, $14.95)

Note: Not all manufacturers and publishers will
accept single orders for a product or book. Always write to them first, before sending
money, to be sure that they will take your
order. Make sure you've got the most recent
price, including shipping and handling
charges. If the company is in your state, then
you may need to include state sales tax as well.

How Children Learn about Sex & Birth
by Anne C. Bernstein

"To get a baby, go to the store and buy a duck." —
SUSAN, A FOUR YEAR OLD

Every day, thousands of parents sit down to tell their offspring about the birds and the bees. And the cows. And the chickens. And the ducks. Parental descriptions of sex and birth often sound like morning roll call on Noah's Ark. When it comes to people, the lecture suddenly takes on the clinical precision of an advanced anatomy course, as the anxious parent rushes through enough detail to confuse a medical student.

Children take this information, process it through mental Jungle gyms, and create their own versions of who comes from where, and how. The children seem content with their answers, and parents, having provided the answers, are not about to start following up with more questions. Chances are, therefore, that misunderstanding will persist.

The most effective way to tell children about sex is to provide information matched to their level of mental development. But because no one ever asks children what they really believe, as opposed to what they were told, we don't understand how their ability to analyze and assimilate information changes year by year.

As part of my research at the University of California, Berkeley, I decided to find out how children understood the explanations and gossip that form their early sex education. With Philip A. Cowan, I devised an interview plan that amounted to turning back on children their perennial question, "How do people get babies?"

It might seem as if the answer to that question will depend on what a child has been told, but that's not the case. Even when adults give children straight facts, the story of human reproduction often gets twisted into a remarkable version of creation.

Jane, aged four, told me: "To get a baby to grow in your tummy, you just make it first. You put some eyes on it. Put the head on, and hair, some hair, all curls. You make it with head stuff you find in the store that makes it for you. Well, the mommy and daddy make the baby and then they put it in the tummy and then it goes quickly out."

Jane had never been told, by parents, peers or sex-education books, that babies were manufactured, using parts purchased from the store. She put together the answer out of information gathered and given, and held together by a thread of childish logic that reflected her understanding of the physical world.

Jane's story comes from my interviews with 60 boys and girls, all of whom had younger brothers and sisters. They were all white, middle- and upper-middle-class children who lived in a university community. One third of the children were either three or four years old; one third were seven or eight; and one third were 11 or 12. The children's ages corresponded to certain developmental levels suggested by Swiss psychologist Jean Piaget.

Piaget regards each child as a philosopher who works at making his universe intelligible. As the child develops, he shapes the world in terms of his own level of understanding and then restructures his understanding when he gets new information that doesn't fit his old view of the universe.

Answers to my questions fell into six levels of maturity that show a consistent sequence of development. The differences between any two levels reflect a difference in problem-solving strategies. It's the structure of a child's answer, not its content, that distinguishes one level from another.

LEVEL ONE: GEOGRAPHY The youngest children answered the question, "How do people get babies?" as if it were a question about geography. These children, usually three to four years old, told me:

"You go to a baby store and buy one."

"From tummies."

"From God's place."

"It just grows inside mommy's tummy. It's there all the time. Mommy doesn't have to do anything. She just waits until she feels it."

Antonia, who will soon be four, carried on the following conversation:

ME: How did your brother start to be in your mommy's tummy?

ANTONIA: Um, my baby just went in my mommy's tummy.

ME: How did he go in?

ANTONIA: He was just in my mommy's tummy.

ME: Before you said that he wasn't there when you were there. Was he?

ANTONIA: Yeah, and then he was in the other place . . . in America.

ME: In America?

ANTONIA: Yeah, in somebody else's tummy. And then he went through somebody's vagina, then he went in my mommy's tummy.

ME: In whose tummy was he before?

ANTONIA: Um, I don't know who his, her name is. It's a her.

This little girl, typical of level-one children, believes a baby that now exists has always existed. The only real question is where he was before he came to live at her house. She knows that her brother grew inside her mother's body. How and when he happened to grow there is beyond her grasp, but she extrapolates from the information she has: babies grow inside tummies and come out vaginas. Before her brother was in her mother's tummy, he must have been in somebody else's tummy, and that somebody must be female because only big girls can grow babies. Presumably this chain can go on indefinitely, with each mommy getting her baby in turn from another woman.

The level-one child does not understand the laws of cause and effect. His belief that babies have always existed is consistent with his conviction that he and all the people he knows have always existed. He cannot imagine a world without himself in it.

LEVEL TWO: MANUFACTURING This is a level that Henry Ford would have recognized and admired, for these children believe that babies are manufactured by people as if they were refrigerators, TV sets or automobiles. A level-two child knows that babies have not always existed; they must be built.

According to four-year-old Laura, "When people are already made, they make some other people. They make the bones inside, and blood. They make skin. They make the skin first and then they make blood and bones. They paint the blood, paint the red blood and the blue blood." Asked how babies start to be in mommies' tummies, she replied: "Maybe from people. They just put them in the envelope and fold them up and the mommy puts them in her 'gina and they just stay in there." Asked where the babies were before they were in the envelope, she answered, "They buy them at the store."

These children seem undeterred by the fact that they've never seen a baby factory or a rack of diapered infants at the local supermarket. When provoked by curiosity or question, they simply make up answers, fitting what they have been told and what they have seen into their view of the world. Because children at this level believe that everything in the world has been made either by a magicianlike God or by people, they assume that babies are created in a similar way.

These children are still egocentric; they can interpret the world only in terms of events or processes they have experienced themselves. Therefore, they often fall into the "digestive fallacy," and believe that babies are conceived by swallowing and born by elimination. One four-year-old boy uses the digestive process to explain how mommies and daddies get to be parents. He says that God makes mommies and daddies "with a little seed": "He puts it down on the table. Then it grows bigger. The people grow together. He makes them eat the seed and then

they grow to be people from skel'tons at God's place. Then they stand up and go someplace else where they could live."

A few children at level two connect a father with the birth process, but fit what they have been told to a mechanical process. One girl said, "he puts his hand in his tummy and gets it [the seed] and puts it on the bottom of the mommy and the mommy gets the egg out of her tummy and puts the egg on top of the seed. And then they close their tummies and the baby is born." The child believes that the seed and the egg can come together only by manual means. She conscientiously tried to fit what she had been told about reproduction into physical processes, but she had a few doubts. She told me that "the daddy can't really open up all his tummies."

LEVEL THREE: TRANSITIONAL Children at this level explain procreation as a mixture of physiology and technology, but they stick to operations that are technically feasible. A level-three child knows that mommy and daddy can't open and close their tummies, but he may assume that conception is impossible without marriage. He may also take quite literally his parents' explanation of conception as "planting a seed." Jack, aged four, told me: "The daddy plants the seed like a flower, I think, except you don't need dirt."

A child at this level of understanding still believes that the world of nature is alive; he talks about non-living and living things as if they possessed will and acted purposefully. Jeanne, who is seven, said: "The sperm goes into the mommy to each egg and puts it, makes the egg safe. So if something bump comes along, it won't crack the egg. The sperm comes from the daddy. It swims into the penis, and I think it makes a little hole and then it swims into the vagina. It has a little mouth and it bites a hole."

Level-three children may know that three major ingredients go into making babies: social relationships such as love and marriage; sexual intercourse; and the union of sperm and ovum. However, their ability to combine these factors into a coherent whole is limited. These children are in a transitional period between the stages of development that Piaget calls preoperational and concrete operational.

A preoperational child builds mental maps based on his own experiences; he solves problems by intuition. He cannot assign objects to categories. Asked to define an apple, he's likely to say, "It's to eat." As he moves into the next stage, which can happen any time between seven and 10 years old, he learns to think systematically and generally about concrete objects. Ask him about an apple now, and he'll say, "It's a fruit."

During this transitional period, children are often aware that their explanations don't quite add up. Ursula, who is eight, describes the father's role in reproduction: "Well, he puts his penis right in the place where the baby comes out, and somehow it [sperm] comes out of there. It seems like magic sort of, 'cause it just comes out."

Asked why the male contribution is necessary, Ursula, who has seen cartons of eggs in the refrigerator, replied: "Well, the father puts the shell. I forget what it's called, but he puts something in for the egg. If he didn't, then a baby couldn't come. Because it needs the stuff that the father gives. It helps it grow. I think that the stuff has the food part, maybe, and maybe it helps protect it. I think he gives the shell part, and the shell part, I think, is the skin."

Her description transforms the father's traditional social role as family protector into a literal protector of the growing baby. His genetic contribution is first a protective shell for the egg, and then the outer covering of the baby.

LEVEL FOUR: CONCRETE PHYSIOLOGY At levels four through six, the eight- to 12-year-old children give primarily physiological explanations. They can think logically about objects and people and can consider past and future. They understand the idea of cause and effect.

Although level-four children may know the physical facts of life, they don't understand why genetic material must unite before new life can begin. One child thought that sperm existed primarily to provide an escort service: "The sperm reaches the eggs. It looses 'em and brings 'em down to the forming place, I think that's right, and it grows until it's ready to take out."

Karen, who is eight, explained: "The man and woman get together, and then they put a speck, then the man has his seed and the woman has an egg. They have to come together or else the baby won't really get hatched very well. The seed makes the egg grow. It's just like plants. If you plant a seed, a flower will grow."

Karen knew that sexual intercourse provides a means for the seed and egg to come together. She knew that both are necessary to create new life, but she had no clear idea of why this was so. Nor did she attempt to reason her way to a solution.

Karen's return to the agricultural metaphor is a reminder that children's thought develops in a spiral, not a straight line. They circle back to the same issues, but deal with old information on a more sophisticated level.

Most of the level-four children I talked to were eight years old. At first, they were embarrassed by

questions about sex. A typical response was, "I don't know much about it." Having disclaimed knowledge, these children would go on to say that the union of sperm and egg or sexual intercourse was the cause of procreation.

LEVEL FIVE: PREFORMATION At level five, children at least attempt to explain the necessity for sperm and ovum to join, but most insist that the baby springs preformed from one of the germ cells. These children, usually 11 or 12 years old, seem to repeat the history of the science of embryology. Like 17th-century scientists, they believe that one germ cell carries a fully formed, miniature person who simply grows to full size in the uterus. They see no need for a final cause.

Some of these children believe that the baby is in the sperm, which is given food and shelter by the egg. As Patrick, who is nearly 13, explains it: "The lady has an egg and the man has a sperm and sort of he fertilizes the egg, and then the egg slowly grows. The sperm grows into a baby inside the egg. Fertilize? It means it gets inside the egg, the sperm does. The egg before the sperm goes in it sort of like, well, I guess it doesn't have anything in it to grow. It just has food and I guess a shell on the outside. It's sort of the beginning of the baby. It has to happen, because otherwise the sperm would just die because it has no shelter on the outside to keep it alive, no food, nothing. And then the egg, there's nothing in it to grow. It has no . . . no . . . no living animal in there."

Twelve-year-old William, on the other hand, believes that the miniature person inhabits the ovum. He describes fertilization: "That's when the sperm enters the egg. I guess the egg just has sort of an undeveloped embryo and when the sperm enters it, it makes it come to life. It gives it energy and things like that."

The child's sex plays no part in choosing the key ingredient of a baby. As many boys as girls believed that the egg was fully responsible. Others of both sexes were convinced that the sperm carried the child. Unlike the three- and four-year-olds who believe that babies come preformed, level-five children embed this notion in a complex theory of causation.

All these children mentioned sexual intercourse or fertilizing the egg by their second sentence, but some seemed embarrassed by the whole topic. A few complained that it was hard to talk about the subject because it required unacceptable language. Another said, after mentioning marriage and affection, "Then . . . I guess uh, they uh, I guess they would . . . go to bed and do something there."

LEVEL SIX: PHYSICAL CAUSALITY About the time

they are 12, children begin to put it all together. They give exclusively physical explanations of conception and birth, and realize that both parents contribute genetic material to the embryo. They are aware of the moral and social aspects of reproduction, but they do not insist that marriage is necessary for conception.

Eleven-year-old Tina describes fertilization: "Well, it just starts it off, I guess. Mixes the genes or puts particles or something into the egg. Genes are the things from the father and the mother, you know, and they put a little bit of each into the baby so the baby turns out to be a little bit like the mother or father or something."

Children like Tina are beginning to move into what Piaget calls the stage of formal operations. They can develop theories and test them against reality; they can think about thinking. Twelve-year-old Michael's account is scientific: "The sperm encounter one ovum and one sperm breaks into the ovum, which produces like a cell, and the cell separates and divides. And so it's dividing, and the ovum goes through a tube and embeds itself in the wall of the, I think it's the fetus of the woman."

Michael's substitution of fetus for uterus leads to an important point. It is the sophistication of a child's reasoning, not simply whether his explanation is correct, that indicates the level of his understanding. Michael's verbal error is like the error of an algebra student who understands quadratic equations but makes a mistake in multiplication.

Not all level-six children gave as thorough an explanation of fertilization as Michael; some said simply, "the two cells meet and start growing."

When questioned, level-six children referred immediately to fertilization or sexual intercourse. None of them seemed embarrassed when I asked, "How do people get babies?"

Few of the parents of the children I questioned had accurate ideas about the extent of their children's sexual knowledge. Parents of children at levels one and six predicted their offsprings' answers with some accuracy; most others expected a greater degree of information than the children possessed. All the parents of level-three children expected that their children knew "the truth," and none anticipated the distortions that turned up. Not a single parent anticipated the level-five child's belief in the existence of a preformed person.

As I talked to children of various ages, it seemed apparent that our present efforts at sex education often confuse children. A four-year-old boy, trying to explain where babies come from, told me, "First they were little, a duck, then they grow older, into a

baby." His solution seemed peculiar, but his source became clear when a level-two girl repeated it. This four-year-old was explicit.

ME: How would a lady get a baby to grow in her tummy?

SUSAN: Get a duck. 'Cause one day I saw a book about them, and they just get a duck or a goose and they get a little more growned and then they turn into a baby.

ME: A duck will turn into a baby?

SUSAN: They give them some food, people food, and they grow like a baby. To get a baby, go to a store and buy a duck.

ME: How did you find that out?

SUSAN: I just saw, find out from this book.

One widely distributed book, which is recommended for children as young as three, starts with a pencil dot (to represent an ovum), then proceeds through the sex lives of flowers, bees, rabbits, giraffes, chickens and dogs before it reaches the human level. Few young children can encounter this kind of explanation without complete confusion.

Another writer, Selma Fraiberg, encountered a four-year-old boy who knew a sex-education book by heart, but insisted that some of the mother's eggs never become babies because the daddy eats them up. "It says so in my book," he claimed, and indeed, it did — in a discussion of reproduction in fish.

Other research suggests a way out of confusion. Lawrence Kohlberg, of Harvard and Elliot Turiel, of the University of California, have studied the development of morality in children. They have found that children can expand their understanding to include concepts that are one level beyond their own.

Using these findings as a guide, we can reduce sex misinformation to a minimum. The level-one preschooler who thinks that babies just grow in mommy's tummy can move up to the manufacturing stage by learning that mommy and daddy make babies. The level-two child, who thinks that babies are manufactured, is ready to learn about the meeting of sperm and ovum. He is not ready for information about dividing cells and the genetic contribution of both parents.

Parents can use their child's curiosity as a guide to the amount of detail he is ready to absorb. By asking the kinds of questions I used, they can find out the level of their child's understanding and begin to provide information geared to the next level. Specific suggestions are listed on the following page.

Children are not miniature adults, and will not think like adults until they grow up. My talks with children have shown that educators need to find out just how children adopt, adapt, and distort information, and then talk to children about sex in new ways. Until they do, our young philosophers will keep on creating unnecessarily confused accounts of the beginnings of life.

Talking to Your Child about Sex and Birth

Never inundate a child with information, but tell him what he wants to know in terms he can understand. The child's own curiosity should be a guide to the explicitness of your explanation. Begin by asking questions that will elicit the child's beliefs without leading his reply. In that way, his level of understanding will become apparent. Some of the questions I asked were: How do people get babies? How do mommies get to be mommies? How did your daddy get to be your daddy?

Children usually are ready to hear explanations of sex in terms that are one level beyond their present understanding. If parents communicate their own comfort, the child will feel he has permission to ask what he wants to know.

Never make a child feel stupid or foolish because he looks at reproduction in a fanciful way. It is important to support the child's problem-solving effort without confirming his erroneous information.

LEVEL-ONE CHILD. This child believes that babies have always existed. Speaking in level-two terms, a parent might tell him: "Only people can make other people. To make a baby person, you need two grown-up people, a woman and a man, to be the baby's mommy and daddy. The mommy and daddy make the baby from an egg in the mommy's body and a sperm from the daddy's body."

LEVEL-TWO CHILD. This child believes that babies are manufactured. The parent could say: "That's an interesting way of looking at things. That's the way you'd make a doll. You would buy a head and some hair and put it all together. But making a real live baby is different from making a doll or a cake or an airplane."

This child can be led to understand that while a factory may have a wide range of components at its disposal, babymakers have only certain ingredients from their own bodies as materials. The parent might continue: "Mommies and daddies have special things in their bodies that they use to make babies. Mommies have tiny eggs and daddies have tiny sperms. When an egg from a mommy and a sperm from a daddy join together, they grow into a baby. The baby grows inside the mommy's body."

The level-two child who speaks of opening tum-

mies might be told: "Can you put your hand inside your tummy? Then do you think the mommy and daddy can really put their hands in their tummies? There must be another way. Do you want to know how they get the egg and the seed together? The daddy's sperm are in his testicles and they come out through his penis. The mommy's vagina is a tunnel to where her eggs are. So if the daddy put his penis into her vagina, the sperm could go through the tunnel to the egg."

LEVEL-THREE CHILD. This child already restricts himself to reproductive processes that are technically possible. The task of the level-three's parents is to clear up misapprehensions, explain why some of his beliefs are mistaken, and provide other physiological explanations.

The child who described the sperm biting a hole with its little mouth to gain access to the vagina can be led to understand that while sperm move in a way that resembles swimming, the sperm is not a whole animal. Unlike a fish, it has no mouth with which to bite. She can be told why a sperm doesn't need a mouth to get into the vagina, which is like a tunnel.

One level-three child described conception in the following manner: "I guess it's like mothers and fathers are related, and their loving each other forms a baby. I don't know how it really comes just by loving and stuff. I guess the love forms the beans and I guess the beans hatches the egg."

This child's parents should agree with him, that loving is an important part of making babies. His statement shows that they have already given him an integral part of their value system. They could say, "It's really important for a baby that mothers and fathers love each other and love the baby, so that when the baby is born they can take good care of it. But loving is a feeling and can't start the baby all by itself. A baby is a living creature and it starts growing from living material. When the mother and the father make love, a sperm from the father goes through his penis into the mother's vagina. When the sperm joins with an egg from the mother, the sperm and the egg form one new thing, which grows into a baby."

LEVELS FOUR AND FIVE. In talking to level-four and level-five children, the objective is the same, although the level-four child may take longer to understand why genetic material must unite to produce a baby. The level-five child believes that the whole baby exists in either the sperm of the egg, needing the other only to promote its growth. Children at levels four and five need to learn that the baby has not begun to exist until the sperm and egg meet and fuse. They can learn that the seeds of life come from both parents, from whom the baby inherits its physical characteristics.

A useful way to explain genetic contributions is to talk in terms of information. A parent might say that both sperm and egg contain coded information about the baby they will grow to be. He can go on to talk about facial features, color of eyes, hair and skin. It is important to stress that neither the sperm nor the egg has the entire code until they unite. Together, they complete the message to develop into a baby that is the child of a particular set of parents.

Anne C. Bernstein grew up in New York. "When I was just past four," she writes, "my parents added my brother Andrew to our family, kindling my interest in how people get babies." Bernstein's parents responded to her questions by reading her a sex-education book. When she shared her book with neighborhood children, the resulting flood of indignant phone calls temporarily ended her exploration of human reproduction. A number of years later, after she had received a B.A. from Brandeis University, she returned to the topic of where babies come from in her doctoral research at the University of California, Berkeley.

BOOKS FOR YOUNG CHILDREN ON BIRTH AND SEX

Every parent has different preferences. Some will want books that demonstrate matters very clearly, while other parents may feel more comfortable with a less explicit book. Your public library is usually a good source for finding books that suit your preferences. It would be wise to take a look at a book before ordering it to be sure that the wording and pictures seem right to you. (I have purposely quoted the more explicit descriptions in the books reviewed in this chapter to aid you in making your choices.)

There are a few criticisms that I have about sex and birth picture books for children that I want to share with you. First, most are entirely too wordy for their preschool audience. A page shouldn't have more than four or five sentences if it is to hold the interest of a child. Second, the diagrammatic approach, using cross sections of the human body, simply isn't effective with literal-minded preschoolers. Some diagrams, such as the one-legged cross section of a mother giving birth, which appears in *How We Are Born* by Julian May, may even frighten a child. Third, many books wander too long around the barnyard before getting down to people. The child is expected to understand pollination, seed bearing, egg laying, and more and then be able to apply all of this to human pregnancy and birth.

We have become overly concerned with the anatomical workings of the body and not concerned enough about the human being who owns the body. I particularly object to sex being defined in terms of "the male" and "the female." It's not that a child shouldn't have some basic facts from which to operate, but the reality of human sexuality is so much more basic and profound than "man, the machine" concepts convey.

What should we tell our children? Maybe we shouldn't tell them as much as we show them. We communicate that we like kissing and hugging. That we like our own bodies and their bodies. We give back scratches on Saturday morning, take baths together once in a while, and let our kids climb into bed with us some mornings to share in the warmth and tenderness of waking up together. Sex at its best is a feeling, a sharing, the "warm fuzzies" to borrow a term from *T. A. for Tots*. Physical love is delighting in another human being and sharing together in a very special way. I'm convinced that if parents are loving and physically demonstrative toward their child, the sexual part of their youngster's life will be fulfilled gracefully and with joy when the time comes for it.

The following books are for use with three- to eight-year-olds in discussing sex, pregnancy, childbirth, and jealousy over a new baby. The first four books are my favorites.

Where Do Babies Come From?
Margaret Sheffield
Illustrated by Sheila Bewley
Alfred A. Knopf, 400 Hahn Road, Westminster, MD 21157 ($3.95)
Soft, gentle paintings illuminate a very carefully worded book about sex, childbirth, and the differences between boys and girls, men and women. This is my favorite of all the sex explanation books because of its clarity, beauty, and color. It may be most useful to adoptive parents, also.

The True Story of How Babies Are Made
Per H. Knudsen
Children's Press, Inc., 1224 W. Van Buren Street, Chicago, IL 60607 ($3.95)
A father's book written and illustrated for his own child. Smiling, cartoonlike characters illustrate intercourse, growth of the baby inside the mother, the birth of the baby, and breast feeding. "Because they made love, they are going to have a baby. They are very, very happy." Excellent in its clarity and simplicity.

Where Did I Come From?
Peter Mayle
Lyle Stuart, Inc., 120 Enterprise Avenue, Secaucus, NJ 07094 ($5.95, paperback)
At first I did not like the book and now I do. The cartoon characters that portray the naked mother and father are fat and somewhat ugly. As you get into the story, its lightheartedness is catching. Sex is described as scratching an itch but much nicer . . . "that ends in a big lovely shiver for both of them." Sperm are portrayed as pollywog-looking fellows, belly buttons are explained, and breast-feeding is shown.

Making Babies: An Open Family Book for Parents and Children Together
Sara Bonnett Stein
Walker and Company, 720 Fifth Avenue, New York, NY 10019 ($5.95)
The book has a dual text — one for parents alone and one to be read to young children. It focuses on the feelings and fears of young children about birth and sex. There is an excellent explanation of the physical differences between boys and girls, color photographs of a newborn baby and scenes of animals mating and nursing. A sensitive, helpful book.

A Baby Is Born: The Story of How Life Begins
Milton I. Levine and Jean H. Seligmann
Western Publishing Company, Inc., 1220 Mound Avenue, Racine, WI 53404 ($1.00, paperback)
Although the book is dated, its clarity is superb. It answers questions typically asked by four- to nine-year-olds. Vocabulary includes *uterus, testicles, male, female, semen, fertilized.* "Every baby begins its life in its mother's uterus, which is the special part of the mother's body just for babies."

They are followed, in alphabetical order, by other titles that are also helpful for this age group.

Unfortunately, there is no really good book that I know to explain sex and childbirth to an adopted child that incorporates the concept of alternative parents. *Where Do Babies Come From?* by Margaret Sheffield is a factual book that emphasizes the processes without making a big to-do about parents, which might best suit the needs of an adopted child.

A Baby Starts to Grow
Paul Showers
Thomas Y. Crowell Company, 666 Fifth Avenue, New York, NY 10003 ($1.25, paperback)
An excellent book for introducing a mother's pregnancy to a two- to four-year-old. Brief words describe life within the womb with the umbilical cord clearly shown. "The baby is ready to be born. It comes slowly out of its mother's body into the world." The baby is shown nursing.

The Beginning of Life: How Babies Are Born
Eva Knox Evans
The Macmillan Publishing Co., Inc., Riverside, NJ 08075 ($3.95)
Brief chapters with sensitive, realistic drawings of adult bodies. The "embryo" (a term used throughout the book, even at birth) is shown at different stages. Both breast-feeding and bottle-feeding are portrayed. An explanation of twins. Comparison of animal and human families.

The Birth of Sunset's Kittens
Carla Stevens
Addison-Wesley Publishing Co., Inc., Jacob Way, Reading, MA 01867 ($5.50 book, $1.00 poster)
A sequence of photographs with a simple, factual text about a cat giving birth. The poster, which can be ordered separately, has no text, but shows the cat's birth sequence. (A similar book, *My Puppy Is Born*, is written by Joanne Cole and published by William Morrow and Company.)

A Child Is Born: The Drama of Life Before Birth
Lennart Nilsson, Photographs
Axel Ingelman-Sundberg and Claes Wirsen
Delacorte Press, Distributed by Dell Publishing Company, 1 Dag Hammarskjold Plaza, 245 E. 47th Street, New York, NY 10017 ($11.95)
Stunning photographs of embryos and fetuses *in utero* by Lennart Nilsson. The text is written for expectant mothers, but the photographs are so remarkable that you and your child will be able to trace the development of your unseen baby month by month.

Gabriel's Very First Birthday
Sherrie Farrell
Pipeline Books, Box 3711, Seattle, WA 98124 ($3.95, paperback)
Black-and-white photographs of Gabriel's home delivery showing the nude pregnant mother pushing Gabriel out with the comforting closeness of her husband. Clipping the umbilical cord. Breast-feeding. Quite a realistic picture of actual childbirth that may make some parents uncomfortable.

How Babies Are Made
Andrew C. Andry and Steven Schepp
Time-Life Books, Distributed by Little, Brown & Co., 34 Beacon Street, Boston, MA 02106 ($3.50, paperback)
Paper sculpture in color is used to illustrate the fertilization of flowers, the mating of chickens and dogs. Adults are shown minus pubic hair and making love under blankets. The baby is shown growing and being born. "You began just this way. A sperm from your father joined with an egg from your mother. You began to grow while you were in your mother's uterus." Excellent for three- to five-year-olds.

How Was I Born?
Lennart Nilsson
Delacorte Press, Distributed by Dial Press, 1 Dag Hammarskjold Plaza, 245 E. 47th Street, New York, NY 10017 ($5.95)
The book describes for a child what it was like when he was inside his mother's womb. It uses the beautiful color photographs of embryos and fetuses that have made Mr. Nilsson famous. An excellent photograph of a mother giving birth and of a sperm touching an egg. Family groupings of nude girls and a woman, nude boys and a full-grown man to demonstrate bodily growth and changes. A bit wordy, but the photographs make it worthwhile.

My Childbirth Coloring Book
Laurence K. Scott and David Baze
Academy Press, Ltd., 360 N. Michigan Avenue, Chicago, IL 60601 ($2.95)
Excellent line drawings of lovemaking, the birth of a baby and breast-feeding. The text may be too wordy and sophisticated for a young child, but the pictures by themselves with your own wording would provide a good, clear explanation.

Show Me! A Picture Book of Sex for Children and Parents
Will McBride, Helga Fleishhauer-Hardt
St. Martin's Press, 175 Fifth Avenue, New York, NY 10010 ($6.95, paperback)
The book's large pages are filled with black-and-white photographs of nude children and adults. Masturbation, pregnancy, intercourse, and breast-feeding are shown with close-ups so extreme that you can view every hair and goose pimple. You might want to use the book to explain anatomical differences, but on the whole, the book's attempt at realism makes it grotesque. Other books are realistic in a more aesthetically pleasing way.

That New Baby: An Open Family Book for Parents and Children Together
Sara Bonnett Stein
Walker and Company, 720 Fifth Avenue, New York, NY 10019 ($5.95)

Deals with the jealousy and fears that a young child
feels when a new baby is born. A thoughtful
discussion for parents and reassurance in simple
words for the child to make her feel she still has a
place in the family. "To Charles, as to all children, it
seems that a new baby replaces the old one. And
why would a mother want a new baby, unless the
old one were not good enough? That is the starting
point: jealousy begins before the new baby is
born."

We Are Having a Baby
Viki Holland
Charles Scribner's Sons, Shipping and Service
Center, Vreeland Avenue, Totowa, NJ 07512 ($6.95)
Four-year-old Dana is portrayed in a photographic
essay about the birth of a new baby in her family.
There's no picture of childbirth, although Mom is
wheeled into the operating room. Poof! the baby is
shown in an incubator. The jealousy that a young
child feels is well portrayed. Daddy's attention
helps Dana to accept the new baby.

What Is a Girl? What Is a Boy?
Stephanie Waxman
Peace Press, Inc., 3828 Willat Avenue, Culver City,
CA 90230 ($3.95, paperback)
Ms. Waxman, a teacher of young children, states: "I
wrote this book to end the battle between the sexes
in my classroom. It worked. When the children got
the information they needed, they didn't have to
exclude and stereotype each other to form a secure
sexual identity." The book uses black-and-white
photographs to portray clearly for young children
the differences between boys and girls, men and
women. "A boy is someone with a penis . . . a girl
is someone with a vagina." Children's stereotypes,
such as that boys are stronger, girls have long hair,
boys wear pants, etc., are laid to rest. Includes
suggestions for teaching activities at the end of the
book. Excellent.

Wind Rose
Crescent Dragonwagon
Harper & Row, Pubs., Inc., Keystone Industrial
Park, Scranton, PA 18512 ($4.95)
A poetic story of pregnancy and childbirth as told
by the mother. The spiritual, feeling side of birthing
a child is communicated here more deeply than
through the physical descriptions available in other
books.

The Wonderful Story of How You Were Born
Sindonie Matsner Gruenberg
Doubleday & Co., Inc., 501 Franklin Avenue,
Garden City, NY 11530 ($1.95, paperback)
Published over twenty-six years ago, this book has
endured over generations. The artwork in the new
edition makes it appealing to young children. It is a
gentle story without startling ideas or illustrations.
The text may be too long to hold the attention span
of a preschooler in one sitting, but it has the feel of
a well-told story. Comfortable, but not very explicit.

GUIDEBOOKS FOR PARENTS ON BIRTH AND SEX

How to Tell Your Child about Sex
James L. Hymes, Jr.
Public Affairs Pamphlet #149
Public Affairs Committee, 381 Park Avenue South,
New York, NY 10016 (35¢)
A well-stated, helpful booklet about answering
young children's questions. Dr. Hymes suggests a
relaxed approach to talking with children that is
brief and to the point. "You know how a boy's body
is made, how he has a penis. And you know what a
girl's body is like, too. She doesn't have a penis but
she has an opening. The two fit together. That is
why people are made that way, so that babies can
be started."

"Sex Education at Home"
Order from: The Community Sex Education Center,
Planned Parenthood Center of Syracuse, Inc., 1120
E. Genessee Street, Syracuse, NY 13210 (50¢)
Describes the development of sexuality from infancy
through adolescence. Answers typical questions
from young children. " 'How did I get inside,
Mommy?' All babies need a Mommy and a Daddy.
When two grown-ups, a man and a woman, love
each other very much they put their bodies close
together. The man's penis goes inside the woman's
vagina. Then a seed from the man may meet an egg
inside the woman. It is a very tiny little dot of an
egg, not big and hard like a chicken egg. The seed
and egg join inside the mother and start a baby
growing." Suggests books on the subject for parents
to read.

Talking to Children about Sex
Edna Lehman
Harper and Row, Pubs., Inc., Keystone Industrial
Park, Scranton, PA 18512 ($4.95)
A year-by-year suggestion book for parents and
teachers, giving sample dialogues and phrases to
help in communication. For a five-year-old: "The
sperm cell goes through a very special tube in the
penis and enters the mother's vagina. Fathers and
mothers do this when they want to have a new child
of their very own to love and care for."

When Children Ask about Sex
Joae Graham Selzer, M.D.
Beacon Press, Inc., 25 Beacon Street, Boston, MA
02108 ($3.95, paperback)
A useful handbook listing typical questions of very
young and preschool children up through
adolescence. Provides a brief discussion of the
questions with a sample answer: "Well, where do
babies come from? They come from a mother's
uterus. It is as simple as that. And so the answer
should be something like this: 'A baby comes from
a special place inside its mother.' "

TOYS TO EXPLAIN BODY CONCEPTS

Dressing-Undressing Puzzle
Children's clothes are the puzzle pieces.
Assembling the puzzle the child gains a sense of the
function of clothing and an increased awareness of
the body. The 12 x 9½-inch puzzle is brightly
painted and contained in a wooden tray. Fourteen
pieces. From the Childcraft "Special Education
Materials" catalog. Price subject to change.
Childcraft Education Corp., 20 Kilmer Road,
Edison, NJ 08817 ($4.95 + $1.95 shipping and
handling)

Monkey Birthing Doll
A handmade sock doll that gives birth to a tiny
baby. The umbilical cord snaps off and the baby
may be snapped to the mother's breast to nurse.
The company also offers a tiny backpack for the
mother to carry the baby and a backpack for a child
to carry both the baby and mother. Directions for
making your own dolls, $1.25. Dolls demonstrating
a caesarean delivery and specific operations such as
a tonsillectomy or appendectomy can be ordered.
Please send a stamped, self-addressed envelope for
more information.
Monkey Business, Rt. 3 Box 153A, Celina, TN 38551
(Finished doll, $15.00; Backpack set, $2.00)

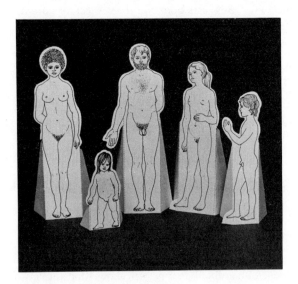

One Big Family Dolls
There are thirteen paper dolls in this set. People of
different ages and races are represented. The dolls
are part of a multimedia curriculum entitled *The
Haunting House* by Barbara Hollerorth. Order from:
Unitarian Universalist Association, 25 Beacon
Street, Boston, MA 02108 (Dolls only, $4.00)

Note: Not all manufacturers and publishers will accept single orders for a product or book. Always write to them first, before sending money, to be sure that they will take your order. Make sure you've got the most recent price, including shipping and handling charges. If the company is in your state, then you may need to include state sales tax as well.

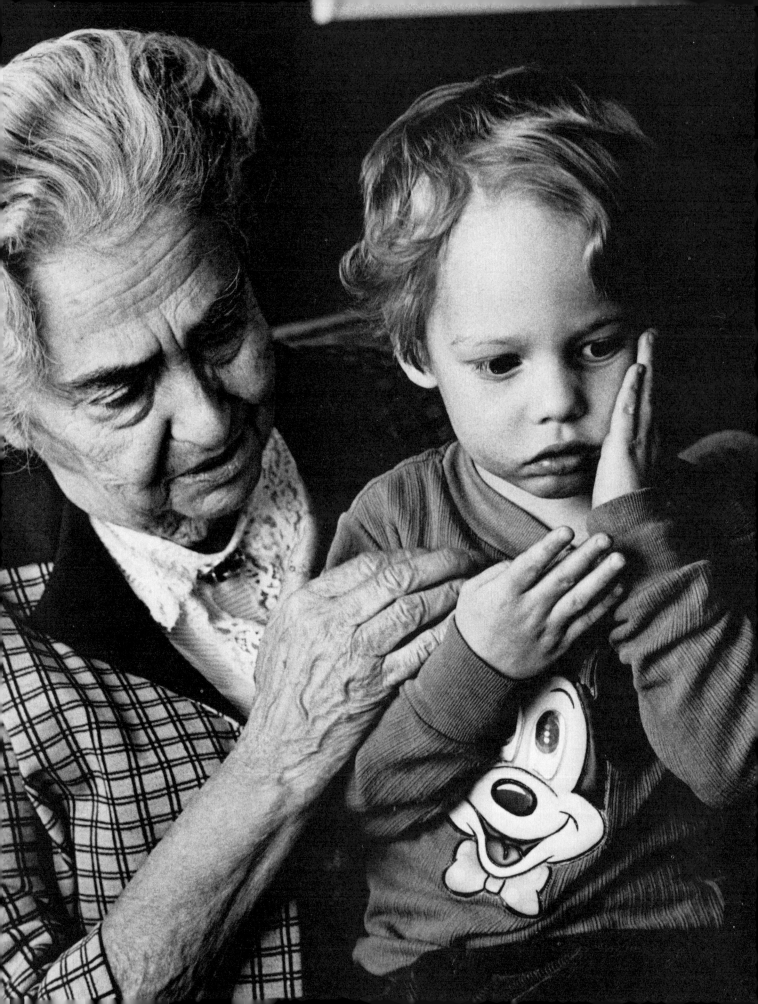

Talking about Death

8

"What does 'dead' mean, Mommy?" The question shocked me coming from Marcie. To be honest, I don't really know what "dead" means as far as people are concerned. I've been to a few funerals. My grandmother probably knew a great deal more about death than I do, because in her day people died at home surrounded by loved ones. I'm a member of the hospital generation where death and birth take place in sterile rooms defensively insulated from children and the public. Dr. Edgar Jackson in *Telling a Child about Death* says: "When anything as prevalent as death is excluded from easy communication, it creates an emotional vacuum into which fear and anxiety, mystery and uncertainty come."

My one most profound memory of death comes from when I was Marcie's age. So often adults make the mistake of presuming that young children can't remember or understand what is happening around them! My uncle, a newly married young man, was killed in an airplane crash. I can remember pleading to be told what had happened. All around me there was crying and tension. The only response I got was, "Nothing's wrong. Now go out and play." It was that gap in communications — the silences in my presence, the whispering behind closed doors, that made death a deeply frightening concept for me. I sensed something was wrong — was it my fault? Had I committed some unforgivable sin? Perhaps my family had genuinely hoped to spare me the pain they were feeling. Or, perhaps, what had happened to them was unspeakable. They just weren't up to having to deal with me.

What my family failed to realize is that I was a member of the family, too, and that it was far more painful for me to be excluded from the family circle than it would have been to be invited to share the realities of what was going on. Everyone went to the funeral but me. I stayed with an aunt. I can only begin to reconstruct the anxiety of the exclusion caused by the giant vacuum of not knowing.

Now it's Marcie's turn to learn about death. And it's a good time, too. There's no stress or real crisis. Just the leisure of a young child's growing and questioning. All right, I said to myself, let's look at what Marcie understands about death. Paul and I frequently use phrases like, "Save me from a fate worse than death!" when Marcie tries to avoid taking a bath, and we say, "It tickled me to death," or "I'm scared to death." And there was a dead starling that she found on the ground one day. She picked it up by the feet, and I found myself aghast, but holding back so that she could begin to understand that the bird was dead. There were dead bees that wouldn't sting and squashed crickets that would never jump again.

My young child hardly knows the difference between what is alive — humans, animals, and plants — and what is inanimate — cars, trucks, and rocks. She lives in a world where dreams and wishes are separated from reality by a very thin curtain as witnessed by the monsters that come to visit in the dark. Her biggest fear is separation from the people that she is so utterly dependent on for survival. How then shall I explain death to her in terms that she can understand while not threatening her sense of security in life?

The concept of death is not a simple one. It's made up of many layers of understanding — in my case it's been a lifetime of experiences, reading, and self-exploration. The most basic understanding seems to be the physical reality of death. Next there is a spiritual, or religious, understanding, when one is able to put death into a perspective about life and human destiny. Probably the most complex understanding is the awareness of one's own limited life-span and the reality of personal death.

To explain death to Marcie, I begin with the basics: "Death is stillness. When something is dead, it doesn't move. It doesn't breathe, or fly, or eat." We examine dead bugs and other dead things.

The next concept is that death is irrevocable.

"When something is dead it doesn't come alive again. Death is not like going to sleep." Many children become frightened when parents use the term "laid to rest" or "gone to sleep" to describe death. How frightening it must be to repeat the phrase: "Now I lay me down to sleep, I pray the Lord my soul to keep. If I should die before I wake, I pray the Lord my soul to take." How difficult it would be to relax and go to sleep with the thought that you might die in the process!

The child must be helped to understand that she cannot wish something or someone to die. Grownups have no control over death either. Sometimes a young child will have strongly murderous wishes about friends or parents. "I'm going to kill you!" "I wish you were dead!" When a child experiences the death of a loved one, it's important that he understands that his wishes had nothing to do with the death.

Finally, a child can be helped to understand that people live even after death in our memories of them. Constructing a memory book in which parents and child share memories of a pet or a relative who has died can be helpful. You can write the words while your youngster draws the illustrations of her memories.

Above all, a child needs to feel that he is safe. To a young child, death is synonymous with separation. A child fears that Momma or Daddy will go away and never come back. We can say, "My husband is taking a trip, but he will be quite safe and he will return on Monday." It's much more difficult for a young child to whom one day is like a year in grownup time. To her, every separation from an indispensable adult that lasts longer than one day brings deep fears. We must gently assure the child that neither he, nor his mother or father will die any time soon. We may feel better about adding that people usually die when they become very old — which can be translated into children's language as "very wrinkled and white-haired."

The quotation, "as adults we do not so much understand death, as gain the courage to confront it," has wisdom in it. As parents, we can grow with our children by taking the courage to examine with them what is fearful to us. And maybe, just maybe, we ourselves will come to see that death is not the horrible enemy we think it is, but a gentle friend that can be faced with dignity and openness.

"When Pets Die"
by Linda Jane Vogel

Recently I got a call from our veterinarian's office. "Your guinea pig is deceased," she said.

"We'll be after him as soon as the children come home from school," was my reply.

It was a cold, rainy November day when the three of us went after Mr. President. We had often laughed about how he reminded us of Theodore Roosevelt in the film at Mt. Rushmore. Peter, age eight, held the dead weight of our one-year-old guinea pig in his hands and then turned away so no one would see his tears. Kris, age six, looked but didn't want to touch the stiff, cold body.

We brought Mr. President home, dug a grave under the lilac bush at the corner of the garage, and stood in the cold drizzle. We put Mr. President in the hole we had dug and gently covered him with wet, black dirt. As we worked, we prayed a remembering kind of prayer.

"Thank you, God, for all the fun we had with Mr. President."

"Remember how he squeaked whenever you opened the refrigerator, Mommy?"

"He always wanted a carrot!"

"Remember that time when we were cleaning his cage and he got away from Kris and ran into the fireplace and came out gray instead of black because he was all covered with ashes?" We laughed through our tears as we all remembered.

"Remember how we moved him home from Minnesota, and there was no room in the car for our feet but we didn't care because we got to keep Mr. President?"

"Please, God, take care of Mr. President!"

"Now Thomas Jefferson Tiger Cat won't be so lonesome, Mommy."

We put a piece of rose quartz we had brought back from the Black Hills on top of the grave and ran in out of the cold. Mr. President had joined two gerbils, a cat, and another guinea pig under the lilac bush.

We had faced the fact squarely — Mr. President was dead. We were sad and we cried. But we laughed too as we remembered funny things about him. We buried him simply, but reverently.

I still remember, though, what the woman at the veterinarian's office said to me: "You'd be surprised how many parents can't bring themselves to tell their children a pet has died. Sometimes they tell them the Vet gave their pet to someone else. What, we may ask, does this say to the child about veterinarians, and parents, and truth-telling?"

This reminded me of a woman I knew who rushed out to buy a new parakeet while her children were sleeping, so they wouldn't know that their own had died. She missed an important opportunity for helping her children face death. Ignoring death won't work in the long run.

Often a pet's death is the first chance we have to help children come to terms with the meaning of death. It can be the basis for a healthy, growing understanding of life and death.

But it can also be, as we have seen, the beginning of a deceitful, denying, and dishonest approach to the meaning of death. We dare not let this happen if we want to develop an open and honest atmosphere for exploring the meaning of death with our children.

What we may take to be "kindness" and "sparing them needless heartache at such a young age" is really more harmful than helpful. Speaking the truth in love and sharing the sadness it brings when a pet dies is the best approach in helping a child face life. It is not always easy; but in the long run it is best.

Sometimes it's hard to help our children face the truth. When we back the car over the puppy or when the neighbor runs over our cat, it hurts us to hurt our child with the truth. But what are the alternatives and where do they lead?

"The puppy ran away."

"But why? I loved him!"

Is this really less painful? And in the long run, might we not wish we had shared the truth together? I still wonder at the parents who often take this "less painful approach" and then cannot understand when their teen-agers don't level with them. Is it any wonder?

My friend's three-year-old daughter saw her kitten hit on the highway in front of her house. What is one to say to a three-year-old's plea? "But Mommy, I know she didn't want to die. She looked right in my eyes and I could tell!"

There isn't much we can say. We can hold the child. We can be there. It's hard! But that is life! And death! Denying or ignoring it won't help.

The man who hit the kitten stopped. He was distraught to see the child so upset. He apologized, though it wasn't really his fault. And then, because he felt so helpless standing there with a mother he didn't know, a sobbing child, and a dead kitten, he gave the child fifty cents, patted her on the arm and left.

I could not fault this stranger who cared enough to stop; at least he did *something* at a time when he did not know what to do or say. But neither did I know how to answer the mother when she asked me, "What could I reply when my daughter looked up at me and said, 'Why did that man pay me to kill my kitty?'"

Sometimes it hurts a lot to be truthful when a child's pet dies. But facing death as a part of life and sharing the burden of sadness can provide a solid foundation for the child's developing attitude toward life and death.

Our job is to help children face the fact of death. This means we must also help them work through any feelings of guilt or resentment they might feel.

The child might be angry with himself — "If only I'd called Bouncer in when Daddy told me to. It's my fault." He might feel resentment toward the neighbor — "Why did dumb old Mrs. Brown run over my kitty? She's just a mean old lady." At such a time of loss and anger we need to love the child, accept his feelings, and help him gradually work them through.

Painful though it is, a pet's death can provide the opportunity for developing a healthy and accepting attitude toward death. To deny children this confrontation with death and to refuse to help them meet the situation in truth will cripple them later when they cannot escape the reality of the death of someone they love.

I would be less than truthful if I did not admit that once we opt for the "face death in truth" approach, we're bound to be asked some hard questions. Children have a way of going right to the heart of the issue.

Let me share some simple guidelines I have found helpful in answering children's questions — on any subject. You may want to alter them for yourself or come up with an entirely different list. But I am convinced that guidelines are the key. Never in a million years can we anticipate the questions children ask! There's no way we can be prepared with all the answers! Our only hope is to have some principles at hand to guide us when the hard questions are asked.

Be accepting. Any question, honestly asked, deserves a serious answer.

Be honest. I try never to give an answer that I can't accept and believe.

Be straightforward. I try to answer the question that is asked as simply as possible. Then stop. If the child wants more information, he'll ask.

Don't lecture. This is one of the most difficult guidelines for me to follow. It's all too tempting to make a point or moralize.

Say "I don't know" when you don't know. This, of course, can be a cop-out unless you're willing to help the child try to find an answer. A teacher I once knew recommended, "If you don't know, bluff!" But this is never helpful and can destroy relationships almost beyond repair.

These guidelines are often easier to repeat than to implement. How they actually operate may become clear in the illustration that follows. My answers obviously will be different from yours. My purpose here is simply to illustrate a method that, appropriately adapted, can be used to answer difficult questions.

The question comes! "But, Mommy, will Bouncer go to heaven?"

Guidelines flash — be accepting . . . honest . . . straightforward . . . Then answer: "I don't really know. But I do believe that God will do whatever is best for Bouncer." Now I have to remind myself and even fight — to avoid lecturing. What I've said is not enough — for me. I'm not ready to stop but, hopefully, I will.

I've answered the question. If the child is satisfied, that is good. If not, she may continue, "But how do you know that, Mommy?"

"Well, Jesus once told his disciples that God knows and cares about the sparrows. I believe God cares about everything in his world. He cares about you and he cares about Bouncer, too. I trust God to do whatever is best for Bouncer."

"But, Mommy, will Bouncer go to heaven?"

"I don't know, honey."

Now if you really believe Bouncer will go to heaven, then, by my guidelines, you should say so. But if you don't, then saying, "Yes, sure, honey!" may seem easier at the moment, but it's potentially more harmful than helpful. There's lots more at stake than just sadness because Bouncer died.

Think about this. In the long run you are either saying, "Yes, you can trust me to answer your questions honestly" or you are saying, "You can see that I'll tell you whatever is easiest at the moment." The approach we adopt — the guidelines we choose to follow — will have a long-term effect on our relationship with our children as they mature.

Linda Jane Vogel is a graduate of Boston University and Andover Newton Theological School. She is the mother of three children and teaches Christian education at Westmar College in LeMars, Iowa.

BOOKS TO HELP ADULTS EXPLAIN DEATH TO A CHILD

About Dying, An Open Family Book for Parents
Sara Bonnett Stein
Walker and Company, 720 Fifth Avenue, New York, NY 10019 ($4.50)
A sensitive, honest book about death for parents and children to share together. The book contains a discussion for adults about children's feelings as they face death, along with a story for young children on the death of a pet bird, Snow, and the death of a beloved grandfather. Beautiful full-page photographs portray death from the eyes of a young child.

A Child's Parent Dies, Studies in Childhood Bereavement
Erna Furman
Yale University Press, 92A Yale Station, New Haven, CT 06520 ($15.00)
A serious study of the process of grief in young children from the psychoanalytic point of view. The book emphasizes the need for honesty, sensitive helping, and a secure family situation to lessen the effects of loss on the child. Terms such as "oedipal phase" and "cathexis" make reading more difficult, but the case studies will help parents who are anticipating death make the transition easier on their children.

The Bereaved Parent
Harriet Sarnoff Schiff
Crown Publishers, Inc., One Park Avenue, New York, NY 10016 ($7.95)
A mother who has lost a young son writes a useful and practical guide for other parents who must cope with the death of a child. Free from sentimentality and shallow reassurances, Ms. Schiff lets you know that you are not alone in your loss. She gives practical, bootstrap ideas for finding direction out of grief, including seeking and finding friends to share it with, and taking those first steps back to normalcy.

Helping a Child Understand Death
Linda Jane Vogel
Fortress Press, 2900 Queen Lane, Philadelphia, PA 19129 ($2.50)
From her personal experiences with death, the author guides adult readers using Christian concepts. The book is helpful in advising parents to be honest and aware of their children's needs when explaining death and suggests ways that adults can explore their own attitudes toward death.

"Helping Children Cope with Death"
Don Carter
Order from:
The Cooperative Extension Service, Bulletin Room, UMC 49, Room 102, Utah State University, Logan, UT 84322 (20¢)

The importance of including children in the talk about an impending death is explained. The book suggests that care-givers recognize the importance of play as a way in which preschoolers can express their feelings about death.

Learning to Say Good-By: When a Parent Dies
Eda LeShan
Macmillan Publishing Co., Inc., Riverside, NJ 08075 ($6.95)
A sensitive, tender book about grief for children who have lost a mother or father. Although it's intended for older children, it's most helpful for parents in becoming aware of the fears and hurt that are a natural part of grief. An excellent gift for a bereaved family.

Life After Death
Raymond A. Moody, Jr.
Bantam Books, Inc., 414 E. Golf Road, Des Plaines, IL 60016 ($1.95)
The experiences of over one hundred people who have been declared clinically dead but then brought back to life. The startling similarity of the death experiences of these people leads to a realization that perhaps human awareness reaches beyond the life of the body. The book will help you to become more comfortable with what death may feel like so that you can face it openly with your children.

On Death and Dying
Elisabeth Kübler-Ross
Macmillan Publishing Co., Inc., Riverside, NJ 08075 ($1.95, paperback)
Dr. Kübler-Ross discusses the stages of awareness of death — denial and isolation, anger, bargaining, depression, and finally acceptance on the part of the dying person. Interviews with terminally ill patients help the reader understand the agony but also the final victory that lies in facing death.

Should the Children Know? Encounters with Death in the Lives of Children
Marguerita Rudolph
Schocken Books, Inc., 200 Madison Avenue, New York, NY 10016 ($8.95)
Aimed at parents and teachers of three- to five-year-olds, the book offers constructive, practical advice about dealing with the questions and problems that children face when a death occurs. The author advocates sharing grief with children rather than shielding them from it with the belief that experiences with death can add to the strength and spirit in one's life.

Talking about Death: A Dialogue Between Parent and Child
Earl A. Grollman
Beacon Press, Inc., 25 Beacon Street, Boston, MA 02108 ($3.95, paperback)
Rabbi Grollman draws from his rich personal experiences as well as his knowledge of the psychology of children to provide a superb sourcebook for parents.

Telling a Child about Death
Edgar N. Jackson
Hawthorn Books, Inc., 260 Madison Avenue, New York, NY 10016 ($1.95)
A sensitive guidebook that includes advice on how to talk about death to children of different ages. The author discusses how children show their grief, the need for honesty and openness, and he emphasizes the importance of closeness, reassurance, and warmth to children during mourning.

BROCHURE

"Helping Your Child to Understand Death"
Anna W. M. Wolf
Child Study Press, Div. of Child Study Association of America/Wel-Met, Inc., 50 Madison Avenue, New York, NY 10010 ($1.50, paperback)
An exquisite brochure! Helps you find words to describe what death is. Answers from parents — when a child loses a pet, when a five-year-old's playmate dies, when a grandfather dies.
Suggestions for dealing with your children when you yourself are faced with grief.

CASSETTE TAPES

Talking to Children about Death
Death and the Child
The Charles Press Publishers, Inc., A Div. of the Robert J. Brady Co., Bowie, MD 20715 ($15.00 ea.)
Dr. George G. Williams of the University of Minnesota discusses ways to open the channels of communication between parent and child on the sensitive issue of death in "Talking to Children about Death." In "Death and the Child" Dr. Edgar N. Jackson directs his remarks to care-giving professionals who will shape children's attitudes on death. (Lengths: 57 minutes and 45 minutes respectively)

BOOKS FOR CHILDREN ON DEATH

The Dead Bird
Margaret Wise Brown
Young Scott Books, A Division of Addison-Wesley Publishing Co., Inc., Jacob Way, Reading, MA 01867 ($4.50)
Four children find a dead bird. They take it into the woods where they bury it and have a funeral. A simple story with artistic and poetic beauty. The final illustration shows children playing in the field near the bird's grave, as if to suggest that life goes on in spite of death.

Growing Time
Sandol Stoddard Warburg
Houghton Mifflin Company, Two Park Street, Boston, MA 02107 ($1.50, paperback)
Jamie's beloved dog, King, dies. The boy feels a deep sense of loss and loneliness, through which he is helped by the sensitive caring of the adults in his life. The unique contribution of the book is in its recognition of the pain of loss that a young child feels when first faced with the reality of death. The book is too long to keep the attention of most preschoolers, but the valuable message makes simplifying the book worthwhile.

My Grandpa Died Today
Joan Fassler
Human Sciences Press, 72 Fifth Avenue, New York, NY 10011 ($5.95)
Grandpa taught David how to play checkers, showed him how to hit a curve ball, and read him stories. They shared a very special kind of love. When Grandpa dies, David's loss is acknowledged and the rich relationship that he shared and will remember is emphasized.

My Grandson Lew
Charlotte Zolotow
Harper and Row, Pub., Inc., Keystone Industrial Park, Scranton, PA 18512 ($4.95)
A book of memories about a grandfather who has died. A small boy and his mother share their memories. A brief little book that might inspire you to begin your own memory book with your child.

Nanna Upstairs and Nanna Downstairs
Tomie de Paola
G. P. Putnam's Sons, 200 Madison Avenue, New York, NY 10016 ($4.99)
The story of a little boy's relationship with his elderly great-grandmother who is bedridden. We share the joy of a simple, childlike relationship that unites the two generations.

Nonna
Jennifer Bartoli
Harvey House, Inc., Publishers
℅ E. M. Hale and Co., 1201 South Hastings Way, Eau Claire, WI 54701 ($4.79)

A child tells the story of his grandmother's death and its effect on his family. There are brothers and sisters, cousins and uncles who help to lessen the sense of loneliness, of the personal loss that the boy feels. The family harvests Nonna's garden in the summer and at Christmas they enjoy cookies like those Nonna used to bake.

The Tenth Good Thing about Barney
Judith Viorst
Atheneum Publishers, Distributed by: Book Warehouse, Inc., Vreeland Avenue, Boro of Totowa, Paterson, NJ 07512 ($3.95)
A boy's cat, Barney, dies. He tries to think of ten good things about Barney for the funeral but can only think of nine. Together, he and his father plant flower seeds on the grave. The more subtle aspect of the story is the caring parents who support the child and encourage his dealing with the cat's death.

When Violet Died
Mildred Kantrowitz
Parents' Magazine Press, 52 Vanderbilt Avenue, New York, NY 10017 ($5.50)
Young children hold a funeral for a pet bird that dies. "Nothing lasts forever . . . nothing," Amy says sadly, but Eva thinks about Blanche the cat who will soon have kittens who will then grow up to have more kittens. Together they catch a glimpse of how life goes on.

Why Did He Die?
Audrey Harris
Lerner Publications Co., 241 First Avenue N., Minneapolis, MN 55401 ($3.95)
Although the book awkwardly attempts to rhyme, the explanations of death are clear and uncompromisingly honest. "All things must die and pass away" is the message.

PARENT GROUPS

Candlelighters, 123 C Street, S.E., Washington, DC 20003
(For parents of children with potentially fatal conditions.)

The Compassionate Friend, P.O. Box 3247, Hialeah, FL 33013
A support organization for parents whose child has died.

National Foundation for Sudden Infant Death, 1501 Broadway, New York, NY 10036
Offers solace to parents and up-to-date information on the Sudden Infant Death Syndrome.

Note: Not all manufacturers and publishers will accept single orders for a product or book. Always write to them first, before sending money, to be sure that they will take your order. Make sure you've got the most recent price, including shipping and handling charges. If the company is in your state, then you may need to include state sales tax as well.

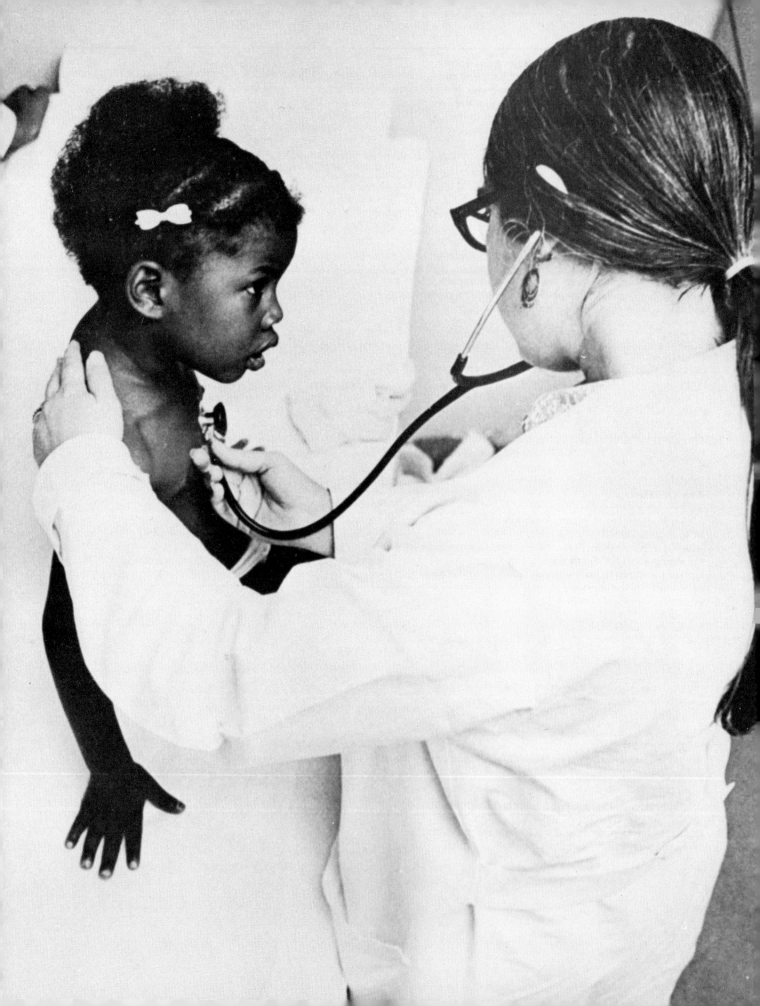

Dealing with Illness
and Other Medical Problems

9

THE SICK CHILD

Don't be surprised if your sick child shows a change in behavior. She may have a shorter attention span, be whiny and generally irritated and quick to cry. It's not unusual for children who are sick to regress to clingy, demanding, babylike behaviors that you thought were long behind. It's hard to be faced with this change without getting angry and feeling that you might succeed in punishing your child back to her old self. Forget it. Punishing will only make matters worse.

It's important to be kind to yourself if you're nursing a sick child. Taking care of a child who is ill is probably one of the most difficult (and unappreciated) tasks that you have as a parent. There's always the uneasy feeling of life being out of kilter, and maybe even a tinge of guilt about it. You need to give yourself some rewards, take opportunities for moments of refreshment to keep tension and fatigue from building up as the day wears on. A long hot bath, a relaxing book, asking someone to relieve you for twenty minutes for a brisk walk around the neighborhood, all these things can help keep your batteries charged for the giving that you're having to do.

Thinking positively about yourself and your child helps too — reminisce together about pleasant experiences that you've had and anticipate holidays and vacations that are yet to come. Send yourself and your child fresh flowers. Think about sprucing up the bedroom — new curtains, attaching a bird feeder to the windowsill, hanging a pot of greenery at the window, buying a goldfish.

If the illness is going to last longer than a few days, then it helps to plan special events to punctuate the day-to-day sameness. Perhaps it's a special party held in the bedroom, or a family storytime. Maybe it's a favorite TV program, complete with popcorn and sodas as a momentary splurge, or even a show of home movies or slides.

It helps to rearrange your child's room so that her bed is close to the window and she can peer out. Bring in a bedside table and lamp to make reading and in-the-bed projects easier. A shelf within reaching distance is helpful, too. This would be a good time to buy or rent an adjustable hospital-type table that extends over the bed. Or you can make your own bed-top table from three pieces of plywood (a top and two sides). You can also make a table using the bottom of a corrugated cardboard box. Measure it so the box fits comfortably over your child's legs. A table leaf resting on the rungs of ladderback chairs on either side of the bed will do.

A grocery bag rolled down and pinned to the side of the bed is a handy bedside trash basket or can be used to hold odds and ends. You can construct a handy pocket out of durable fabric with a cardboard-filled flap to tuck under the mattress and secure it to the side of the bed.

It might be worthwhile to fix up a sickbed downstairs, so that your child can have a change of scenery and so you can do the chores that you need to do while still being close at hand. Who says sick kids have to stay indoors? If it's spring or summer, why not prepare a cot or a quilt outside on the ground? One mother I know who had a chronically ill child would pack up her sewing and her child and go to a nearby park with a lake. They would spend several hours watching the light sparkle on the water before returning refreshed to the four walls of home.

Give a sick child useful tasks to do that will help you with chores: sorting socks, folding laundry, polishing silver, sewing on buttons, polishing shoes, preparing vegetables such as peeling potatoes or carrots, snapping beans, or shelling peas.

Keep in mind that prolonged TV viewing can arouse tension rather than relieve it. A regular schedule limited to two favorite programs a day would be wisest, giving the shut-in child something to look forward to during the long day. A record player, or cassette tape recorder-player offers the child a variety of choices and gives him a sense of mastery over what is heard. Many libraries offer record collections. If your child qualifies for the Talking Book Program (available in all states) because of blindness, reading disability, or physical handicap, he may be eligible to receive a record player and free mail service of recorded books. For more information write the Library of Congress, Division for Blind and Physically Handicapped, Washington, DC 20542.

HOUSEHOLD THINGS FOR PLAY

Old alarm clock to take apart with a container for the parts
Hole puncher
Tracing, writing, coloring, cutout, and pasting materials
Small magnets
Paper clips
Can of Play-Doh (work it well before using, it crumbles into little pieces that are hard to clean up)
Small blackboard and chalk
Box of toothpicks, styrofoam cups and balls to stick them in
Package of balloons
Magic slate (erases when the cover sheet is lifted)
A deck of cards
A kaleidoscope
An ink pad and moveable date stamp, or a toy printing set
Box of macaroni (for stringing and glueing to paper)
Pipe cleaners
Paper dolls

STEPS IN PREPARING A CHILD FOR HOSPITALIZATION

If your child must be hospitalized, when do you begin to tell her what's going to happen to her? The older your child is the more she will be able to tolerate the time between being told and the actual hospitalization. For preschoolers, two to three days before entering the hospital is early enough to broach the topic, but general preparation about doctors and hospitals should begin as soon as you expect that hospitalization will be necessary. (Even if you don't think your child will ever go to the hospital, it's valuable to familiarize her with this often unexpected experience.)

Reading is a good way to begin. A child can become familiar with what hospital beds look like, what injections are for, what an operation is. If you have memories of hospitalization yourself, you can share them — the funny smell of a hospital, what your room looked like, what it's like to use a bedpan, the way you called the nurses when you needed them. Having your child talk with other children who have had good hospital experiences is an excellent means for her to see that the experience can be positive.

Play-acting provides a good vehicle for becoming comfortable with procedures and instruments such as face masks, shots, and the frightening feelings they provoke. Perhaps you and your child can play doctor with a favorite doll or stuffed animal. Hand puppets and dolls enable you to communicate the child's own negative feelings — "I don't want to go! I'm so scared!" — so the child herself can play the role of comforter and clarify within herself the reason why people have operations.

Taking a tour of the hospital while secure in the presence of a parent can also ease a child's adjustment to where she will be. What may not seem important to an adult, such as the smell, may be very important to a small person. A hospital bed may appear strange in relation to a child's bed. Young children are put in high metal cribs with bars on the side, even though they may have outgrown their crib at home, and beds for preschoolers usually have a guardrail raised on both sides as a safety precaution. An introduction to these things before the child is a patient can help in the gaining of mastery over fears.

When it comes time to discuss your child's own hospitalization, one simple way is to make a storybook from blank pages stapled together: "Jennifer's Trip to the Hospital." You can supply the words and your child the pictures, or you can draw the pictures yourself. Explain how her room will look, how she won't be able to eat before the operation even though she's hungry, how she might have an injection that will hurt a little, how she will put on a "space mask" and breathe air that will make her want to go to sleep so that she won't feel any discomfort while the doctor fixes her, and that she will wake up with the expected discomfort after surgery. It's essential to stress the coming home aspect of the experience — that she tells the people at the hospital good-bye and goes back home to her brother, sister, or favorite pet.

It's important that you recognize a child's anxiety about the unknown and her fear of being abandoned can cause more discomfort to her than the actual hospital procedures. If you can help her to understand what the experience will be like, even the pain of it, you can help to provide a means for her to relate to the experience and a shield from the deep anxiety caused by being faced unexpectedly with a strange, new situation.

A simple calendar can be put on the wall to help the child to understand time concepts. The child can cross off days until hospital day. Each day in the hospital can be accounted for with drawings by the child and then the day for coming home clearly delineated to help the child grasp the departure, hospital stay, and return cycle.

Let your child help pack her own suitcase and select toys and books to bring with her. You'll want to pack her own pajamas, at least for the first night, a toothbrush and paste, a collection of favorite toys and books that should be labeled with the child's name, and clothes to wear home.

Some parents feel so threatened by their child's hospitalization that they feel uncomfortable about events that are frightening. Sometimes you may have the feeling that you might lose control in front of your child and begin crying. These are normal reactions: You care very much for your child and you want to protect her from unpleasant experiences. Even if you do cry, you will open between your child and yourself a channel for communication that permits the healthy expression of fears and negative feelings.

If you can, adopt a positive, hopeful attitude about the experience. Portray the hospital staff in your own mind and for your child as being caring people who want to help. Try to avoid communicating your own fear unconsciously to your child through tension and abruptness, moving quickly, or talking rapidly to other adults about the situation when your child is present.

When your child returns from the hospital, she may show signs of anger with you for what happened to her, feeling that you betrayed her trust by putting her in the hands of doctors. This is to be expected when her body has been turned over to strangers. Recognize these reactions rather than pretend that they are not there. "You really feel angry with me, don't you?" Make-believe can help. Set up a situation in which your child can let her dolls or stuffed animals portray some of the rage. Returning to babylike behavior, clinging, thumb-sucking and bed-wetting and nightmares may also temporarily occur as the child's way of expressing her anxiety. These behaviors can best be dealt with indirectly by offering physical closeness, rocking, reading stories — love and support, the age-old remedies for healing the spirit.

There's much that can be learned from hospitalization. Above all else, it can teach us that we are able to cope with stress and that sometimes what hurts can also help. We can learn to trust strangers. After all of the negative elements have been sifted out, it's valuable to look back with your child on the positive strength and forbearance that she was able to show and the way that you and she dealt with the problem together.

Rooming-In: My Experience with My Son
Erma Walsh

When the doctor told us that James, our six-year-old, was going to have to enter the hospital for brain surgery, both my husband, Michael, and I were shocked and frightened. Ever since he had been four, James had suffered a series of seizures. He had undergone a lot of tests and x rays but doctors had never been able to pinpoint the source of his problem. Finally, his seizures had gotten to the point that something had to be done.

That night I lay awake in my bed remembering the time I had hepatitis as a child. I was hospitalized for three weeks. I spent most of my time in the hospital alone, since there were very strict visiting hours. Painful memories flooded me of the doll my brother brought me to cheer me up, and of my crying every time my family left to go home. I determined then and there that I was going to stay in the room with James and be by his side as much as I could during his ordeal.

We had only two weeks to get ourselves and our son ready for his upcoming surgery. Fortunately, this was not to be his first trip to the hospital. The year before he had undergone a hernia operation. We had prepared him very carefully for his first visit by reading children's books on hospitals from the library and by talking honestly with him about what was going to happen to him. We realized that it was important not to gloss over what the experience was going to be like. We didn't want to arouse too much anxiety in him, but we were careful to explain to him that it would hurt and that we would be with him to comfort him. What would be done to him would help him feel better in the long run. He didn't seem overly upset by that first operation, and I sincerely feel that my being continually present with him helped him to come through his surgery without undue fear.

We told James's older sister, Michelle, what was going to happen, and we let her help us in planning for what she would do during this time. We feel that it is very important that other children in the house have a chance to participate and to help make decisions that are going to affect them. In our case, we were able to arrange for Michelle to go to her aunt's house in Philadelphia for two weeks. This suited Michelle, and she came back happy and a bit fatter than when she had left.

When it was time to pack for the hospital, I let James pick out his three favorite stuffed animals to bring with him. I felt that it was important for him to have a part of home with him — something familiar to play with. We also packed his own pajamas even though hospital pajamas were available. I packed enough clothes for myself for one week, along with the toiletries and self-care things that I felt I would need. It's important, too, to remember to pack a robe for yourself that gives you good cover since doctors are in and out constantly. (You'll find that you don't get much more privacy than the patient.)

One of the most difficult parts of James's hospitalization was the long hours of waiting. For example, when we went for James to be admitted, a lady took our name and then promptly passed us on to someone else. We sat and waited. Then we were called to a desk to give information. Then we sat and waited some more. All in all, we waited several hours. There were no toys, or any play area to accommodate children waiting to be admitted. That was to be just the beginning of the waiting. We waited for tests, waited for results, waited for the operation to be over, and waited while he was in intensive care. It's difficult to explain to someone who hasn't experienced it — the anxious loneliness of being separated from someone you love at the very time when you feel the strongest need to be with them. The painful good-bye as they are wheeled away from you and the shock of bandages and tubes when the ordeal is finally over.

Sometimes the hospital made no provision for the waiting of loved ones. When James had tests, I was left to wander back up three floors to my son's empty room. I'm sure I would have felt less tension if I had been able to wait on the floor, or been able to look in a window or door at my son once in a while just to reassure myself that all was well with him.

Hospital personnel assume that a child will respond better if the parent isn't there. But what I saw convinces me that the opposite is true. The children whose parents weren't with them, in some cases, were aggressive and disruptive to the nurses trying to carry on their responsibilities. I would see small children crying inconsolably through the night, and children wetting their beds while waiting for nurses to come and take them to the bathroom. Some children adapted to the stress of hospitalization by becoming totally passive with a glazed look in their eyes. I suppose that the casual observer would say that the child was doing fine since he or she made no demands on anyone. But as a mother of two children, I could tell that all of these children needed the physical closeness of the important people in their lives to reassure them of their own safety in a strange, and sometimes hurtful, situation.

Your most valuable ally during your child's hospitalization is a doctor who is willing to talk with you. We found one who came on duty on the evening shift who was willing to sit down and explain things in detail to us. He tried to answer our questions as honestly as he could. Taking a piece of paper, he diagrammed for us where James's cyst was on his brain and told us exactly what was going to be done in surgery. We were concerned about the side effects of James's medication. Other doctors told us not to worry about it, or that the side effects were rare. This doctor dealt with our question openly, telling us exactly what the side effects would be, even though they probably wouldn't occur.

I have stayed continually with my son during both of his hospitalizations. The first hospital did very little to provide for me to stay with my son. I spent a week sleeping on a narrow reclining chair in his room. There was no place to put my clothes. I had to use the ladies' room down the hall to brush my teeth and take care of my personal needs. I was made to feel that I was an intruder, when, actually, I was providing free nursing care for my son and trying to help him get well, just as the medical staff was.

The second hospital was much better prepared. I was willing to fight if I had to for the right to stay with my child, but, with great relief, I found that I didn't have to. The hospital provided me with a comfortable fold-away bed. The room had a closet where I could hang my clothes and its own bathroom. Down the hall was a shower and dressing room that I could use.

The hospital didn't provide me with anything to eat, though. So I waited until James was fed and his medicines all administered before I went downstairs to the cafeteria to eat my meals. I always took time to explain to James where I was going and that I would be back as quickly as I could, because I knew how a

few minutes to a grownup seem like hours to a young child.

I was surprised at how poor James's hospital food was from a nutritional standpoint. It was shocking to see the amount of junk cereals, doughnuts, Jell-O, and sodas served routinely. Vegetables were clearly the canned variety, heavy in salt and low in the necessary vitamins needed by the body for rapid healing. Most meals contained two or more carbohydrates.

I suggest that you bring nutritious snacks such as nuts, dried and fresh fruits into the hospital with you for yourself. (For some reason, I found myself very hungry between meals when I was just sitting.) I also brought vitamins for James. You might want to take time to read Adele Davis's book *Let's Get Well* about the role nutrition plays in healing. I followed her suggestions and felt that supplying his body with vitamins contributed to his speedy recovery. I was also glad that I brought a good supply of James's regular medicines since it took several days for the hospital to get through the red tape for approval from James's doctor to administer drugs that he was already taking.

You are not going to get much sleep in the hospital. Nurses come in at least twice a night to take temperatures and blood pressure. I found that I awoke each time the nurse arrived. James would wake up, too, and be unable to go back to sleep.

It's important to snatch naps whenever you get the opportunity. I slept while James played in the playroom down the hall where teachers and aides provided activities for him. My husband, Michael, relieved me for a whole day on weekends, so that I could go home and take a leisurely bath, wash and set my hair, and have some time to relax before returning to the hospital. In both cases, taking naps and taking time to go home, helped renew my spirits so that I could cope better. If the hospital is too far from home for you to do this, a hotel room for a day might be the next best.

I surprised myself at how well I was able to cope with being confined in a hospital room with a restless six-year-old who had to be helped and entertained continually. But I would be less than honest with you if I made you think that I was always the ''perfect mother'' (if there is such a thing!). At first my patience was marvelous. It took no effort to give myself to James and his needs. He needed me, and I was there. It was as simple as that. But as James began to recover, I found my patience beginning to wear thin. I became short-tempered and fatigued.

James was restless, too, as he began to feel better. He wanted to go home and play with his friends.

It really helped me, during these times, to have something to do. It was a good opportunity to catch up on books that I had always wanted to read. I found that doing work with my hands — crocheting, knitting, embroidery, or needlepoint — had a calming effect on me and helped take my mind off my problems for a while. If you decide to do handwork, I suggest that you find something to keep it in, since little children frequently wander from room to room, and you don't want anyone to be hurt by your scissors or needles.

When we first got home from the hospital, I found it difficult to treat James normally. He expected that we would give him as much attention at home as he received in the hospital. Michael and I had gotten conditioned, too, to waiting on him hand and foot. It's important, I think, to remind yourself that your child is well now and does not need constant attention, that he can do some things for himself. Once your child has adjusted to being back home and seems happy, there's no reason he can't wait his turn like everybody else. Given plenty of love and attention when needed, he should fall back into the normal family pattern quickly.

For several weeks after coming home, I found myself "gun-shy" as my husband termed it. Every time James made a loud noise while playing, or dropped something, I would jump up thinking something had happened to him. At the sound of any noise, my insides felt like my heart had fallen to my stomach. I found myself exhausted all of the time, a natural letdown, I think, from the stress we'd been through.

A few weeks before school was to start, with the doctor's approval, I took the kids and went on a quiet camping trip. Michael couldn't get time off from work, so he joined us on the weekend. The change of scenery worked wonders for all of us. We relaxed, had a lot of fun and came home feeling that we were able to cope with whatever lay ahead.

Now, as I look back over our hospital experience, I think the thing that James and all children need during this difficult time is the closeness and reassurance of the important people in their lives. (I am not convinced that the person who stays with the child has to be the mother — particularly if the child has a close attachment to the father or some other person in the family.) I want to emphasize how essential I think it is to be honest with your child. Don't overstate the pain, but if it will hurt, even a tiny amount, tell him. It's important to your relationship with your child that he feels that he can trust you, and that you won't lie to him. If it hurts, let him cry. Tell him that it's O.K. to cry rather than trying to make him hold his feelings in. What you can give to your child is your physical closeness, holding him, stroking his face — just letting him know that you are there. It will be your job to sympathize with him even when no one else will. I don't regret a moment of the time that I spent with James in the hospital, and I feel that many children and their parents would benefit from rooming-in during hospitalization.

Erma Walsh is actively involved with the La Leche League International as a district advisor. She and her husband, Michael, are parents of Michelle, twelve, and James, six.

CHILDREN IN HOSPITALS

Children in Hospitals (31 Wilshire Park, Needham, MA 02192) is a nonprofit organization of parents and health-care professionals organized to educate and support parents who wish to keep in close touch with their children during the experience of hospitalization. The organization offers personal counseling to parents, a newsletter, information sheets, and meetings. Membership is four dollars a year. They have the following suggestions based on the experiences of many parents:

1. Trust your instincts. You know your child better than anyone else does. If you feel he needs you, stay with him as much time as you can. You have the right to stay with your child whatever hours you wish to stay no matter what visiting hours have been established by the hospital. This is true whether you are a clinic patient or a private patient.

Children become fearful of even routine tests and exams without the reassuring presence of a parent. Often they withdraw and become silent and "good." Hospital staff often interpret this as adjusting, but medical literature tells us this is a sign of emotional upset, requiring more parental contact.

You are experienced in the care of your child and can help in her care. Usually you can continue the routine things you do for your child at home. She will react well to familiar handling. The nurses will tell you of special precautions that may be necessary. Medical sources report that children recover faster and with fewer complications when cared for by parents.

2. Shop for a doctor. Find one sympathetic to your being with your child as much as you feel the child will need you. If you cannot agree on this perhaps you will work better with another doctor. Letting your doctor know how strongly you feel may be all that is necessary for winning his or her support.

3. Shop for a hospital. Call and ask about policies regarding visiting and rooming-in. Your child may need you full time especially if she is too young to understand explanations, or is in pain, or is upset by being separated from you. A breast-fed baby will also need you beyond regular visiting hours so as not to interrupt her customary feeding routines.

4. Prepare yourself. Find out in advance about tests, procedures, surgery, future restrictions on the child, and special care so you can explain these things simply to your child in language she will understand. Read, ask questions, talk with other parents about their experiences. If your child is an infant, your preparation will help you cope with the experience and be calm and reassuring with your child. Discuss with the doctor and nurses how much of the regular care of the child you can continue to provide.

5. Prepare your child. Be honest with her. Tell her the reason for the hospitalization in terms she will understand. Assure her that you know these doctors and nurses have helped other children and will also be able to help her. Be sure to tell her there may be pain or discomfort for a short time, but that each day she will feel better and be getting ready to come home.

Some children will ask no questions or will refuse to talk about a planned hospital stay but continue to mention the subject in the days before they are admitted.

Be honest about how much time you will spend with her. Always tell her when you are

leaving. Let the nurses know when you are going so they can offer some comfort to the child. It may seem easier to slip away when she is playing happily, but when she finds you gone she will feel more confused than if she had seen you go. Children often are afraid you won't come back or that they won't go home again.

After a hospitalization, parents often notice signs of upset that continue for days or weeks. Some children wake at night, cling more by days, fear doctor visits, and wet their beds. Some try hard to behave perfectly fearing a return to the hospital as punishment.

6. Work for changes. Write to the hospital and to the doctor after a hospitalization to let them know what you liked and disliked about your child's hospital experience. Request any policy changes that you would like to see made. Send Children in Hospitals an account of your experience to share with other parents.

7. Be present at the important times. If you cannot be in the hospital full time, you should try to be there the first night of a stay, as well as just before and after surgery. Find out when major tests and procedures are being done so as to be there during them or to offer support to the child immediately afterward. Many members have gone with their children while anesthesia was given at such hospitals as Massachusetts General and Children's Hospital in Boston. Parents have also been with their children in the recovery rooms in some hospitals. These can be scary times for children and they can benefit from the presence of their parents.

PARENT SUPPORT GROUPS

The following organizations are made up of parents and professionals working to liberalize and humanize hospital policies to the benefit of children and their parents. Many offer counseling to parents who will be facing the hospitalization of their children, as well as newsletters and group meetings.

Associaton for the Care of Children in Hospitals
P.O. Box H, Union, WV 24983

Candlelighters
123 C Street, S.E., Washington, DC 20003
(For parents of children with potentially fatal conditions.)

Children in Hospitals
31 Wilshire Park, Needham, MA 02192

Family Centered Parents
Box 142, Rockland, DE 19732

National Association for the Welfare of Children in Hospitals (NAWCH)
Exton House, 7 Exton Street, London SE180E, England

Total Parent Education of Greater Cincinnati
P.O. Box 39382, Cincinnati, OH 45239

Mothershare
P.O. Box 694, Huntington, NY 11743

Virginia Rae
615 Henley Avenue, Pine Beach, NJ 08741

Children in Hospitals, Minneapolis
Mrs. Ed Golly, 8001 30th Avenue N., Minneapolis, MN 55427

Maine Children in Hospitals
Linda Hadley, 91 Broadlawn Drive, Brewer, ME 04412

Parents Concerned with Hospitalized Children
Jody Grove, 176 N. Villa Avenue, Villa Park, IL 50181

Children in Hospitals, New Hampshire
Amherst, NH 03031

Consumers for Family-Centered Health Care
P.O. Box 165, Union City, CA 94587

Children in Hospitals, Butler
Jackie Hoeflinger, 14 De Bow Terrace, Butler, NJ 07405

Parents for Family-Centered Health Care
Mrs. Richard Garey, 10 Main Street, Walden, NY 12586

Children in Hospitals, Vermont
Susanna Griefen, 35 Lexington Avenue, Brattleboro, VT 05301

Children in Hospitals
Mrs. Larry Palm, 856 N. 12th Street, Reading, PA 19604

BOOKS FOR ADULTS ON CHILDREN'S HOSPITALIZATION

**Emotional Care of Hospitalized Children:
An Environmental Approach**
Madeline Petrillo and Sirga Sanger
J. B. Lippincott Company, E. Washington Square, Philadelphia, PA 19105 ($6.25, paperback)
Written primarily for the professional health-care worker, I find this book very useful from the parent's standpoint. It is an excellent guidebook for preparing a child for surgery. Specific examples are given for preparing a child for a tonsillectomy, a hernia operation, correcting crossed eyes, and a number of other common operations for children. Suggestions for stimulating imaginary play so that children can act out their fears and anxieties about injections and operations.

Children in the Hospital
Thesi Bergmann in collaboration with Anna Freud
International Universities Press, Inc., 239 Park Avenue S., New York, NY 10003 ($3.45)
The authors are child therapists who describe their work with children and the emotional effects of hospitalization upon them. Techniques for comforting and giving support to young patients are offered, as well as close observations of how individual children cope with the stresses of hospitalization and surgery. Helpful if your child is facing long-term confinement.

"In Hospital: The Child and the Family"
(Publication #143)
Betty Ann Countryman
La Leche League International, Inc., 9616 Minneapolis Avenue, Franklin Park, IL 60131 (30¢)
A frank discussion of the rights of parents to be with their babies and children during hospitalization. "Is the hospitalization really necessary?" Discusses what behavior to expect when the child comes home.

"When a Child Goes to the Hospital"
Ann Leslie Moore
Eliot-Pearson Alumnae Association, Inc., Tufts
University, Medford, MA 02155 ($1.00)
A very practical brochure that explains how to
discuss hospitalization with your child.
Occupations and toy suggestions for all ages from
babies to fifteen-year-olds. Suggests ways of
helping to eliminate children's fears through
reassurance and honesty.

"When Your Child Goes to the Hospital"
Children's Bureau
Order from:
Superintendent of Documents, U.S. Government
Printing Office, Washington, DC 20402 (85¢)
A helpful brochure that encourages parents to seek
more information about the upcoming
hospitalization of their child. Suggests books and
films for children and adults. One quote in the
booklet worth knowing: "As you make your
decisions about staying with the child, it's possible
that some doctors or nurses will tell you that
children are better off, even in the first few days, if
parents don't stay with them. *There is no justification*
for telling parents that. Much research over the past
twenty-five years has shown that the old way of
simply telling arriving parents to 'go home and
wait, the child will cry less if you're not there' is
wrong and *especially* when children younger than
four or five are involved."

BOOKS FOR YOUNG CHILDREN ABOUT DOCTORS, ILLNESS, AND HOSPITALIZATION

Books showing women in the role of physician are
noted. Unfortunately, almost all picture books dealing with the medical professions, although excellent
in every other respect, have presumed that only men
are doctors and women are nurses. It's important
that you point out to your child as you read these
books that both women and men can be either doctors or nurses to help free your child from the mis-
conception that roles are solely determined by
gender.

A Visit to the Doctor
Knute Berger, Robert A. Tidwell, Margaret
Haseltine
Grosset & Dunlap, Inc., 51 Madison Avenue, New
York, NY 10010 ($2.95, paperback)
A reprint of a 1960 book with dated illustrations.
Deals with taking weight, temperature, a
stethoscope, brief discussion of the circulatory
system, and getting a shot.

A Visit to the Hospital
Francine Chase
Grosset & Dunlap, Inc., 51 Madison Avenue, New
York, NY 10010 ($2.50, paperback)

Originally published in 1957, this second printing
retains the somewhat dated illustrations. It is the
story of Stevie who goes to the hospital to have his
tonsils removed. Although it dwells only
momentarily on the discomfort of the operation and
tests, there are clear explanations about hospital
beds, uniforms, and the anesthesia mask.

Betsy and the Chicken Pox
Gunilla Wolde
Random House, 457 Hahn Road, Westminster, MD
21157 ($1.95)
Betsy's baby brother gets itchy red spots. Dad takes
a rectal temperature, the baby has a fever. Betsy is
jealous of all the attention her baby brother is
getting until she gets chicken pox, too. Then she
doesn't like them.

Curious George Goes to the Hospital
Curious George Takes a Job
H. A. Rey and Margaret Rey
Houghton Mifflin Company, Two Park Street,
Boston, MA 02107 ($1.50 ea., paperback)
George, the ever curious and sometimes naughty
monkey, undergoes surgery after swallowing a
piece of a puzzle (*Curious George Goes to the
Hospital*). Hospitalized for a broken leg, George gets
into the ether (*Curious George Takes a Job*).

Danny Goes to the Hospital
James Lincoln Collier
W. W. Norton and Company, Inc., 500 Fifth
Avenue, New York, NY 10036 ($3.50)
Danny undergoes surgery to correct crossed eyes
(strabismus).

"Danny's Heart Operation"
"Dee Dee's Heart Test"
Public Relations Department, Children's Hospital of
Philadelphia, 34th Street and Civic Center
Boulevard, Philadelphia, PA 19104 (Single copies
free; 15¢ ea. additional copy)
Clearly written accounts of a cardiac catheterization
and the experience of heart surgery. Includes tests,
intensive care and a mention of postoperative plans.

Elizabeth Gets Well
Alfons Weber
Thomas Y. Crowell Co., 666 Fifth Avenue, New
York, NY 10019 ($4.50)
A very descriptive book about Elizabeth's
hospitalization and appendectomy. Includes
injection, stitches, blood tests, and other medical
procedures.

Good-Bye Tonsils
Anne Guy
Western Publishing Company, Inc., 1220 Mound
Avenue, Racine, WI 53404 (39¢)
Mary Ann has her tonsils out. The story is too
cheerful to be realistic, but taking a blood sample
and other aspects of hospitalization are mentioned.

A Hospital Story: An Open Family Book for Parents and Children Together
Sara Bonnett Stein
Walker & Company, 720 Fifth Avenue, New York, NY 10019 ($5.95)
Jill goes to the hospital to have her tonsils taken out. An honest account of the fears and discomforts a child feels during hospitalization. Illustrated with photographs.

Have a Happy Measle, a Merry Mumps and a Cheery Chickenpox
Jeanne Bendick
McGraw-Hill Book Company, 1221 Avenue of the Americas, New York, NY 10036 ($3.50)
For children who are sick at home with common childhood illnesses — stories, poems.

I Think I Will Go to the Hospital
Jean Tamburine
Abingdon Press, 201 Eighth Avenue S., Nashville, TN 37202 ($4.50)
Susy has a tonsillectomy. Well-done book is honest and presents a number of hospital procedures realistically, including blood tests and going to the operating room.

"I Went to the Hospital"
Tompkins County Hospital Auxiliary, P.O. Box 23, Ithaca, NY 14580 (35¢)
A child describes his hospital experiences — taking a "sleepy" pill and a "sleepy" injection, having a blood test, sleeping in a hospital bed. Simple, easy-to-understand language.

Jeff's Hospital Book
Harriet Lansam Sobol
Henry Z. Walck, Inc., Div. of David McKay Company, Inc., Promotion Department, 750 Third Avenue, New York, NY 10017 ($6.95)
Jeff has an operation to help correct his crossed eyes. A well-written book that includes the child's admission, experiences in the operating and recovery rooms.

Let's Find Out about the Clinic
Robert Froman
Franklin Watts, Inc., Subs. of Grolier, Inc., 845 Third Avenue, New York, NY 10022 ($3.75)
Written for young readers to read for themselves, this book talks about medical professionals and some equipment and procedures such as blood tests, scales, stethoscope and blood pressure.

Let's Go to the Doctor's Office
Billy N. Pope and Ramona Ware Emmons
Taylor Publishing Company, ℅ Newsfoto Publishing Company, Box 1392, San Angelo, TX 76901 ($3.00)
Full-color photographs show a doctor's and a dentist's offices. Children get immunizations, have their blood pressure taken. Dentist gives toothbrushing demonstration, and takes x rays.

Madeline
Ludwig Bemelmans
Viking Press, Inc., 625 Madison Avenue, New York, NY 10022 ($1.25, paperback)
Madeline has her appendix taken out. Little resemblance to an actual hospital situation but an enjoyable story nonetheless.

Mr. Rogers Talks About . . .
Platt and Munk, Div. of Questor Educational Products, 1055 Bronx River Avenue, Bronx, NY 10472 ($4.95)
A discussion in clear language about going to the doctor, along with moving, a new baby, getting a haircut, and other concerns of preschoolers. Color photographs.

Mom! I Broke My Arm!
Angelika Wolff
The Lion Press, Inc., Distributed by Sayre Publishing, Inc., 111 E. 39th Street, New York, NY 10016 ($3.95)
Steven breaks his arm and has a cast put on. Discomforts of the cast are openly discussed along with x rays and cast removal.

My Doctor
Harlow Rockwell
Macmillan Publishing Company, Inc., Riverside, NJ 08075 ($4.95)
A child's visit to a woman doctor and clear illustrations of the tools that she uses: blood pressure cuff, scale, syringe.

My Friend the Doctor
Sylvia Tester
David C. Cook Publishing Company, Elgin, IL 60120 ($1.95)
A large-sized book created for telling groups of children about a visit to the doctor. It makes an interesting picture book as well. Excellent full-color illustrations tell the story from the point of view of the child. Shows the child being weighed, having blood pressure taken, ears and throat examined.

My Friend the Doctor
Jane Werner Watson, Robert E. Switzer and J. Cotter Hirschberg
Golden Press, Western Publishing Company, Inc., 1220 Mound Avenue, Racine, WI 53404 ($1.95)
A read-together book for parents and children written in cooperation with the Menninger Foundation. A visit to the doctor: physical examination, finger prick, injection, rectal temperature. Home visit by a doctor.

Pop-Up Going to the Hospital
Bettina Clark and Lester L. Coleman
Random House, Inc., 457 Hahn Road, Westminster,
MD 21157 ($2.50)
Accepting the fact that pop-up books are fragile and
quickly torn up by young hands, this book about
Andy's tonsillectomy is excellent. Discussion of
mask for anesthesia, procedures such as blood test,
and not being allowed to eat.

Richard Scarry's Nicky Goes to the Doctor
Richard Scarry
Western Publishing Company, Inc., 1220 Mound
Avenue, Racine, WI 53404 ($1.95)
Colorful, detailed pictures tell about a routine visit
to the doctor by Nicky the bunny.

Tommy Goes to the Doctor
Gunilla Wolde
Houghton Mifflin Company, 2 Park Street, Boston,
MA 02107 ($1.65)
An excellent little book! A visit to a woman
doctor — usual examinations and an injection.
Realistic reactions by Tommy.

What Happens When You Go to the Hospital
Arthur Shay
Reilly and Lee Company, Distributed by Henry
Regnery Company, 114 W. Illinois Street, Chicago,
IL 60610 ($5.95)
Karen, a black child, has her tonsils out, is
realistically upset by the x ray machine and her
parents leaving, dislikes the sides of her bed, but in
the end is shown going home with her parents.
Black-and-white photographs.

Play Family Children's Hospital
The front of the box opens to reveal a hospital
setting with an x ray machine, an ambulance, a
wheelchair, two beds and chairs, medical personnel
including one wearing a mask, operating table, and
a mother, father, child, and baby. Twenty pieces in
all. Available in toy and department stores.
Manufactured by:
Fisher-Price Toys, A Division of The Quaker Oats
Company, East Aurora, NY 14052 ($20.80)

PRODUCTS

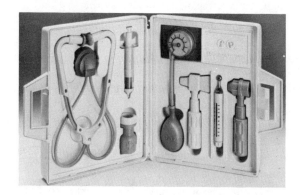

Medical Kit
Kit includes seven make-believe medical
instruments, including a stethoscope that can detect
heartbeat and a play syringe with a medicine bottle
that gives the appearance of medicine flowing into
the syringe. Available in toy and department stores.
Manufactured by:
Fisher-Price Toys, A Division of The Quaker Oats
Company, East Aurora, NY 14052 ($12.65)

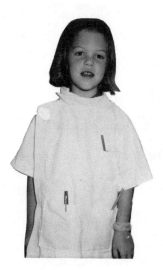

Child-Sized Doctor's Smock
Your child can pretend being "doctor" herself with
this handmade copy of a real doctor's smock. White
polyester and cotton with Velcro closures. Also
available for a 10- to 12-inch doll (Barbie size), or for
a 14- to 16-inch doll ($1.50 each). The "Toys That
Care" catalog (50¢) has an authentic stethoscope for
$6.50, and anatomically correct boy and girl dolls for
children.

Toys That Care, P.O. Box 81, Briarcliff Manor, NY
10510 (Size 4 and under [small], $11.00; sizes 4–7
[medium], $11.75 + 15% postage and handling.)

"The Doctor" Floor Puzzle

A giant, full-color puzzle measuring 2 x 3 feet.
Printed in bright colors on heavy, plastic-coated
board that can be cleaned easily with a damp cloth.
Consists of approximately fifteen pieces, depicting a
medical clinic with a waiting room, an examining
room, x ray, a child getting a shot, a laboratory.
From the Judy Company, makers of excellent
puzzles for young children. Order from:
Barclay School Supplies, 26 Warren Street, New
York, NY 10007 ($9.95 + $2.00 postage and
handling)

Medicine Spoon

A lighted, indexed spoon that makes it simple to
measure out a dose and to keep it level from bottle
to mouth. Intrigues a young child enough to make
medicine-taking a little nicer. (Remember *always* to
turn on the bathroom light to select and measure
drugs.)
Gus File, Inc., P.O. Box 3006, Albuquerque, NM
87110 (Approx. $3.00)

THE HANDICAPPED CHILD

Being the Parent of a Special Child
by Janis Ellis

I first began to suspect that something was wrong
with my son Billy when he was just a baby. He was
much slower in doing things like sitting up and
walking than other babies I had watched. He just
seemed more floppy. Our pediatrician would always
soothe my fears and tell me just to wait. Finally,
when he was two years old, the orthopedist we were
going to for Billy's feet noticed that when Billy
reached for a cookie his hand trembled. He over-
reached for the cookie and then moved his hand back
to grasp it. She wanted Billy to see a neurologist.

The neurologist spent only a short time with Billy
before he called us into his office to announce to us
that our son was functioning on a ten-month-old's
level even though he was twenty-six months old. As
much as we tried to get more information from him,
the physician coolly and aloofly refused to commit
himself but referred us to an institute for further
tests. My husband thought the news was optimistic
in that the doctor didn't want to alarm us unduly. I
felt just the opposite. In time we learned that Billy
was retarded. That word chills me even now when I
hear it. He was also hyperactive so that we had to
hold his hand constantly in order to control him.

Billy is almost eight now and lives in a residential
treatment center for trainable retarded children during the week. I would like to share with you what we
have been through. The stages I describe are very
similar to those Elisabeth Kübler-Ross found in patients accepting their own deaths (see the review of
On Death and Dying, page 107). The difference for
parents of a disabled child is that the grief never
ends as it does with death.

The first stage is *shock.* There is a numbness that
takes over, which allowed me to keep on doing routine chores. It all seemed very unreal, as though I
were watching a movie rather than learning that my
own child was retarded. Very quickly after shock
comes *denial.* I just couldn't believe that what was
being said about my son was true. I found myself
running to the library to try to diagnose for myself
what was wrong with Billy. I came up with ten different conditions I was sure applied to him. First I
thought he was autistic, then I thought he had cerebral palsy.

Looking back now I see that this information-seek-
ing, although it gave me something to do in the un-

certainty of those first days, was also harmful. The many different case histories and their diagnoses frightened me more than they helped me. Deeper than that, I developed a cool, intellectual façade that made me seem as though I understood everything while inside I was emotionally torn up and needing help. I found that I assimilated information intellectually almost a year before I began to work through my inner feelings.

Since that time I've seen other parents show their emotional denial of the crisis they are going through in different ways. One mother carried her child from one doctor and clinic to another in hopes of finding a miracle cure. Another suddenly became very religious, and found great meaning in having been blessed with her handicapped child. I sense that each of us has our own characteristic way of dealing with the inner turmoil necessary for the true acceptance of this deeply painful experience.

Along with denial came *anger*, deep, raging anger that struck irrationally at everything and everybody. I found that I was deeply angry at the doctor who first gave us the news about Billy's condition. I have since found that almost every parent of a disabled child feels that resentment toward the news bearer. I was angry with parents of normal children, even though I had a normal child, too. I was angry at parents of handicapped children. When I went to a meeting of a parent-support group at the suggestion of my social worker, I found myself silently seething and refused to tell them about Billy. Schools that refused to take Billy into their preschool programs also were the targets of my wrath. It is important during this stage of denial and anger to be able to talk with someone about your feelings, rather than let these emotions eat you up inside. I fortunately found a sensitive former learning-disabilities teacher of mine who agreed to work with me over a period of time.

One of the most constructive things that my counselor did was to carry on a desensitizing program to help me deal with my anxieties and fears. She asked me to make a list beginning with the things that made me the most anxious and ending with what made me the least anxious and even happy about Billy. At the bottom of the list was the great joy I feel when Billy sees me and runs to hug me. The list included my fear that Billy would forget us or that we would forget him if he went into a residential treatment program, or my anxiety over the feeling that other people were judging me. First on the list was the fact that I am the mother of a retarded child. When I got stuck on one of the problems, it was a signal to go back and work on earlier ones before

moving ahead. While I still have trouble now and then dealing with these same problems, being able to check off my progress helped me to see that I could begin to cope with this crisis in my life. I found that my fears about Billy's future — what he would be like as a teen-ager or what would happen when we died — were really covers for my present anxieties about Billy's head-banging and destructiveness and the fact that I couldn't cope with him.

The most practical advice I can give to parents who are dealing with a disabled preschooler is to find some form of care for the child — even if it's just a baby sitter for an hour a day — so that you can have time for yourself, perhaps just to go upstairs and read a book. Concentrate on yourself, not just on your child. I know parents who feel that every single minute of the day must be devoted to their special child even at the expense of other children. It seems to me that this kind of total effort, making your child your life's work, is a form of self-imposed punishment. You need to have a hobby. You need someone to keep your child on occasional weekends so that you and your spouse can get away and recharge yourselves for the day-to-day coping.

Time is the greatest healer. The pain of the early experiences of finding out about your child and seeking answers to dealing with his problems will diminish in time just as grief does. That's not to say that you will ever get over it. Even now I find myself hoping that I will wake up to discover it was all a dream. The stages of adjustment that I thought I had mastered have to be worked through all over again, especially in times of new crises about Billy, but the anxieties and fears don't have as strong a hold on me as they did in those first years.

I'd like to reassure you that there does come a time when you will be able to take what you have experienced and use it in a positive way. You will find that life goes on in spite of tragedies. My husband and I have been drawn closer together because of Billy, while weaker marriages have been pulled apart by having a disabled child. I've come to appreciate truly what it's like to have a normal child — something so many parents take for granted. And I've found a new career as a teacher in a nursery school that accepts special children.

I've stayed with my parent-support group through these years and now I find myself able to help other parents who are experiencing what I went through. We are working together to try to make doctors and medical students sensitive to the feelings of parents during those crucial first interviews. So often the doctor, who has no interviewing training, is just as upset as the parents and rushes to get the session over with, hoping not to have to see the parents again. On the other hand, parents are furious at having to receive this news and become unable to hear what the doctor is saying. We were fortunate in having a doctor who realized this and so set up another appointment a week later to answer our questions. Professionals dealing with parents need to understand that each person can be at a different point in accepting and coping with his or her child's handicap. What might help one parent may hurt another.

I think that teachers of special children have a long way to go, too, in learning to relate to parents. Perhaps it's that they don't know what to say, or what to do with the child. To the other extreme, there are teachers who feel that they have all the answers and become hostile toward parents who don't carry out their programs at home. It's important for outsiders to realize that the few moments of interaction that they see between the parent and the child each day are not the true indicators of how a parent and child interact at home. Some teachers are quite concerned about how a handicapped child seems to manipulate a parent. Putting the relationship of a parent and child into a manipulative frame of reference overlooks the emotional ties that make a home an entirely different place than a school. Perhaps a mother can't carry out an intensive behavior modification program at home while carrying out the multitude of other duties she performs for her family. I feel that this is no reason to stand in judgment against her. There needs to be more sensitivity — more caring and sharing back and forth. If we as parents can reach the professionals who so often treat anguished parents with aloofness and abruptness, or who judge us harshly, as though we were at fault for our child's handicap, then we will have done something to help parents and professionals who come after us!

Here is a list of several books that helped me:

A Child Called Noah: A Family Journey
Josh Greenfield
Holt, Rinehart and Winston, Inc., 383 Madison Avenue, New York, NY 10017 ($5.95; also available in Warner paperback)
A touching and sensitive story by a father about his autistic child.

David
Nancy Roberts
John Knox Press, 341 Ponce de Leon Avenue, N.E., Atlanta, GA 30307 ($3.95, paperback)

A photographic story about a young child with Down's syndrome (mongolism) written by his mother and photographed by his father.

Is It Well with the Child? A Parent's Guide to Raising Mentally Handicapped Children
Susan Strauss
Doubleday & Co., Inc., 245 Park Avenue, New York, NY 10017 ($7.95)
A mother talks about her own experiences with her child. She discusses diagnosis of the problem, reactions and some solutions to dealing with a handicapped child.

Thursday's Child Has Far to Go
Kathleen Lukens and Carol Panter
(Out of print but available in many libraries)
Four stories about handicapped children written by parents.

Janis Ellis is the mother of two children, Jimmy, twelve, and Billy, eight. She has a master's degree in Early Childhood Education and directs and teaches a nursery school for three- and four-year-olds. She also teaches a course on the hospitalized child at Villa Julie College in Baltimore, Maryland.

EDUCATION FOR HANDICAPPED CHILDREN

The Education for All Handicapped Children Act, which went into effect nationwide in September of 1978, is now having a big impact on education, particularly on special education. One of the law's provisions is that handicapped children may not be segregated from nonhandicapped children except when the nature or severity of their handicaps prevents them from being served in a regular classroom with the help of supplementary materials. States are now required to provide a free public education for all handicapped children between the ages of three and eighteen (except where state laws conflict on the age range). Parents are given the right to examine all school records relating to their child and no child can undergo assessment without written permission from his or

About Handicaps: An Open Family Book for Parents and Children Together
Sara Bonnett Stein
Walker and Co., 720 Fifth Avenue, New York, NY 10019 ($5.95)

Claire and Emma
Diana Peter
John Day Co, Inc., 666 Fifth Avenue, New York, NY 10019 ($5.95)
A simply written explanation of children's hearing deficiency. Hearing aids are described, as are the extra lessons needed by deaf children. Full-color photographs are used.

Don't Feel Sorry for Paul
Bernard Wolf
J. B. Lippincott Co., 521 Fifth Avenue, New York, NY 10017 ($6.95)
A photographic essay about an eight-year-old boy whose hands and feet are incompletely formed. With the help of artificial feet and a hand like a two-part hook, Paul is shown living, working, and playing with other children. The text of the book is too long and wordy for preschoolers but the photographs are self-explanatory.

He's My Brother
Joe Lasker
Albert Whitman and Company, 560 West Lake Street, Chicago, IL 60606 ($4.75)
A simply written book — no moralizing — about a boy's brother, Jamie, who has the "invisible handicap" (as explained in the back of the book) of uneven growth and development. Jamie took a long time to learn to tie his shoes and school is hard for him. The book communicates a family's acceptance of a slow and somehow different child.

Howie Helps Himself
Joan Fassler
Albert Whitman and Company, 560 West Lake Street, Chicago, IL 60606 ($4.50)
The small victory of Howie, a boy whose legs and arms were weak and who rides in a wheelchair. He goes to special classes and finally is able to make his wheelchair move himself after great effort. The inner feelings of joy and pain about a handicap.

I Have a Sister, My Sister Is Deaf
Jean Whitehouse Peterson
Harper and Row, Pubs., Inc., Keystone Industrial Park, Scranton, PA 18512 ($4.95)
A six-year-old's younger sister is deaf. Explains deafness in a way that young children can understand — she has trouble talking, she cannot hear when someone is at the door, she can watch TV without the sound on. She is shown as a part of a loving relationship which has its own ways of communicating.

her parents. Parents cannot be asked for permission to place a child in special education until they have been fully informed of the results of their child's evaluation. If the parents are dissatisfied with the test results, they can get an independent evaluation of their child. This second evaluation may be used in an impartial hearing at the request of the parent.

If you would like more information about special education and the new federal law, read Kate Long's book, *"Johnny's Such a Bright Boy, What a Shame He's Retarded"* (Houghton Mifflin Co., Two Park St., Boston, MA 02107, $4.95, paperback). A brochure, "How to Look at Your State's Plans for Educating Handicapped Children," is available free from The Children's Defense Fund, 1520 New Hampshire Ave., N.W., Washington, DC 20036.

Like Me
Alan Brightman
Little, Brown and Co., 34 Beacon Street, Boston, MA
02106 ($2.95, paperback)
Explains in children's language the meaning of
retarded. Emphasizes the importance of trying rather
than whether one is fast or slow. The book is aimed
at helping normal young children overcome their
biases against those who may be slower.

Lisa and Her Soundless World
Edna S. Levine
Human Sciences Press, A Division of Behavioral
Publications, Inc., 72 Fifth Avenue, New York, NY
10011 ($4.95)
Although somewhat condescending of Lisa as a
child "who is not as lucky as you," the book
explains about hearing aids, lip reading, learning to
talk, and finger spelling for deaf children.

My Brother Steven Is Retarded
Harriett Lansam Sobol
Macmillan Publishing Co., Inc., Riverside, NJ 08075
($5.95)
Eleven-year-old Beth explains about her mentally
retarded brother with the help of sensitive
photographs of the two of them. It speaks out loud
the secret fears and pain of siblings of a special
child.

One Little Girl
Joan Fassler
Human Sciences Press, A Division of Behavioral
Publications, Inc., 72 Fifth Avenue, New York, NY
10011 ($6.95)
Laurie is a "slow child" although she can do things
like brush her hair and jump rope fast. When the
doctor emphasizes that the most important thing is
that Laurie is happy to be herself, her parents and
other grownups seem to be able to accept her better.

Rachel
Elizabeth Fanshawe
Bradbury Press, Inc., 2 Overhill Road, Scarsdale, NY
10583 ($4.95)
A simply written text with large type about a small
girl in a wheelchair. She goes to school with other
children who are not handicapped. She feeds the
gerbils, paints, and helps around the house. The
book communicates hope about the child and about
her future.

Tracy
Nancy Mack
Raintree Editions, Distributed by: Children's Press,
1224 W. Van Buren, Chicago, IL 60607 ($6.60)
A photographic essay about a girl who has cerebral
palsy. The emphasis is on what she can do rather
than her limitations. "I'm Tracy. I get around."

ORGANIZATIONS

The following organizations are sponsoring research
in their particular areas, offering information to the
public, and direct help to those seeking it.

Alexander Graham Bell Association for the Deaf
3417 Volta Place, N.W., Washington, DC 20007

Allergy Foundation of America
801 Second Avenue, New York, NY 10017

American Association on Mental Deficiencies
520 Connecticut Avenue, N.W., Washington, DC
20006

American Diabetes Association
18 E. 48th Street, New York, NY 10017

American Foundation for the Blind
15 W. 16th Street, New York, NY 10011

American Speech and Hearing Association
9030 Old Georgetown Road, Washington, DC 20014

Arthritis Foundation
1212 Avenue of the Americas, New York, NY 10036

Association for Children with Learning Disabilities
2200 Brownsville Road, Pittsburgh, PA 15210

Children's Bureau
U.S. Dept. of Health, Education and Welfare,
Washington, DC 20201

Council for Exceptional Children
1920 Association Drive, Reston, VA 22091

Deafness Research Foundation
366 Madison Avenue, New York, NY 10017

Epilepsy Foundation of America
1828 L Street, N.W., Washington, DC 20036

Muscular Dystrophy Associations of America
1790 Broadway, New York, NY 10019

National Association for Retarded Citizens
2709 Avenue E, East, Arlington, TX 76011

National Cystic Fibrosis Research Foundation
202 E. 44th Street, New York, NY 10017

National Easter Seal Society for Crippled Children
and Adults
2023 W. Ogden Avenue, Chicago, IL 60612

National Foundation for Sudden Infant Death, Inc.
1501 Broadway, New York, NY 10036

National Foundation — March of Dimes
Public Education Dept., P.O. Box 2000, White Plains, NY 10602 (The prevention and treatment of birth defects.)

National Hemophilia Foundation
25 W. 39th Street, New York, NY 10018

National Kidney Foundation
315 Park Avenue S., New York, NY 10010

National Society for Autistic Children
169 Tampa Avenue, Albany, NY 12208

Osteogenesis Imperfecta Foundation
% Mr. C. C. Neely, 1231 May Court, Burlington, NC 27215

United Cerebral Palsy Associations, Inc.
66 E. 34th Street, New York, NY 10016

Two other sources of information deserve special mention. *The Exceptional Parent* is a magazine for parents of disabled children. Activity ideas, discussions on special education, advertisements for products, and an excellent bookstore with selections on mental retardation, learning disabilities, emotional problems, epilepsy and deafness. Back issues are most valuable for information and are available in college libraries. A subscription costs $12.00 per year. Order from P.O. Box 641, Penacook, NH 03301.

Closer Look, National Information Center for the Handicapped, provides free information services for parents of handicapped children and to parent groups. To be included on the mailing list for the newsletter, write Closer Look, Box 1492, Washington, DC 20013.

The Special Child Handbook
Joan McNamara and Bernard McNamara
Hawthorn Books, Inc., 260 Madison Avenue, New York, NY 10016 ($12.50)
An excellent sourcebook. Out of the McNamara's family of six children, four of whom are adopted, five have disabilities. And so, the suggestions offered by the book have the soundness of actual experiences behind them. You'll find reviews of helpful books, a list of support organizations, discussions of legal rights, financial planning, and suggestions for coping with your disabled child.

THE ABUSED CHILD

A recent study by Richard J. Gelles, a University of Rhode Island sociologist, has shown some startling statistics about child abuse in America. After sampling 2134 representative American families, he estimates the parents of between 900,000 and 1.8 million children stabbed or tried to stab or shot or tried to shoot their children. He found that an estimated 3 or 4 million children had been kicked, bitten, or punched by their parents in 1975, and between 1.4 and 2.3 million children had been beaten up by their parents.

If you are a parent who abuses your young child (children between three and five years of age run the greatest risk of being abused), there is an organization that may be able to help you. It's called Parents Anonymous and it has groups in cities all over the United States. Parents Anonymous is a self-help program that includes weekly meetings and telephone support for parents who abuse their children. It will also guide parents to sources of long-term help. For further information write:
Parents Anonymous
2810 Artesia Boulevard, Redondo Beach, CA 90278

Note: Not all manufacturers and publishers will accept single orders for a product or book. Always write to them first, before sending money, to be sure that they will take your order. Make sure you've got the most recent price, including shipping and handling charges. If the company is in your state, then you may need to include state sales tax as well.

What is art for young children? It is mushing, pushing, molding, mixing, cutting, and swishing. Moving, working, painting, or making something. Who cares what? But there is great joy in the doing!

Watch a child paint. You see immense seriousness and concentration. There is freedom, too. Splotching paint here and there, brushing here and there with abandon. Such freedom to get lost in colors! A child can naturally concentrate within himself. He enjoys the experience for its own sake — not for what people will think or what the finished product will look like.

At various points in my adult life, I have tried to paint. But always there was the feeling of being *judged*. We grownups are caught up in the competition of wanting something to look right. We have an internal rule that clicks off "good" or "not good" — and sometimes, we even take the liberty of forcing these limits on our young, free children. We must comment on the painting and find out what it is. (What if it isn't *anything?*) The child drops the paintbrush to go on to something else with the same self-centeredness that he had at the easel. If we adults could just capture that wholeness of the self again. If we could only hold the child together until he is grown in the unity that he has within himself and his works!

How to Talk to a Scribbler
by Joseph J. Sparling and Marilyn C. Sparling

A young child draws wiggly-looking marks on paper (or on less approved places) and derives much joy and satisfaction from the experience. These marking or scribbling experiences can be the child's first steps in visual self-expression. Understandably, we adults want to clear the way for "first steps" of any kind and to lend a helping hand if possible. One way to help the scribbler is by offering an occasional, well-chosen comment as the child finishes a scribble.

But just how many sensible things can one say about a scribble? The random markings of a one- or two-year-old can tax the imagination of the most resourceful adult. Even the more controlled scribbles of a three- or four-year-old do not present an easy topic of conversation between adults and children. Yet the beginner in art needs encouragement in the form of verbal approval and respect. He benefits also from language which stimulates him to be aware of the creative process and product, and of his own thoughts and feelings. The gaining of new names or labels for things gives the child a way of recalling and reusing an experience, and skill in concept formation has been shown to be linked to the acquisition of language, particularly to labeling (Kendler & Kendler, 1961). Adults might well view language stimulation as helping the child to gain some of the basic equipment needed to grow toward more mature forms of thought.

What principles can guide an adult who wants to improve his or her communication with scribblers? First, communication must be geared to the developmental level of the scribbler. Comments which are appropriate for a child who scribbles without control are hardly adequate for a child who has gained good control of his crayon. Second, comments must relate specifically to what each child has done. Most of us as adults have been guilty at one time or another of not really looking at what a child has done or not noticing what type of experience he has had. When this happens our responses are often stereotyped phrases which do not provide rich language stimulation. These two principles ("gear to developmental level" and "be specific") are the source of the positive suggestions and examples in this article.

Since the young child does not have a high degree of control over his motions, the first drawings are usually little more than a few random marks.* The physical process of scribbling is fascinating to the young child, while the marks which are made are of less interest to him. In talking about the very first scribbles, an adult can mention (1) the child's movements, (2) the way the scribble looks and (3) the way the child probably felt as he made the drawing. There are, of course, many things which could be said under these three headings, but in each of the following sections only one or two samples are provided. Hopefully, these will stimulate the reader to think of many other possible choices. The best remarks are simple and to the point. In each exchange with a young child, usually no more than one or two individual comments are appropriate, and there are many instances when the adult may wisely remain silent.

* This is the first of three levels of scribbling, each a little more advanced than the previous level (Lowenfeld & Brittain, 1964, p. 95).

Commenting about movement emphasizes the actual physical process, the act of creating, and helps the child to be more aware of his own movements. The development of motor coordination is a major task of the child during the scribbling period. Thus, comments such as this one are appropriate and make sense to the child: "Look how fast your hand is jumping back and forth!" One could mention instead something positive about how big or small a child's movements are, or how light or hard he is pressing with his crayon.

Comments which center on the visual features of his work help the child to be more aware of the various kinds of things he has spontaneously created. An appropriate comment here might be: "You've made some little dots and a long curvy line." Besides describing some of the actual marks, one could talk about the placement of the marks on the paper or about the colors used.

It may be helpful at times to point to that aspect of the child's work to which a comment refers. For example, when talking about a particular line in the child's drawing, it is appropriate to touch or trace it with a finger. This helps to guarantee that the child understands what the adult is referring to.

By providing language models, an adult can help children to be more conscious of the way they feel during and after creation and can lead children to independently verbalize these feelings. Clues to a child's feelings can be "read" in his facial and body expressions, and noted in his preferences for certain activities, colors or ways of working. Comments such as "You worked a long time on your painting — you must have enjoyed it very much," help the child realize that what he is doing and what he is feeling are understood and valued.

After many experiences, a child will gradually develop visual and motor control over his scribbles. As with the very first scribbles, comments can be made regarding movement, the visual aspects and feelings. Most children will begin to spend a little longer time on their work now, and will be more interested in the actual marks they have made. Again, one or two comments are adequate. Sometimes, however, several comments and questions may be effectively used if a child seems particularly responsive.

Comments about developing motor control and increasing ability to devise a variety of movements are now of special significance to children. They will be able to keep their marks more on the paper, and to repeat certain movements, such as up and down and circular scribbles (de Francesco, 1958, p. 251). Comments such as "See how you make your hand go around and around — like a merry-go-round!" can focus attention on these newly acquired skills.

Adults can strengthen a child's self-confidence and stimulate his thinking by encouraging him to look more carefully at what he has done. Comments and labels can help a child realize that he has made a certain mark many times or that he has created a great variety of lines and closed shapes. One specific comment might be: "See how well you've drawn a small circle right inside this big one. That's hard to do." Other appropriate comments concerning the visual features of a child's work might refer to contrasting colors and values, comparisons or descriptions of different lines or shapes, and the relationship of various marks to each other.

The scribbler who is gaining fine motor control develops feelings of pride which are the topic of some important adult comments. This pride is seen in the child's satisfaction over his increasing skills and his growing ability to control his movements and markings. A comment such as this focuses attention on feelings that go with new accomplishments: "It's exciting to find new ways to use a crayon!"

One day the child will discover for himself that the various lines and shapes he has drawn "look like" something he has seen around him. A person will often be identified first, and the child may call his drawing *a man* or *my mommy* (Lowenfeld & Brittain, 1964, pp. 116–117). This new development (of relating marks on paper to things in the visual world) usually stimulates the child to show and talk to others about his work. At this point a rich opportunity for communication exists.

Unfortunately for the adult, these named scribbles will not look much different from earlier markings. Children will further confuse us by rapidly changing the ideas and meanings that they read into their pictures. Thus a particular shape may at one time be called a ball, five minutes later a sun, and perhaps the next day a flower. For these reasons, adults are rather presumptuous if they attempt to guess or name a shape in a child's art work. Adults need to listen carefully to the child's comments and capitalize on the meaning *to the child* at that moment. Whatever the statement by a child about his picture (and some statements may be not at all what the adults expect), we can do no more or less than to accept these meanings which are personal to the child and respond to them sincerely.

The following suggestions to adults are divided into two categories: (1) how to respond to a child who initiates a conversation, and (2) what to say when a child is reluctant to discuss his work.

Some children are ready to name or comment about their work without any questioning from adults. When the child does offer some comment about his work, the adult then has a clue to the child's thinking and can ask a leading question to help expand the child's thinking even further (Lowenfeld & Brittain, 1964, p. 102).

These leading questions should include both aesthetic and personal ideas. If a child says "See my big man," the adult could stimulate awareness of aesthetics by asking about the colors, shapes or repetition of lines. To encourage awareness of the personal aspects, the adult could ask about the child's relationship to the man (as a Daddy) or the child's thoughts about the man. For example: "Your man is so big he fills up the whole paper! Is he someone that you know?"

Such comments and questions help carry the child's thoughts in the direction *he* initiated and are therefore likely to have meaning for him. But the child must feel free also to disregard adult comments and questions and adults must willingly accept rebuffs at their attempts to stimulate discussion.

Sometimes a child may hesitate to talk about his work. At such times, an adult might encourage conversation by asking questions such as "That looks like fun. Would you like to tell me about some of the things you've made?"

Sometimes a child may appear confused by a request such as "I'd like to know more about your drawing." This probably means that the child is still at an earlier scribbling level and has not yet begun to name his markings. At other times, a child may simply be unwilling to enter into a conversation. In either case, the adult should then make a positive comment to the child such as "I'm glad you're having fun drawing," or "You're making lots of nice lines go all around your paper." Comments such as these offer reassurance that the adult understands and respects the child's way of working and does not intend to try to force him to comment. Everyone has the right to at times enjoy his own private world. With continual support and through many opportunities to create, more children will gradually want to talk about their work. The adult can then respond to that need and strengthen it through appropriate questions and comments.

A few children will be inhibited in their visual self-expression, or will seem reluctant to scribble. In such situations an adult may want to initiate some special stimulation. Motivational techniques such as this may be of some help:

Let's try drawing together today. We can each pick out some special paper and a crayon to use. Oh, you chose a bright red crayon. That's a beautiful color! Now, I'm going to let my crayon move all around my paper. Like this. It feels good to move it all around. Sometimes I like to close my eyes when I draw. Then I just let my hand move anywhere it wants to. Let's try it together now. Want to close our eyes? Okay. Now open them. Wow! Look at all the things we made. I like the way your lines go around and around . . . You might like to draw again sometime.

This approach provides encouragement and approval for the creative act itself. This procedure is generally to be used with a single child but might prove effective at times with a small group of children. The adult should praise even the smallest effort and should keep trying a little each day. It takes a while for a child to build up courage and confidence, especially when the child has had a bad experience before or is fearful of trying anything new or different. If the adult is unable to get the child to participate, he should let the child go on to something he likes and give a positive statement such as "I enjoyed sitting down with you. Maybe we can do something special again tomorrow." Through such stimulation, we hope to gradually involve even the most reluctant scribbler in satisfying motor activities.

Children need to gain satisfaction from their work without constant adult approval. Thus, comments and questions need not be given every time a child does something. In fact, adults should look for appropriate opportunities to be silent and should frequently remain away from children while they are working.

Some children hum to themselves as they scribble. This is a natural response to the rhythm of the scribbling activity. Usually it is an indication of involvement in the experience, and so the child should be left to himself at this time.

Other children stare off into space as they scribble contentedly. This, too, is reasonable since the motor activity predominates, especially in the first two levels of scribbling. At such a time children are not usually interested in the actual marks they are making. It is the process of scribbling itself which is immensely satisfying. During this occurrence nothing needs to be said and the adult can leave the child alone to finish at his own pace.

When a child is fully involved in his activity, it is best not to interrupt him with a comment. When the child puts down his crayon or brush, looks up, or otherwise takes his attention from his work, the time is ripe for communication. The adult can then show interest in the child and his work by making a thoughtful, sincere comment. Additional respect can be shown by using the child's name when talking to him. Of importance to many children is actual physical contact. So, when speaking, a thoughtful adult may put a hand on the child's shoulder, sit or kneel to his level, and direct all attention for a moment to the child and his work.

Comments and questions, to be appropriate and effective, must be open-ended and help to heighten the sensitivity of each child to what he is doing or has done. Therefore, adults should avoid questions such as "What are you drawing?" "Is this a house?" or "What's this?" This type of question puts the child on the spot, leaving no room for varied interpretations and often closing the door on creativity and further exploration.

Instead of asking a child what he is making, one might comment first on the nice bright red color used and then ask if he or she would like to tell about something special in the painting. This approach emphasizes the importance of a positive initial statement to let the child know that the adult accepts what the child is doing and finds meaning in some part of the child's creation. The follow-up question is then an expression of genuine interest and is worded in such a way that the child can choose freely whether or not to respond.

Why all this fuss about talking to a scribbler? Hopefully, the kinds of conversations suggested here will result in young children who are more enthusiastic about expressing themselves through art and who are motivated to continue and expand their art activity. In addition, the general awareness that is built up through language is the catalyst which enables the young child to translate art experiences into art concepts. This general awareness is the forerunner of a critical awareness the child will need if he is to reach later stages of his development where he must *evaluate* his own work and the work of others by applying aesthetic concepts.

Clearly, the comments given here cannot be picked up and used verbatim by other adults. These sample comments can act only as a stimulus to the thinking of others. Communication is an important matter, and anyone who reaches out to another human being must be ready to expend effort in the process. Parents, teachers and day care workers cannot expect to "turn on" a scribbler with a casual glance at his work and a stock or pat phrase.

The thoughtlessness of this approach was pointed out in an eye-opening classroom experience. Smiling at a child's drawing, a teacher said "That's nice." With painful honesty, the little girl replied "Oh, Mrs. Merrill, you say that to everybody!"

References
Bland, J. C. *Art of the Young Child.* New York: Simon & Schuster, 1969.
de Francesco, I. L. *Art Education, Its Means and Ends.* New York: Harper & Bros., 1958.
Kellogg, R. & O'Dell, S. *The Psychology of Children's Art.* San Diego: CRM-Random House, 1967.
Kendler, H. H. & Kendler, T. S. Effect of verbalization on discrimination reversal shifts in children. *Science*, 1961, 134, 1619–1620.
Lowenfeld, V. & Brittain, W. L. *Creative and Mental Growth.* New York: Macmillan, 1964.

Joseph J. Sparling, Ph.D., is an assistant professor in the School of Education, University of North Carolina, Chapel Hill. Marilyn C. Sparling has been an art consultant to public schools and an instructor in Art Education at the University of North Carolina. Dr. & Mrs. Sparling write and give workshops on child development and art.

CRAYONS AND MARKING PENS

Crayons come in two sizes: large, pressed crayons for younger children and the dime-store variety small-sized ones. The value of the large crayons is that a young child can grasp them easily and they are more difficult to break. The small crayons are more "waxy" and come off on the paper more readily. They have more colors to choose from and are more brilliant than the big ones. They also break easily. (My little girl broke every one just to hear the loud cracking sound they make.)

It's important to have an easy way to store crayons so they don't end up littering the house: a plastic index-card box with a snap-down lid, a clear plastic bag tied with a piece of wire or a rubber band, a one-pound coffee can with the plastic lid on, an oatmeal box, an old-fashioned cigar box. The original box isn't any good after the first use since *nobody*, not even parents, can fit them back in again.

Broken crayons can be recycled in several interesting ways. They can be slowly remelted together in a plastic egg carton placed on a cookie sheet in the sun. Or they can be melted in a muffin tin in a warm oven with the heat turned off. Chips of color can be mixed and melted until they stick together for an interesting drawing effect. *Never* heat wax directly over the heat of a burner; it's extremely flammable. If you must be fast about it, use a double boiler for heat.

Some other ideas for using crayons:

• Melted crayon wax can be applied to tough, textured paper with a brush, a stick or a palette knife to resemble an oil painting. Clean the brush by dipping it in a pot of boiling water and then washing it with soapy water.

• Scrape shavings from several different colors of crayons on to a sheet of waxed paper. A flat stick, such as a tongue depressor or a dull knife, makes an excellent scraper. Place another sheet of waxed paper over the shavings. Cover the waxed paper with a piece of newspaper and press the sheets together with a *warm*, not hot, iron. The crayon shavings will melt and flow together creating a beautiful transparent effect. Cut in the shape of a butterfly or put in a black construction paper frame and hang in front of the window. Autumn leaves, bits of fabric, or tissue paper can also be mounted this way.

• Peel off the paper and try using the crayon on its side. For best results, use a stack of papers underneath or some other padding. Try going around in circles, or outlining a flower or a tree this way.

• Try drawing on things other than paper. (Please, my little Rembrandt, *not* on the wall!) Interesting surfaces: cardboard, corrugated board, wood, sandpaper. Patterns can be created by putting paper over leaves, or fine twigs while rubbing it back and forth with the side of a crayon. Try changing directions and crayons.

There's a lot of controversy in the art education world about the use of coloring books. Some teachers believe that coloring books stifle a child's creativity and intimidate the child because of their "letter perfect" nature. Others, particularly teachers of children with motor difficulties, feel that coloring books are good for helping children to learn better hand coordination. My feeling is that coloring books are O.K. but that a blank piece of paper is even better. A coloring book tells a child exactly what to do. A blank piece of paper lets a child use his imagination to come up with anything he wants to draw.

Marking pens are also excellent for young children to draw with. It's wise to select the nonpermanent water-based pens since the ink from the permanent type is difficult to get out of clothes. Keeping the little white caps on the pens is a real problem. One night with the cap off is enough to dry the pen up completely. Perhaps a good, clear explanation about keeping the tops on will help. So will storing the pens top up so that you can see that they're covered. Marking pens used on paper towels have a nice spreading effect that looks pretty in the light. (Don't let them stain through to your rug, though.)

CHALK

Chalk comes in thin or fat sizes. The large, kindergarten chalks are easiest for a small child to manage. The joy of using chalk on small home blackboards is that it can be erased and redone over and over again. Blackboard paint is available in some school supply stores. It allows you to paint masonite or any wall surface to make it suitable for use as a blackboard. Blackboards are fun to paint with water, too. A child can practice painting strokes without the mess of dripping paint.

Chalk is also fun to use on paper — the more textured and "toothy" the paper, the better. A chalk drawing can be made more permanent by spraying it with hairspray or ironing it with a piece of waxed paper on top.

Here are a variety of things you and your child can do with chalk:

• Try using chalk on wet paper. You can either dip the paper in a pan of water, or you can sponge the paper down. Another alternative is to dip the chalk in water or liquid starch before using it.

• Soak chalk sticks in a solution of ⅓ cup of sugar to 1 cup of water for five to ten minutes before using. The colors will seem much more brilliant.

• Try drawing on paper dampened with blobs of buttermilk, or a combination of canned milk and liquid starch.

• Don't forget the great outdoors! Chalk can be used for sidewalk art, on blacktop, and even smooth walls. It washes away with the next rain.

FINGER PAINTING

Finger painting is an excellent experience for heightening a child's awareness of his fingers and his hands. Sometimes younger children may have resistance to doing it, perhaps because it seems too much like being dirty, or because they don't like having their hands, one of their most valuable sensory tools, coated with anything. The best way to overcome a child's resistance to finger painting is simply to sit down and do it yourself. Talk about how smooth and cool it feels. Wait for your child to ask you to let him finger-paint rather than trying to coerce him into doing it.

Finger paints can be bought commercially in kits or in individual jars from dime stores and art or teacher supply stores. Finger painting paper is also available in packages, but it's quite expensive. You can mix up your own finger paints (see page 145).

The best finger painting paper has a shiny, glazed surface. "Butcher" meat wrapping paper is excellent. Shiny shelf paper can also be used. Paper towels provide an interesting change. Sheets of cardboard, gift-box tops, and the insides of cereal boxes also can be used for finger painting.

Another alternative is to allow your child to finger paint directly on the kitchen table (if it's formica), or on an enamel baking sheet. Or you can let your naked child finger paint on the sides of the bathtub with a fluffy soap paint. Use a bath mat or a damp towel on the bottom of the tub to prevent slipping.

How to do regular finger painting on paper:

1. Put an apron or an old shirt on your child, buttoning it up backward.

2. Moisten the paper on both sides with a sponge. Put the shiny side up on a smooth table. Gently press out the wrinkles and bubbles by lifting the paper and then patting it down. The best table is one that lets your child stand while working, leaning over slightly. That way, he can use more muscles.

3. Put a bowl of water and a sponge nearby for hand cleaning.

4. Put about a teaspoonful of paint in the middle of the paper and then let your child spread the paint completely over the paper using both of his hands.

5. If the paint begins to get too dry, drip water down onto the painting from the sponge.

6. It's best to begin with just one color — but later you may want to add one other color so that your child can see the effects of blending colors. Too many colors result in a very dull, murky painting.

7. When the painting's finished, put it on newspaper to dry flat.

8. After it's dried, it can be ironed with a warm iron on the back to flatten it out.

The painting can be made more permanent by lacquering it or putting shellac on it and mounting it with rubber cement on poster board, or by covering it with clear contact paper.

Your child will begin to develop many different hand techniques in time: making thumbprints, using just the fingers, using the base of the palms, the fist, the fingernails, the side of the hands, even his elbow! You can encourage him to explore using his hands by asking him, "What happens if you use your fist? Just your thumbs?"

Some other interesting finger painting techniques include:

• Making a picture with colored crayons on the paper first, and then finger-painting with a thin paint.
• Transferring the finger paint to another piece of paper by putting a clean sheet of paper directly over the finger-painted paper and then peeling off. Using just half of the paper and then folding over and opening back up gives an inkblot effect.
• Objects can be drawn through the paint to make designs: a comb, a fork, a brush, an eraser. You can make your own wide-toothed comb by cutting chunks out of the end of a piece of cardboard.
• Flour dusted over the bottom of a baking sheet or flat pan with sides can be drawn on with fingers for a quick art diversion.

TEMPERA PAINTS

Tempera paints are excellent for the beginning painter because their color is so brilliant and they cover the paper so well. Tempera can be bought in small jars at the dime store, or in ready-to-make powdered form from art and some office supply stores. The premixed tempera paints are more expensive but their colors are more brilliant and they're less likely to be powdery when they dry. Unfortunately, they often dry up in the bottle before you buy them,

so you have to add water and wait for them to "melt" before your child can use them.

Powdered tempera paint is more economical if you plan many painting experiences for your child. Red, blue, yellow, and green are good basic colors to begin with. Powdered tempera should be mixed with water until it is the consistency of heavy cream (about two parts paint to one part water). The paint should be thick enough that the paper won't show through it. A few drops of rubbing alcohol will speed the mixing of the colors with water. Liquid dishwashing detergent can be added to the paint for thicker, richer color that washes off more easily. You can make it by the cupful with only two or three tablespoons of powder at a time, or you can make larger quantities and store them in jars with screw-on lids. Large, wide-mouthed peanut butter jars are excellent for this. Tempera can also be used for an interesting effect by dipping the brush in water first and then into the powder each time.

Containers for your child to paint from can be baby food jars, frozen orange juice cans, paper cups, milk cartons with the top cut off, or muffin tins with one color in each hole. It's wise to stabilize the jars somehow so that they won't tip over while they're being used. You can set the jars in a shoe box or a shoe box lid, or you can put orange juice cans in a six-pack carton.

The best paintbrushes for a young child are big enough to cover a lot of territory. Firm bristle brushes with one-inch flat ends are good for beginners. You will need a brush for each color your child is using, or else he'll end up with nothing but jars of mud-colored paint from the colors mixing together.

Don't try to use beat-up old brushes with bristles sticking out all over since all they do is frustrate a child. You can try to improve an old brush by cutting straight across the straggly end with a razor. When you're through with the brushes, be sure to wash them with soap and warm water. (Hot water will melt the glue that holds the bristles in.) Store them lying flat or with the bristles up so that they won't get pressed out of shape.

Using a paintbrush properly isn't an easy task for a child to learn. If the brush goes into the can too far, paint drips all over the place and even down his hand. If he gets too little paint, it won't cover the paper enough. A parent can help by putting only an inch or so of paint in the container. When the paint level gets too low, you can add more. In time your child will learn how to scrape the brush against the inside of the jar or container to get rid of excess paint.

Some enjoyable brush alternatives:
• A twig with the end frayed by a kitchen knife.
• A sturdy stick about a foot long with one end split about three quarters of an inch. Insert a piece of kitchen sponge or a gauze square folded over into the slit. Wind string around the slit to hold the "brush" in. A spring-type clothespin makes a good sponge holder, too.
• Sponges or foam rubber with the paint in a saucer.
• Small-sized paint rollers made for painting trim. A small baking pan can hold the paint.
• Household brushes, a whiskbroom, and even a feather duster if you're careful just to dip the feathery ends without letting it get too soggy.
• Cotton balls or squares, Q-tips, or crumpled newspaper.

There are a variety of materials that a young child can paint on with satisfying results. All kinds of paper can be used (see page 142). Wood — sticks, scraps that have been glued or nailed together, leftover pieces from a lumberyard or carpentry work, clothespins, spools, and pine cones. Cardboard — small boxes, corrugated cartons, flat pieces of cardboard from laundered shirts, or pieces cut from the side of a carton. Rocks are fun to paint, and can be made into monsters and smiley faces.

Your child's first painting experience is best done on the kitchen floor on a large piece of paper. Spread out the classified section of the newspaper and let him paint on that. A single color is all that's needed while he becomes familiar with how to use a brush. Have a sponge or a mop ready for quick clean-up afterward.

An old shirt buttoned up backward with the sleeves rolled up or cut off makes a good smock. You can also make a protective painting poncho from a rectangle of oilcloth with a hole cut in the middle to slip over the head. If you're more daring, and don't expect a neighbor to drop in, let your child paint naked. Child to the tub, mop to the floor, and everything's cleaned up in a jiffy.

Other places to paint besides the floor:
• Tape paper on the refrigerator.
• Cover the kitchen table with a plastic tablecloth and paint there. A lower table that allows your child to stand on the floor is even better.
• Buy a sheet of wallboard to be used on the table or floor for a protective backing. You can stand it against the wall, up on a kitchen chair, or carry it outdoors with the paper pinned on it. An inexpensive bulletin board serves the same purpose.
• You can make a slanted easel by cutting a large cardboard carton in half diagonally so that it sits like a pyramid on the table.

Other exciting ways to use tempera paint:
• Pour a small puddle of paint in the middle of a piece of paper and then blow the paint around on the paper with a straw for a splashy pattern.
• Dip a length of string into the paint and then drag it across the paper, or fold the paper over the string and then pull the string out slowly while the paper is held down firmly.
• Trace your child's body on a large piece of paper. Then let him cut it out and paint it.
• Squeeze paint thickened with liquid starch out of a plastic mustard or ketchup container onto the paper, or spray thin paint from a liquid detergent bottle. Try shaking and dripping

thin tempera from a wet brush down onto paper at your feet.

• Try texture painting with paint thickened by Elmer's Glue-All and with sand added. Sugar added to paint gives a shiny, grainy texture.

• Use heavy, tough paper and color it with brightly colored crayon marks or use a candle stub. Paint over the crayon with black or other dark colored tempera. Because the wax of the crayon resists the liquid of the paint, a beautiful stained-glass effect results. Be sure the crayon streaks are bold and very waxy. You'll probably have to experiment to get the tempera paint to the right consistency to "resist."

• Paint dark construction paper with a thick mixture of tempera paint and liquid starch, then drag a fork or comb across the paint for interesting designs.

• Cut out a cardboard stencil of an apple, a valentine, a Christmas tree or other simple object. Tape the stencil to the paper with masking tape. Let your child dab a sponge dipped in paint over the stencil and then remove it.

• Use thin paint in an eyedropper (the plastic ones used for baby vitamins are best) and drip it on to a paper towel.

WATER-COLOR PAINTING

Water-color paints available in metal boxes at the dime store are an easy way of providing painting experience for your child. Fill a paper cup or coffee cup with water, dip the brush into the water and put a drop of water into each color cup. Let the water sit for a few minutes until the paint has softened. Remind your child to rinse his brush in the water after each stroke. Almost any paper can be used with water colors, although most papers will crinkle. Professional quality water-color paper gives beautiful, brilliant results and can be bought in tablet form. It's helpful to tape the paper to the table with masking tape so that your child doesn't have to worry about the paper slipping.

Other water-color techniques:

• Wet the paper first and then dab, brush, or drip colors down onto it.

• Paint blobs of color and then lift the paper up and let them drip down. Turn the paper sideways and watch the drips change direction.

• Fold the paper over onto itself for a butterfly effect when it's opened back up.

• Draw a design by squirting a thin line of Elmer's Glue-All onto the paper and then dab water colors directly on top of the wet glue. Let the glue dry and then paint again around the dried glue lines.

PRINTING

Printing is a simple art activity that is enjoyable for young children because of its repetitive nature. It also can be used to help children understand how newspapers, books, and fabric designs are printed.

Spread newspapers on the floor or table where your child will be working. You will need a good thick paint that will stick to the surface of the printing object. You can use poster paint, finger paint, tempera paint thickened with Elmer's Glue-All, liquid starch or Ivory soap flakes, or a tube of water-based ink or acrylic paint available from an art store. You can also buy a regular stamp pad from an office supply store for under a dollar. Their colors are not as bright, though.

The paint can be brushed directly onto the printing object, or you can make your own "ink" pad to work from. You can use moistened folded paper towels, a moist flat sponge, a moist folded washcloth, or a small damp carpet scrap. For a single color use a pie pan or a saucer. If you plan to have several colors on hand then use an aluminum T.V. dinner plate or a muffin tin. Each section should have an absorbent "pad" to hold the thick paint.

Spread the paint across your pad with a

brush or the back of a spoon and then wait a few minutes for it to soak in.

Paper to print on can be anything: an opened up paper bag, the classified section of a newspaper, nonerasable typing paper, even onionskin. If you want to make cards, then a thick paper such as rice paper is excellent. If you want to make your own wrapping paper then use tissue paper. Green tissue paper with red stars, trees, and circles is good for Christmas.

Printing with parts of yourself is an excellent way to get an idea of the process and pressure needed for good prints. First start with fingerprints. Using a Magic Marker to make stems, fingerprints can make colorful flowers. Mouthprints can be made using lipstick. Footprints are great fun but messy. If you have a roll of shelf paper, you can cut a length, put the paint pan at one end, and a pan of water and paper towels at the other end. Handprints are fun to make and mail to grandparents.

OBJECT PRINTING

Any gadgets that you can round up around the house can be used to provide interesting patterns for printing on paper. Your child can either paint the side of the gadget to be printed, or he can use a homemade stamp pad described earlier. Here are some ideas: tongue depressor, pretzels, scissors, keys, clothespin halves, forks, paper clips, toy tractors (roll the wheels across the paper), pencil erasers, nuts, and bolts.

You can also design your own printing objects:
- Crumpled paper
- Pieces of sponge
- Yarn glued zigzag fashion around a tin can
- Plasticene clay with grooves and holes in it (It can be folded over and used again and again.)
- Toilet paper roll with holes cut out, or with rubber bands around it

- Elmer's Glue-All squirted on a piece of wood or a block and allowed to dry
- Patterns cut out of corrugated cardboard or inner tubes or made from pipe cleaners can be glued onto wooden blocks or small gift boxes for printing. (Remember, they'll come out backward.)
- Flocked contact paper can also be cut into designs or numbers and mounted on a block or box bottom.
- Vegetables and fruit can be cut in half and designs cut in relief for printing: potatoes, carrots, turnips, radishes. Others have patterns of their own when halved: cabbage, citrus fruit.

SIMPLE SILK-SCREEN PRINTING

Silk-screen printing consists of squishing thick paint through a thin fabric onto paper. To do screen printing with your child, mount organdy (cotton, nylon, or silk) onto a small picture frame or a canvas stretcher available from an art store. The fabric can either be tacked onto the sides of the frame or pulled tightly across and stapled to the sides of the frame with a heavy-duty stapler. Your child then cuts out designs from construction paper or tears them. He can also use yarn for a pattern. The designs are laid over clean paper and the framed fabric goes face down on them. Several "glops" of paint are put on the fabric. Then, using a rubber squeegee, the end of a windshield scraper, if it fits in the frame, or folded-over cardboard, firmly scrape the paint through the fabric onto the paper below. If your child wants to experiment, he can rearrange his paper pieces and rescreen the same paper for a variety of paint densities. The screen can be rinsed off under the faucet and saved for use again.

Spatter painting is a similar principle. You need an old window screen or a scrap of screen with duct tape around the edges to prevent getting scratched by the sharp wire edges. Place a piece of colored construction paper over newspapers. Then put a cutout design or a stencil over the paper. Rub an old toothbrush over the screen to make a snowy spattering of paint on the picture. The part of the paper that's uncovered will be outlined neatly with spatters.

CLAY

There's nothing more soothing than pounding, rolling, squeezing, and squishing a ball of clay. Playing with clay is one time in the day when it's O.K. to get messy, or to break something because it can be quickly mended again. There are many different kinds of clay: Play-Doh and its homemade varieties, plasticene clay that has an oil base and never dries out, and water-base clay sometimes called potter's clay.

Flour-based doughs are natural for play in the kitchen. You can buy Play-Doh in cans, or you can make your own (see page 145). Play-Doh comes in brilliant colors and is quite fragrant (which may be a disadvantage because it tempts children to eat it). Its major disadvantage is that it tends to be crumby. I've spent a lot of time on my hands and knees trying to pick up the little pieces of it that get spread around the house and ground into the rug. Play-Doh will dry up in the can unless it's well covered, so it's a good idea to put it in a plastic sandwich bag with a twist tie before putting the top on the container to make it last longer. Works of art will dry to a hard finish in about two weeks.

Homemade doughs are more fun because they're more pliable and closer to the real thing. Dough lends itself to kitchen table fun: rolling with a rolling pin, cutting it with cookie cutters, pressing patterns in it with buttons, a potato masher, and other interesting things. Some doughs can also be baked slowly in the oven to a hard finish which makes them fun for making Christmas tree decorations, Mother's Day handprints, and doll dishes and fruits.

Water-based clay, sometimes called firing or pottery clay, can be bought in a ready-to-mix powder or in five-pound premixed chunks. It's less expensive than plasticene and oh so cool and squishy for playing with. It usually comes in a gray or dull brown color. It's much easier to mold and work with than other clays, but it's also the messiest, just one step above playing in mud.

If you decide to try the powder, you'll need to allow several days after mixing for the clay to sit in order to get a good, smooth texture. Some powders come in a plastic bag that can be used for mixing — just add water and squish around until the right texture is achieved. Other storage possibilities are a gallon pickle jar, a crock with a top, or several thicknesses of plastic bags fastened tightly with a twist tie. It's important that the stored clay not be too wet because it will get moldy and smell. On the other hand, if it gets too dry, it will become hard like cement. To prevent dryness, check the clay every week or so and add water by poking a hole in the center with your finger. Fill the hole with water.

When your child is working with the clay, he needs a bowl of water for moistening it when it begins to get crumbly. A roll of paper towels is useful, too, for cleaning hands off when they get too mucky. If the clay is too sticky and wet, you can work it on an unfinished wooden board or concrete until it dries up. Too much water and it turns into mud — which is great fun to play with, too, especially if you're not the one who's got to clean it up. The best place to play with the clay, weather permitting, is outside on a tray or on a picnic table. That way, when the project's over, you can take a hose or a bucket of water and simply wash it all away.

Projects made of potter's clay take a long time to dry — sometimes weeks. Once they are dry through and through, they can be painted with thick tempera paint. Do it quickly so that the surface doesn't get mushy. A shiny finish can

Tools for Clay Play

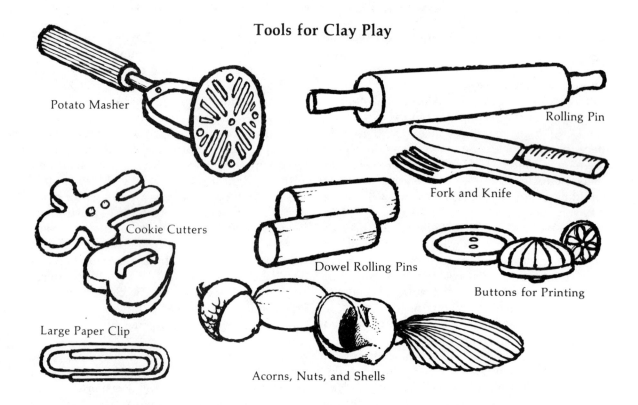

Potato Masher

Rolling Pin

Fork and Knife

Cookie Cutters

Dowel Rolling Pins

Buttons for Printing

Large Paper Clip

Acorns, Nuts, and Shells

be added by painting over it with clear fingernail polish. Shellac can also be used, but be sure to have some denatured alcohol for cleaning the brush, or it will be ruined after one use. Smooth projects can be sanded and then shined up with floor wax or clear shoe wax. Remember, none of these things can hold water or be washed. Potter's clay can also be glazed and baked in a kiln much hotter than the kitchen oven for the beautiful shiny finishes that you often see on handmade ashtrays and vases, but most people don't have access to that process.

Children develop their clay skills gradually. For a long time, most are concerned just with enjoying the feel of clay. Later they begin to construct simple bowls by imprinting their thumbs in a ball of clay or trying simple sculptures. Little children will call what they are making one thing one minute and another thing another minute, depending on how it looks to them that instant. It's important that grownups don't try to make children label what they're doing. Avoid demonstrating what to do with clay or forcing your child to come up with a particular object. That's taking all the fun out of it for him. Instead, sit down and play with the clay yourself to satisfy your own creative urges, but be discreet about what you're making so your child won't get intimidated by his own lack of skills.

ART MATERIALS FROM RANDOM OBJECTS

Bags Small paper bags can be used to make hand puppets. Grocery bags are good for making masks, and can be cut open to provide paper to paint or color on. Burlap bags can be used for sewing with yarn, a background for chalk sketches and crayon rubbings. It can be unraveled for interesting weaving effects, and the extra strings used for puppets' hair.

Bottles Plastic squeeze bottles can be used for novel painting effects. They can be used as bases for homemade dolls.

Boxes and bins Shoe boxes can be used to make small dollhouses, make-believe Christmas scenes, and can be taped together for building blocks. Appliance cartons from furniture stores can be made into forts and playhouses. The sides of cartons can be cut apart for painting. A shape mobile can be constructed from pieces of cardboard cut into a circle, a square, a rectangle, a triangle. Cardboard lids can be used as the base for clay sculptures and constructions. Ice-cream bins from ice-cream stores can be decorated with magazine cutouts and painted over with diluted Elmer's Glue-All for a child's own trash can. Cardboard centers from fabric bolts can be used to paint on or to build with.

Charcoal A soft black substance for drawing, it can be bought in pencil form, by the stick, and in a block; pieces broken off a partially burned log, or burned matches can also be used. Shading can be created by rubbing the charcoal with the finger. You can purchase special charcoal paper or use any heavy drawing paper.

Cloth Cloth can be used for beginning stitchery projects. It makes puppet bodies, simple fabric dolls, beanbags, and pieces for gluing onto a collage. Scraps can often be obtained from clothing factories, textile manufacturers, tailors, and fabric stores.

Cork Cork can be found in a number of textures and shapes. Pieces can be used for making toothpick sculptures, gluing onto collages, and printing on paper. Wine bottle corks can be used to make three-dimensional sculptures with wire and pipe cleaners.

Egg cartons Tops or bottoms can be used for the main piece of a mobile. Good for storing small items. A row of cutout cups make a caterpillar. Single cups make tulips and Christmas tree decorations.

Glue Mucilage is easy for young children to use for gluing paper because of its rubber applicator top. Elmer's Glue-All is good for gluing wood and styrofoam in three-dimensional structures. It can be used to thicken tempera paint and for making masks, paper puppets, paper jewelry. A diluted mixture can be painted on collages made from magazine pictures to make a smooth surface. Cotton string soaked in diluted Elmer's can be wrapped around a balloon to make a lacy globe. When it dries, the balloon is removed. Rubber cement is best for putting paper on paper, since it doesn't make paper crinkle. It's useful for pasting photos in an album. It has strong fumes so should be used outside if possible.

Meat trays Can be used for beginning stitchery with yarn. A base for seed mosaics and mobiles. A simple loom for weaving.

Paper Paper is the indispensable basic material for art experiences. It can be used to draw on, paint on, and in making three-dimensional sculptures. It can be cut, torn and glued onto a background to make compositions. Some varieties of paper:

NEWSPRINT. A thin, inexpensive paper that can be used with pencils, chalk, and crayon. It's not good for painting. If you're lucky, your newspaper publisher will let you have the end roll of a run — which is the end of a huge roll of newsprint used in printing the paper.

CONSTRUCTION PAPER. Lots of colors, sizes, and weights are available. It's best for use with chalk and for beginning practice in cutting skills. Tolerates paint well.

BOGUS. A heavy gray paper used for charcoal and chalk projects.

BUFF MANILA. A heavy, rough-surfaced paper that can be used for crayon, pencil, charcoal, chalk, and tempera painting.

TAGBOARD. A stiff paper that can be used for paper sculpture or for painting and drawing.

TISSUE PAPER. Art tissue, gift-wrapping paper, and cosmetic tissues can all be useful. Tissue paper can be cut and folded into forms. It can be glued on gift boxes, cans, and containers, or applied to other backgrounds in collages. It's applied by using a solution of one part Elmer's Glue-All to one part water. Shellac to maintain permanency.

Some inexpensive paper sources are butcher paper by the roll; cereal boxes cut apart to reveal the insides; computer cards; computer print-out paper; grocery and department store bags; unfolded greeting cards; newspapers; old magazines, catalogs, and telephone books; plates; pizza boxes; and wallpaper catalogs.

Pipe cleaners Can be used to make flowers, animals, and people characters. They can be glued onto paper in collages or used to make the features on puppets.

Plaster Can be used to make sand castings. When mixing plaster, add plaster to water rather than water to plaster. Mix in small quantities. The plaster should be the consistency of thick cream. Work all of the lumps out. Plastic pans are good for mixing plaster since they can be flexed to remove dried plaster.

Using wet sand to make a mold. Press out a design or push an object into the sand. It's a good idea to put the sand in a plastic-lined box so that it will have enough support for the weight of the plaster. Gently pour the plaster into your sand mold. Put a bent paper clip in the upper part of the back of the plaster for a hook to hang the casting on when it's dry. Let dry for an hour. *Don't allow plaster to go down the sink drain or it will stop it up.* Dust excess sand off your sculpture — does it look like you thought it would?

Plastic beer can holders Can be used with two pipe cleaners to make goggles or glasses. Can be cut into bracelets, stretched on a frame or box lid for the base of weaving.

Rug samples Can be taped together on the back with duct tape for a multitextured rug. Rug pieces can also form the background for glued-on pieces of fabric, felt, and yarn for a collage. Available in carpet stores and rug outlets.

Sandpaper Can be purchased from hardware stores and lumberyards. It can be cut up and used to provide texture in paste-up pictures. It can create a textured effect in crayon rubbings, and can be drawn or colored on.

Seeds, beans, and macaroni Can be used to make mosaics in meat trays, on the flat part of an egg carton, or a shoe box lid using Elmer's Glue-All. Can be used to decorate boxes, cans, and bins. Macaroni can be used to string necklaces. It can be colored with marking pens or allowed to soak for a few minutes in a jar with rubbing alcohol and food coloring then dried on paper towels.

Sponges Come in many different textures and sizes. Can be used to apply paint, to print designs, or pieces can be glued on paper.

Spools Available from tailor shops and garment manufacturers. Can be used for stringing necklaces, gluing into three-dimensional sculptures, hung from mobiles, and used in printing designs.

Sticks The small sticks that ice-cream bars come on can be bought by the box at craft shops. Tongue depressors are available from drugstores. Both can be used for stirring paint and spreading paste or finger paint.

They can be glued together for sculpture and painted with tempera paint. Can be used to make stick people and small puppets (see page 195).

Straws Plastic straws can be cut into sections for stringing into a necklace. They can be used for paint-blowing in pictures. Small sections can be pasted on paper for straw mosaics. They can be used for blowing mounds of bubbles in a bowl.

Paper straws can be crimped and inserted into each other to make bracelets, necklaces, and crowns.

Styrofoam Is available in many sizes, shapes, and thicknesses. It can be purchased from florist shops and art supply houses and found free when used to pack typewriters and other fragile equipment. It can be painted with tempera mixed with detergent, stuck with toothpicks and wire for sculpture. Styrofoam balls make good puppet heads. Large, dense

sections can be used for sawing and nailing practice for young carpenters.

Toothpicks Can be used as parts of sculptures using clay or styrofoam. Can be used to scrape and punch textures in clay.

Wax From old crayon scraps can be melted in a muffin tin over boiling water and then painted on heavy paper with a brush. Shredded crayon chips can be melted and poured into an egg carton with a pipe cleaner "U" inserted for a handle. When the crayon chunk dries, it's ready to use again, complete with an easy-hold handle. (*Danger:* Never melt crayons or other wax directly over heat. Highly flammable!)

Wire The telephone company has giant cables made of very flexible wire with colored plastic coverings. If you can get scraps, you can use the wire for making jewelry, forming sculptures, and hanging mobiles. Florist wire is thin and very flexible for shaping. Coat hanger wire can be used to support mobiles and can be shaped with pliers into circles and other shapes and then covered with colored cellophane taped on to make "stained-glass" hangings. Be sure to tape over any sharp edges.

Wood Wood blocks and scraps are available in quantity from building sites and lumberyards. Driftwood can be gathered from the beach. As your child works with wood, encourage him to notice the different grains, textures, and colors. Blocks can be glued together to make constructions. Flat pieces can be used to paint on, or to form mosaics.

Yarn and string Can be used for stitching on burlap, painting, hanging mobiles, pasting on paper for yarn pictures, weaving, making puppet hair and features, pasted on a can for printing a design.

WEAVING

Weaving teaches a young child about how fabrics are made. A weaving experience should be simple and easy to complete in one or two sittings. It's quite difficult for a young child to do the over-under sequence demanded for a perfect piece, but still a child is quite absorbed by the effects of his weaving.

Weaving with construction paper provides a simple project. Fold over a sheet of construction paper and cut it in one-inch strips beginning at the fold and stopping one inch from the end of the paper. Let your child cut strips from colored construction paper to weave into your "loom." Strips of paper are woven across the paper — over, under, over, under.

A simple yarn loom can be made by taping yarn zigzag fashion back and forth across a lap-sized picture frame. Zigs and zags should be one inch apart. Duct tape is excellent for this purpose. Fat strips of yarn should be cut to overlap the loom sides by about six inches. Your child weaves one strip of yarn across the loom at a time, varying colors each time. The yarn should be combed downward with the fingers as it is woven in so that it will fit against the end of the loom firmly. When your child has filled up the whole loom, carefully peel off the tape. Now stitch the open sides with the sewing machine so that they can't be pulled out. Voilá, a placemat or a doll blanket! The sides can be clipped to make them even.

Another simple weaving project is to make a small circular loom by taping curler picks, top up, around the empty ring from masking tape or duct tape. A toilet paper roll can also be used. Knitting yarn is woven around the ring going inside one pick and outside the next. A second layer is woven around with the same pattern. Loop the lower yarn up over the upper yarn and over the pick head. Weave the yarn around the circle again, and loop the bottom yarn over the top yarn again. Soon a yarn snake will appear from under the ring. To remove the knitting from the ring, break the yarn about six inches from the knitting and thread it through the loops one at a time. The yarn can be sewn together at the end with a needle and thread if it seems too loose.

ART KIT

You can put together an art kit for your child that will provide many hours of enjoyment. It would make an excellent birthday or get-well gift for a preschooler. Fix up a department store gift box for a carrying case. Cover it with patterned contact paper or brightly colored gift wrapping paper painted over with a solution of half water and half Elmer's Glue-All. Glue the child's name, using felt letters or pieces of yarn, across the side. Tape the top onto the back of the kit with duct tape. Put handles made of fat yarn on the front (opening) end of both top and bottom of box. You can also add yarn for tie fasteners on the front to keep the box from popping open when the child carries it. Some ideas of what to put inside:
- A package of colored construction paper
- A pair of good, sharp scissors with blunt ends (not the dime-store type — they're too difficult to maneuver)
- A box of colored chalk
- A small box of crayons
- A box of nonerasable typing paper or newsprint
- A clipboard to act as an easel
- A box of water-color paints
- A can of Play-Doh or box of plasticene dough
- A small bottle of Elmer's Glue-All
- Some pencils and a little pencil sharpener
- A package of pipe cleaners
- A plastic bag filled with notions: paper doilies, cottonballs, pieces of rickrack, strips of bright yarn, small squares of bright fabrics, pieces of macaroni, feathers and bows from an old hat. (Anything light enough to be pasted onto a piece of construction paper.)

RECIPES

Paste for Paper Projects

1 cup sugar
1 cup flour
1 teaspoon alum (available in pharmacies)
4 cups water
oil of cloves

Mix the sugar, flour, and alum together. Add the water. Cook until thick, stirring constantly. Cool. Add several drops of oil of cloves. Store in a covered jar.

Homemade Play Dough

½ cup salt
1 cup flour
2 tablespoons cream of tartar
1 cup water
1 tablespoon vegetable oil
food coloring

Mix the salt, flour, and cream of tartar together. Add the water, oil, and food coloring. Cook the mixture on medium heat until the dough feels right for use (about three to five minutes). Store in a plastic bag or a coffee can with a lid.

Finger Paint

½ cup flour
½ cup water
1½ cups boiling water
2 teaspoons alum
food coloring or tempera powder

Mix the flour and cold water together in a pot. Stir in the boiling water and bring the mixture to a boil, stirring constantly. Remove from the heat and add the alum and coloring. Paintings from this recipe dry flat. (For an interesting extra dimension, add fragrances for different colors: vanilla extract, peppermint extract, perfume, lemon extract. [No tasting!])

Cornstarch Finger Paint

½ cup cornstarch
4 cups boiling water
food coloring or tempera powder

Dissolve the cornstarch in a small amount of cold water in a pot. Gradually add the boiling water while stirring. Cook, stirring constantly until the mixture is clear. Add the coloring.

Laundry Starch Finger Paint

1 cup liquid laundry starch
6 cups water
½ cup soap flakes (not detergent, too strong)
food coloring or tempera powder

Dissolve the soap flakes in water until smooth. Mix in the starch. Stir in the coloring.

Whipped Soap Finger Paints

⅔ cup Ivory flakes
⅓ cup water
food coloring or tempera powder

Dissolve the soap in water and whip with an eggbeater until the texture is like beaten egg whites, or put into the blender. Whip in the coloring.

BOOKS FOR ART IDEAS

Weaving Is for Anyone
Jean Wilson
Van Nostrand Reinhold Company
Order from:
Order Processing, 7625 Empire Drive, Florence, KY 41042 ($5.95, paperback)
A basic handbook that will give parents many ideas for weaving projects. Making and using simple cardboard looms. Making a loom, from a simple picture frame loom to the more complex wooden looms. How to use stems and other natural materials in a weaving.

Stitchery for Children
Jacqueline Enthoven
Van Nostrand Reinhold Company
Order from:
Order Processing, 7625 Empire Drive, Florence, KY 41042 ($5.95, paperback)
Jacqueline Enthoven is an expert! Beginning with two-year-olds, she traces the levels of children's skills in stitchery. She suggests materials, needles, frames, and hoops suitable for children and gives ideas for stitches to be used in creating yarn pictures. A far cry from the old-fashioned sampler, the child is encouraged to express himself and to design from his own imagination. Many photographs of children's work throughout.

Sticks and Stones and Ice Cream Cones
Phyllis Fiarotta
Workman Publishing Co., Inc., 231 E. 51st Street, New York, NY 10022 ($4.95, paperback)
A good collection of innovative crafts from paper, oatmeal boxes, coffee cans and other around-the-house things. Tells how to make a wind chime from seashells and a plastic coffee can lid, how to dry flowers, how to make a piggy bank from a one-gallon plastic bleach bottle.

What a Child Can Do
Carroll Lambert and Sandra Christensen
Pruett Publishing Company, P.O. Box 1560, Boulder, CO 80302 ($3.25, paperback)
An ideabook especially suited for home use. A very helpful section on using paper plates, egg cartons, cottage cheese and milk cartons, toothpicks, and soap in simple crafts. Making play sandals from construction paper and yarn. A section on simple science and food experiences, too.

Creative Art Tasks for Children
Frank D. Taylor, Alfred A. Artuso and Frank M. Hewett
Love Publishing Co., Denver, CO 80222 ($4.95)
A compendium of 146 tasks, all suited to very young children. Basic art experiences from scribbling to more complex collages, designs, and patterns are included. Soap art, constructions made of toothpicks, finger paint printing, paper bag masks, to name a few tasks.

Art of the Young Child
Jane Cooper Bland
The Museum of Modern Art, 11 W. 53rd Street, New York, NY 10019 ($2.95, paperback)
A discussion of the art of children three to five years of age. Shows with photographs how children progress in their art skills over a period of time. Ways that parents can encourage their children's art development. Gives practical suggestions for materials.

Bear's Pictures
Manus Pinkwater
Holt, Rinehart and Winston, Inc., 383 Madison Avenue, New York, NY 10017 ($1.45, paperback)
A picture book intended for young children but with a lesson for grownups, too. Bear paints a picture just the way he likes it. Two fine, proper gentlemen call it a silly picture. A subtle comment on the way adults are often judgmental about the artwork of children.

Let's Discover Puppets; Let's Discover Crayon; Let's Discover Paper; Let's Discover Watercolor; Let's Discover Mobiles; Let's Discover Tempera; Let's Discover Papier-Mâché; Let's Discover Printing; Let's Discover Weaving; Let's Discover Tissue
Jenean Romberg
The Center for Applied Research in Education, Inc., 521 Fifth Avenue, New York, NY 10017 ($3.95 each)
Arts and Crafts Discovery Units each with many suggestions for use with children. *Let's Discover Mobiles*, for example, has no fewer than fifty different mobiles illustrated, using coat hangers, wooden dowels, plastic straws, twigs, wire, and plastic tubes for arms. A wiggly witch mobile for Halloween, hanging translucent Christmas trees, a colorful butterfly mobile, a stained-glass mobile using tissue paper and black construction paper, to name a few.

Creative Art for the Developing Child
Clare Cherry
Fearon Publishers, 6 Davis Drive, Belmont, CA 94002 ($5.25, paperback)
Written for teachers of preschool children, this is the most comprehensive basic art experience book that I have found. Drawing, painting, coloring, pasting, woodworking, print making, all of the most common art techniques are discussed with suggestions for materials. Very practical.

ART EQUIPMENT

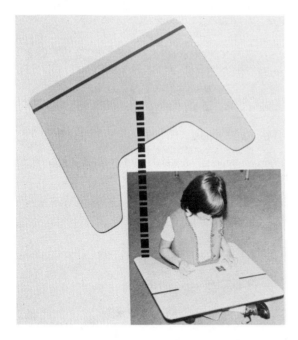

Lapboard
Made with a durable finish fused to a hardboard base that resists heat, moisture, and stains. Measures 31½ x 23½ inches. In gold with a heavy rubber band that acts as a handle and paper holder. Selected from a catalog of arts and crafts materials. Sax Arts and Crafts, P.O. Box 2002, Milwaukee, WI 53201 ($10.80 + 15% postage and insurance)

Sunshine Sketcher
Finished one masterpiece? Tear it off and start another! This bright yellow painting and drawing board has a seemingly endless roll of paper (60 feet). Simplifies artwork while traveling and provides a steady surface on which to work. Measurements: 10½ x 12½ inches. From the "Childcraft Toys that Teach" catalog. Price subject to change. Childcraft Education Corp., 20 Kilmer Road, Edison, NJ 08817 ($9.99 + shipping. Extra roll, $2.50)

Messy Tray
The neatest way to play! Children can do anything from finger painting to making mud pies in this self-contained environment without messing up the house. Just work in the 23-inch tray and put the tray aside when it's time to stop. Made of durable plastic that's easy to clean. From the "Childcraft Catalog of Special Education Materials." Price subject to change.
Childcraft Education Corp., 20 Kilmer Road, Edison, NJ 08817 ($7.50 + shipping)

Portable Easel and Paint Tote
Use this easel anywhere, on a tabletop, on the floor, in the park or playground. The 24 x 20-inch hardboard panels are hinged at the top with a cutout section to serve as a handle. Paint Tote makes paint storage easy. From the "Childcraft: The Growing Years" catalog. Price subject to change. Childcraft Education Corp., 20 Kilmer Road, Edison, NJ 08817 (Easel and Tote $17.95 + shipping)

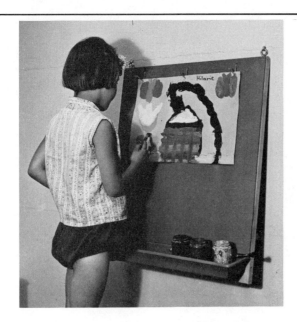

Wall Easel
Hang it wherever you want! Adjust the height as your child grows. It's made with two heavy eyehooks for hanging on the wall, two spring clips for holding paper, and waterproof removable plastic tray. Adjustable arms hold the easel out 4¼ inches from the wall to give your child a comfortable working angle.
Community Playthings, Rifton, NY 12471 ($15.50 + shipping)

Art Smock
A wipe-clean smock that ties in the back. Bright vinyl with elasticized cuffs and a pocket for storing treasures in the front. Large size, suitable for six years old and up, comes in blue with yellow and red

circle pocket. Smaller-size for preschoolers is in red with blue and yellow pocket. An excellent buy! Order from:
Mothercare-by-Mail, P.O. Box 228, Parsippany, NJ 07054 (Large size $3.00; small size $2.50)

Stubby Paint Brush
A big, thick short-handled brush with head designed especially for the young painter. The brush is 7¼ inches long. From a big catalog of school supplies and equipment.
abc School Supply, Inc., P.O. Box 13086, Atlanta, GA 30324 (75¢ each + postage and handling)

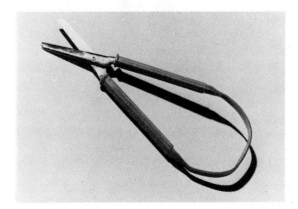

Easy-Grip Scissors
Only the lightest pressure is needed to cut with these scissors, designed with a softly spring-loaded handle to supply the "opening" action. The fine steel blades with blunt ends cut with a gentle squeeze of the red plastic handle that's a continuous loop. Excellent for young children or older children with motor control problems.
Developmental Learning Materials, 7440 Natchez Avenue, Niles, IL 60648 ($5.00)

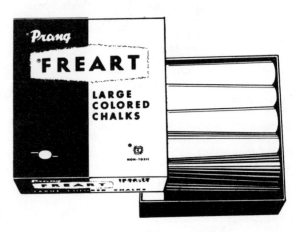

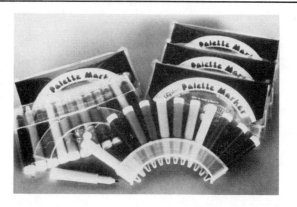

Kindergarten Chalk

Extra large tapered sticks of brightly colored chalk for use on paper. Coated for cleanliness and strength. Ideal for preschoolers. Lift-lid box. Size: 4 inches long, 1 inch in diameter. Colors: red, orange, yellow, green, blue, violet, red orange, yellow green, blue green, red violet, brown, and black. From a catalog of school supplies and equipment. Barclay School Supplies, 26 Warren Street, New York, NY 10007 (Cat. No. 1534, $6.40 per box of thirty-six. $2.00 charge for orders under $15.00)

Rich Art Tempra Marker

The colors on these big markers virtually set themselves down on paper. No dripping, no cleaning, no spilling. A set of six markers filled with Rich Art moist water colors: red, green, blue, yellow, black, and white. Refill colors available by the pint. From the "Dick Blick Catalog for Special Education and Early Learning."
Dick Blick, P.O. Box 1267, Galesburg, IL 61401 ($5.90 a set + postage)

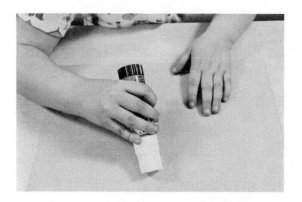

Glue Stick

Just draw it on and press! This neat, new way to glue never leaves a mess and is easy for young children to handle. Nontoxic and washable. From the Growing Years catalog. Price subject to change. Childcraft Education Corp., 20 Kilmer Road, Edison, NJ 08817 ($1.95)

Palette Markers

Solves the problem of lost caps. The special palette container encourages your child to replace the marker when finished. Marker locks in firmly to prevent drying out. Caps can be unsnapped for use separately.
Dick Blick, P.O. Box 1267, Galesburg, IL 61401 ($2.90 + postage for set of twelve markers)

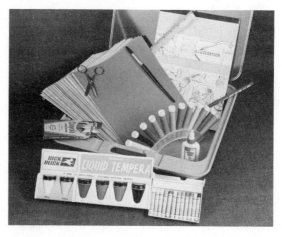

Art-Tote Kit

This plastic tote desk has a transparent 14½ x 16-inch top. The kit contains: six liquid tempera jars, a water-color brush, a box of crayons, a pair of blunt-nosed scissors, a 9 x 12-inch drawing pad, a package of 9 x 12-inch construction paper, a plastic bottle of white glue, a kindergarten-sized pencil, a box of oil pastels, a palette marker set and a 12-inch wooden ruler.
Dick Blick, P.O. Box 1267, Galesburg, IL 61401 ($15.20 + postage)

Spatter Box

A wooden box with a grooved, slip-out bottom and a rust-proof aluminum top for spatter painting by rubbing a rough-bristled brush such as a toothbrush over the screen. Place construction paper inside the box and top it with cutout stencils. Close the box and brush over the screen until the desired

results are obtained. Rinse box in water after using. Excellent for children with limited motor coordination.
Mrs. Virginia P. Harman, 8210 Lighthouse Ct., Annandale, VA 22003 ($8.00)

Payons

When they're dipped in water Payons produce sparkling water-color results. Durable lift-lid box, crayon-size in a protective holder, Colors: red, orange, yellow, green, blue, violet, black, brown. Box of eight. (Also available from most art stores.) Barclay School Supplies, 29 Warren Street, New York, NY 10007 (Cat. No. 341, 75¢ a box + $2.00 charge for orders under $15.00)

Set of Hand Weavers

The set consists of two sizes of weavers made of selected hardwood and birch dowels. Produces 4- or 5-inch squares with one continuous length of yarn. After your child acquires skill on the larger loom, he's ready to move to the smaller size. Set includes Germantown wool, yarn needles, and plastic curtain rings for making pot holders. From a catalog of school equipment and supplies.
J. L. Hammett Co., 2393 Vaux Hall Road, Union, NJ 07083 ($9.75 + $2.00 processing and delivery)

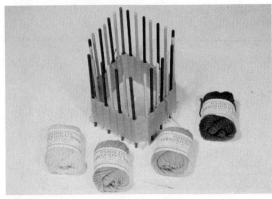

Loom Cage

Made of selected hardwoods, this loom makes stocking caps and bedroom slippers. It's lightweight, portable, and adjustable for the height of the weaving project. Enough yarn is included to complete one project.
J. L. Hammett Co., 2393 Vaux Hall Road, Union, NJ 07083 ($15.00 + $2.00 processing and delivery)

Rake Knitting Frames

Large, easy-to-use frames for making caps, scarves, stoles, and other projects. Sturdy hardwood and veneer to last a long time. Circular knitters: 5½-inch (71480), $3.80; 8-inch (71479), $4.30; 10½-inch (71478), $4.15; 13-inch (71477), $4.30; 15½-inch (71476), $4.40. Straight knitters: Single, 16-inch (71481), $3.45; Double, 15½-inch (71482), $4.20. Designed for rehabilitating the handicapped, but also most suited to the limited dexterity of the young child.
J. L. Hammett Co., 2393 Vaux Hall Road, Union, NJ 07083 (Add $2.00 processing and delivery charge)

So, Sew Stitch Kit
A kit to teach children basic stitching skills. Your
child begins with a large wooden "needle" which is
stitched in and out of a smooth board with large
holes in it. Next comes a smaller metal needle to
stitch on a second, more difficult frame. The kit also
includes two pieces of 4 x 9-inch heavy sewing
canvas, two blunt-tipped needles, three skeins of
bright thread, a spool of extra-strong button thread,
five buttons of varying sizes, and four pieces of stiff
fabric for stitching on. Instruction booklet is
included with suggestions for making a beanbag, a
potholder, a shoe tote bag, a felt change purse, and
a drawstring purse.
Milo Products Corp., Grantham, PA 17027 ($20.00)

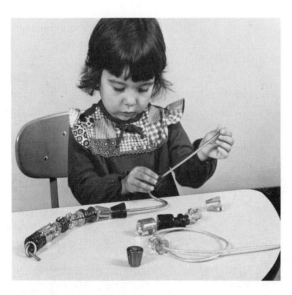

See-Thru Threading Shapes
Coordination and manipulative skills grow by
threading these beautiful transparent plastic beads
on easy sliding plastic tubing. Unusual bead shapes
with only slight variations in each one to encourage
tactile discrimination. Set includes sixteen beads, 1-
inch long, in four colors and four shapes. Two
thirty-inch strings are also included. From the
"Childcraft Special Education Materials" catalog.
Price subject to change.
Childcraft Education Corp., 20 Kilmer Road,
Edison, NJ 08817 ($8.50 + postage)

Picture Lacing Boards
Six photographs of familiar items in full color
mounted on heavy board. The boards vary in
complexity with the position of the holes. Six 54-
inch colored laces and full instructions are included.
An intriguing pastime that develops hand-eye
coordination.
Developmental Learning Materials, 7440 Natchez
Avenue, Niles, IL 60648 ($5.75 set)

Wooden Beads
These brightly colored beads for stringing are just a
sampling of arts and crafts materials for young
children available from this company. Here are
some more: small lace-up change purse kits, $2.16 a
dozen; small wooden sticks for projects, $1.75 for
1000; plastic pop beads, $4.00 for aaproximately
1000; plastic charms like from the bubble gum
machine, $2.95 for 500; alphabet beads like on baby
bracelets, $3.60 per gross; a ten-pound carton of
wooden scraps for carpentry projects, $2.95; a
simple three-legged stool to sand and nail together,
$1.75. Wooden beads vary with the size of the
package and the beads.
S & S Arts and Crafts, Colchester, CN 06415 (Large
wooden beads, $1.35 per package of 100 + shipping
and $1.00 surcharge for orders under $10.00)

Note: Not all manufacturers and publishers will
accept single orders for a product or book. Always write to them first, before sending
money, to be sure that they will take your
order. Make sure you've got the most recent
price, including shipping and handling
charges. If the company is in your state, then
you may need to include state sales tax as well.

There's no better source for learning than the out-of-doors! Watching my preschooler squatting to examine a tiny bug or to pick a dandelion blossom reminds me that the world is filled with tiny things that go unnoticed by adults who are always in such a hurry to get from one place to another. My words: "Come on! Hurry!" Her words: "Stay and look a while!" The beauty of childhood lies in this fresh discovery of life and the world of nature. Did I forget how to blow the puffs off a dandelion and make a wish, or to whistle with a blade of grass, or to make a chain of clover flowers? To lose the sense of joy about the plants and creatures of the earth is to lose connection with all of life.

The Sense of Wonder
by Rachel Carson

A child's world is fresh and new and beautiful, full of wonder and excitement. It is our misfortune that for most of us that clear-eyed vision, that true instinct for what is beautiful and awe-inspiring, is dimmed and even lost before we reach adulthood. If I had influence with the good fairy who is supposed to preside over the christening of all children I should ask that her gift to each child in the world be a sense of wonder so indestructible that it would last throughout life, as an unfailing antidote against the boredom and disenchantments of later years, the sterile preoccupation with things that are artificial, the alienation from the sources of our strength.

If a child is to keep alive his inborn sense of wonder without any such gift from the fairies, he needs the companionship of at least one adult who can share it, rediscovering with him the joy, excitement and mystery of the world we live in. Parents often have a sense of inadequacy when confronted on the one hand with the eager, sensitive mind of a child and on the other with a world of complex physical nature, inhabited by a life so various and unfamiliar that it seems hopeless to reduce it to order and knowledge. In a mood of self-defeat, they exclaim, "How can I possibly teach my child about nature — why, I don't even know one bird from another!"

I sincerely believe that for the child, and for the parent seeking to guide him, it is not half so important to *know* as to *feel*. If facts are the seeds that later produce knowledge and wisdom, then the emotions and the impressions of the senses are the fertile soil in which the seeds must grow. The years of early childhood are the time to prepare the soil. Once the emotions have been aroused — a sense of the beautiful, the excitement of the new and unknown, a feeling of sympathy, pity, admiration or love — then we wish for knowledge about the object of our emotional response. Once found, it has lasting meaning. It is more important to pave the way for the child to want to know than to put him on a diet of facts he is not ready to assimilate.

If you are a parent who feels he has little nature lore at his disposal there is still much you can do for your child. With him, wherever you are and whatever your resources, you can still look up at the sky — its dawn and twilight beauties, its moving clouds, its stars by night. You can listen to the wind, whether it blows with majestic voice through a forest or sings a many-voiced chorus around the eaves of your house or the corners of your apartment building, and in the listening, you can gain magical release for your thoughts. You can still feel the rain on your face and think of its long journey, its many transmutations, from sea to air to earth. Even if you are a city dweller, you can find some place, perhaps a park or a golf course, where you can observe the mysterious migrations of the birds and changing seasons. And with your child you can ponder the mystery of a growing seed, even if it be only one planted in a pot of earth in the kitchen window.

Exploring nature with your child is largely a matter of becoming receptive to what lies all around you. It is learning again to use your eyes, ears, nostrils and finger tips, opening up the disused channels of your sensory impressions.

Rachel Carson was a marine biologist, conservationist, and the author of several books. Silent Spring — *Miss Carson's last, and perhaps most famous, book — aroused much public concern and gave rise to governmental inquiries into the problem of indiscriminate use of chemical pesticides.*

NATURE ACTIVITIES FOR YOU AND YOUR CHILD

Marcie and I went with great excitement to get free scraps of wood from a lumberyard for building a birdfeeder. It was cold outside and soon the birds would be looking for food. We carried our heavy load home, spread out the papers and began to saw and hammer scraps together until we had fashioned a birdfeeder of sorts. There was the flat feeding area with pieces of wood on all sides to keep the seeds from blowing away. A small branch was nailed into the board in an upright position for the birds to land on. A long piece of lumber was nailed under the feeder for a stand. The feeder was then tied on to our apartment balcony with clothesline wire.

I optimistically bought a twenty-pound bag of sunflower seeds. Sunflower seeds attract the beautiful cardinals, bluejays, chickadees and titmouses, while offering no appeal to starlings, sparrows, and more quarrelsome birds. We put a fistful of seeds in the feeder and waited. And waited. I had visions of running a sunflower farm if this project failed. Finally, after three weeks, the chickadees discovered our treasure with excited chirps. Then came the nuthatches and, now, as spring comes, we have old friends — the brilliant red cardinals with the male feeding the female tidbits, proud, beak-stuffing bluejays and a host of passersby like the red-headed flicker who was drawn to a piece of suet we put out in a dish.

Other outdoor activities that lend themselves to happy sharing with your young child are:

Collect fireflies on spring and summer evenings. Fashion a holding jar with holes in the lid so that you can examine them more closely. Is their light hot like a light bulb? When the evening's hunt is finished, open the jar and let them go back where they came from.

Bring a lamp with an uncovered bulb or a strong flashlight outside in the evening and let it sit for a while. What kind of insects have you attracted? Put a moth in a jar and then examine it. Where are the eyes? The antennae? How many legs does it have? Have you got moth "dust" on your hands?

Watch for bats circling overhead on spring and summer evenings.

Try to locate a frog or a cricket that you hear chirping in the grass or by a stream.

Go out in the early morning to look for spiderwebs covered with dew. If you strum the web, will the spider come to see what it is? Can you see where the spider is storing her captured meals?

If you're lucky enough to live near fields with edible wild berries, go on a picking expedition together.

Go on a collection walk to find seeds, feathers, pieces of bark, and interesting rocks. Use a clear plastic bag to carry them home. Make a collage by glueing them onto a shoe box top.

Take a length of string or rope and cordon off a piece of the yard for scientific exploration. Get down on your hands and knees with a magnifying glass. Look for tiny creatures and growing things. Can you imagine how it would feel to be that size? That would make us giants, wouldn't it? Don't forget to smell the soil and grass.

See if you can find an anthill. Try giving some ants a piece of bread. How do they bite it off? How do they carry it? Do you think they can communicate with each other? How do they do it? With a magnifying glass watch them use their feelers.

Take a feeling walk together. What can you find that feels soft? Rough? Smooth? Wet? Take a fragrance walk. Smell the earth, the plants, the flowers. Explain how a dog's sense of smell is much more developed than ours. Dogs that are lost can find their way home by their sense of smell. Do different parts of your neighborhood have different aromas?

Take a leaf-collecting walk in the autumn. Try to find leaves of different colors and different shapes. Press the leaves between two layers of waxed paper to preserve them, or layer them in powdered borax for about four days. When you remove them from the borax, wipe each leaf with liquid floor wax.

If you live near the seashore, collect shells of different sizes and shapes. Try to identify the shells. Put the shells in a large brandy snifter, or suspend them from a dowel for a wind chime. Play sorting games with them: large shells in one place, small shells in another. Practice counting with them. Try lining them up from lightest to darkest.

Go on a winter walk to observe the buds on trees. Keep a sketchbook of the progress of buds as spring approaches. Try "forcing" a bud to bloom early by putting it in a glass of water.

Look for footprints of animals in the snow: bird tracks, the boxy tracks of squirrels with each toeprint showing, the long hind foot tracks of a rabbit. (Warn your child against touching strange animals, since they may be easily frightened and bite.)

Collect dandelion greens in the early spring before they bloom and cook them as you would spinach. Gently dig up the new roots, and peel and slice them. Boil in water and then drain and add salt. A tasty vegetable! Did you know that dandelions used to be thought of as an herb? (When the plant has flowered, it will taste bitter.) Examine dandelion blossoms with a magnifying glass. You will discover that each petal is a separate flower with all the parts of a regular flower. Try germinating the little umbrella seeds indoors by putting them on a moist blotter or sponge. Blow the seeds on prepasted black construction paper to see the pattern they make. Try using the sticky substance from the stem for glue.

Take a nighttime walk together to listen to the sounds. Does the air smell differently than during the day? Is it cooler? Do the trees and familiar things look different? It's valuable to help a young child overcome fear of the dark by sharing the joys of the moon, the stars, and night sounds with her.

Don't forget to stop and savor the fragrances of the earth! Pine needles in the forest, the first rains of springtime, freshly mowed grass, the moist leaves of autumn, the smell of the sea.

Ah yes! I mustn't forget to mention the fine art of cloud gazing. Create pictures and stories from cloud patterns on a blue-skyed day.

Investigate Your Backyard Beasties
by Stephen W. Kress

A Medieval chant pleads for deliverance from "ghosties, ghoulies, long-legged beasties, and things that go bump in the night." While fear of ghosts and ghouls is no longer an everyday concern, the general fear of long- and short-legged beasts has persisted and frequently expresses itself wherever encounters occur with such everyday animals as spiders, insects, and earthworms.

Those who know the least about these animals are generally the ones who experience strong feelings of disgust and revulsion. Even simple investigations of these small creatures reveal that they are gifted with extensions of senses which we have lost or never attained. We should not only recognize their evolutionary success, but should acknowledge them for supporting the life systems above and within the soil which permit our own survival.

Negative attitudes toward these animals result largely from unfamiliarity, misconceptions, and exposure to the prevalent negative attitudes of peers, parents, and teachers. Parents have a very real opportunity to promote the development of positive attitudes toward animals and to encourage feelings of compassion and wonder toward all creatures that co-inhabit the earth,

The activities that follow focus on animals that live near homes and schools. The activities are intended to assist the child and his parents to take a close look at a few of those animals. Glimpses into the lives of such creatures as spiders, grasshoppers, and earthworms will stimulate children's curiosity and permit them to become increasingly familiar with these abundant yet little-known backyard animals.

GRASSHOPPERS

During autumn when grasshoppers are abundant you can conduct some interesting investigations with these common animals. Make a grasshopper cage by rolling a 30 centimeter square of window screen into the shape of a column and fasten the overlapping edges with paper clips. Then place the screen into a pie pan filled with moist sand and cover the top of the cage with a second pie pan.

Collect a grasshopper from your yard and put it in the cage along with some of the plants in which you found the grasshopper. Push the plant stems down into the sand and watch the grasshopper feed. Watch the grasshopper's jaws and carefully observe them to see if one jaw moves (as in humans) or if both jaws move. Do the jaws (called mandibles) move sideways or up and down? Put several different types of vegetation in the grasshopper cage and see which plants the grasshopper eats first. Then repeat the experiment and see if you get the same results.

SPIDERS

Spiders frequently head the list of "most despised animals." This, however, is an unearned notoriety, for few spiders will bite even when coaxed and most could not even penetrate human skin if they tried. (A warning, though: The female black widow spider should be avoided. She is identifiable by the red or yellow patches on the abdomen.) Spiders adapt well to captivity and make interesting subjects for activities. Many spiders construct elaborate webs and perform intricate courtship displays. In addition, their predatory nature makes them excellent subjects for talking about predator-prey relationships.

Children can make excellent spider cages from rectangular plastic boxes such as shoe boxes or vegetable crispers. Cover the bottom of the box with about an inch of dry sand and set a bottle cap or watch glass in the sand for a water dish. Then drill many small holes into the lid of the plastic box with an electric drill for the child. A small tree branch will make the spider home complete. A similarly furnished gallon jar will also make a suitable spider habitat. If you collect a web-spinning spider from your cellar or garden, you'll find that it will be a rather slow-moving animal and can easily be handled. Before placing the spider in its new habitat you can watch its web-spinning behavior by holding it in one hand and letting it lower itself on a dropline of silk. The dropline makes a convenient handle and the animal can be passed among kids by permitting them to hold the dropline while the spider dangles below.

After you have placed the spider in its new home, watch to observe how it spins its web. Careful observation will reveal why the spider does not get entangled within its own web. Touch the web in different places with a broomstraw — look for some strands that are not sticky. Then make a small hole with the straw — does the spider repair the damage? Drop a live fly into the cage and observe the spider's behavior. Does the spider eat the entire fly? Will he capture more than one fly at a time and store some for the future? What happens if you drop a dead fly into the web? How do spiders recognize their prey?

EARTHWORMS

Because earthworms live a secret life, they are frequently overlooked and seldom given credit for their important role as soil conditioners. Good farm soil may contain over a million earthworms per acre and within a single year the earthworms will enrich over seven tons of soil per acre! In the process of passing soil through their bodies, earthworms recycle plant matter and bring rich soil nutrients from deeper layers to the surface. Their tunnels also permit air and water to circulate better through the soil.

The earthworm's capacity for recycling plant matter can be demonstrated by placing at least twenty earthworms in a small brownie pan with an inch of moist soil. Scatter coffee grounds on one side of the pan and spread potato gratings on the other side. Cover the pan with a damp towel and place it in a dark place for a week. Then examine the pan to see what happens to the different foods. How long does it take for the foods to disappear? Where did they go? Can you still smell the coffee grounds after a week?

This miniature compost pile may inspire some of the children to build a larger-scale composting effort at home.

Stephen W. Kress is a science consultant for Instructor *magazine.*

Guess Who's Coming to Dinner?

I'm not suggesting that you collect all kinds of wild living things for pets, but I think it's valuable for a child to get the chance to see small creatures of the earth up close. Teach children to respect them and their right to live unhampered in their own environments. This is the time to examine the creatures closely — then release them with a fond farewell to pursue their own destinies.

Ants Sugar water, diluted honey, pieces of nuts and apples, dead spiders or insects, bread crumbs. Place near where ants live on the soil or in a saucer.

Birds Wild birdseed, peanut butter, pieces of bread, suet, apple, raisins, grit, cranberries, sunflower seeds, peanuts taken out of the shell (unsalted).

Melted bacon or hamburger fat can be mixed with whole wheat crumbs, nuts, seeds, raisins, and chopped apple and put in the bottom of an aluminum pie pan. Spoon peanut butter onto pine cones and roll in birdseed. Hang on tree limbs. Hang out a doughnut or put it onto a tree branch.

Butterflies A thick, fresh sugar water solution. Will sometimes take the nectar out of fresh flowers.

Caterpillars Save the leaves from the plant where you found it. Provide fresh leaves and a moist cotton ball for water daily.

Crayfish Water, plants, small pieces of meat.

Crickets Peanut butter, lettuce, bread, fruits.

Frogs Live insects, worms, raw meat dangled on a thread in front of them, caterpillars, cornmeal. (Don't overfeed!)

Horned Toads Ants, meal worms.

Ladybugs Aphids. Look on the bottom of the yellow leaves of sick plants. Rosebushes are a good place to find them.

Lizards Insects, worms, meat on a stick, Sprinkle water in the cage.

Moths Sugar water.

Mice Uncooked oatmeal, rice, bread soaked in milk, birdseed, lettuce, carrots, celery. A peanut in the shell. Fresh water daily.

Newts Parts of dead insects, ant eggs. Finely ground beef.

Praying Mantis Any live insects.

Salamanders Insects, worms, ground meat, dog food occasionally, raw fish. Must have water constantly to preserve their moist skins. Soak, head out, in barely warm water if the skin seems too dry.

Snails, Land Fresh lettuce leaves, plant material, celery tops, soft vegetables, grapes, apples. Water daily.

Snails, Water Fish food, lettuce, aquarium plants, shredded shrimp. Keep in water.

Snakes Different snakes have different tastes, so it's best to look up your variety in the library. Try live food, roaches, earthworm pieces. Water to drink. Snakes only eat every few days. Some won't eat at all if they're in captivity. If yours won't, be kind — let him go back where he came from.

Spiders Flies and mosquitoes. (Some wait a long time between meals.)

Tadpoles Eats foods available in pond water. Water plants, green scum. Cooked oatmeal, cooked spinach, lettuce or spinach leaves, small bits of hamburger.

Toads Insects, earthworms, meal worms, roaches, ants and other live insects. Water daily.

Turtles (Beware the danger of salmonella infections from commercially purchased turtles!) Meat pieces, vegetables, fruit pieces, worms, insects, snails, bits of hardboiled egg, berries. Put the food in the water dish. Give fresh water daily.

Hiking and Camping with Our Kids
by Norman Baron

Joshua, our oldest child who is now five, first hit the camping trail when he was five months old. Since that time we — Joyce, Norman, Joshua, and now Eliza (age three) — have spent at least a few weeks a year living in our one-room canvas house which can be rolled up, put in a sack and carried to our next adventure. We love camping, and if you like vacations full of fun, adventure, problem solving, learning, and the joy of being close together with your family, it might be just the thing for you.

It's not always easy and there isn't always laughter, but the feelings that go along with being a vagabond family — taking care of your own daily needs, providing your own food, warmth, and shelter, being close to the ground and surrounded by trees — overshadow passing problems.

There is always an infinite variety of activities for children, providing the adults are relaxed enough to follow the kids' leads. There is fire-building, wood-collecting, rock-hunting, campsite-improving, hiking, sunny afternoons by babbling brooks, emergencies like wet sleeping bags and countless other events that our kids seem to love being a part of. We especially love the feeling of knowing that our family is not our house, or our car, or our town, or our friends, but us wherever we are.

When we first started camping with Joshua, although we didn't know it then, we had some of our hardest times. He spent most of his time in a car bed, which became his playpen and dining room as well as his bed in the tent and the car. We simplified the diaper scene by using disposable diapers and often used a small baby food grinder to make his meals from ours. Luckily one of his favorite places to be was in the Gerry pack on one of our backs. Those were the days of carrying everything ourselves and seeing that our joy in the woods was only occasionally shared by Joshua. Somehow it did not seem like twice the work when Eliza came along, perhaps because Joshua was then beginning to be able to take care of some of his own needs. Having two children two years apart means that the limits imposed by one are not unbearable restrictions for the other. For example, hiking this summer we found we could cajole and carry Eliza for about as long a hike as Josh felt like doing himself.

A few tips we have discovered over the years might be worth mentioning. First, suitable clothing can make the difference between a disasterous day and one of warm, dry bodies and loving feelings. When it rains or turns cold suddenly, hauling along comfortable raincoats, boots, and sweaters really pays off. Second, we have found it important not to expect too much from the children when hiking and to avoid giving them the feeling that the hike was a failure if the destination was not reached. Each moment should be accepted and enjoyed for itself. (Remember, getting there is only half the trip: There must be energy reserved for the journey home.) Third, bring along food and drink. Kids like to munch along the way.

This past summer's camping trip included three wonderful days in the White Mountains of New Hampshire. We bought a small trail map at the base of Mount Washington and investigated the cog railway that goes to the summit. Since it was rainy and foggy, we decided to leave that train adventure for another day. Carefully checking the trail map, we found a hike that seemed to suit us and spent the rest of the day in the woods exploring.

Probing into the woods on trails has many rewards. Our country's parks seem to be full of people who are not at all interested in leaving the security of the paved road or the comforts of their cars or campers. One day's hike led us to a beautiful mountain stream and waterfall with many pools for swimming. We spent most of the day swimming, building dams, and following the sun from rock to rock. We were there about four hours and only a few people passed by.

We packed our gear, cleared our campsite, decided to return to the White Mountains next summer, and moved on to Mount Desert Island and Acadia National Park on the coast of Maine. This beautiful and varied island was America's first national park. How nice of John D. Rockefeller to know how much we would appreciate his setting it aside for public use. This type of camping includes somewhat crowded and less scenic campgrounds balanced by countless beautiful, interesting and amazingly varied things to do during the night and day. For us this is the kind of place where we rise early, have a good breakfast, pack a lunch, and leave our crowded campgrounds for the day, knowing that there are endless activities available for us to enjoy. I'll list a few so that you can get the idea: During the day at Mount Desert Island you can hike on carriage paths and trails of different levels of difficulty, canoe on a wilderness lake, bask in the sun at Sand Beach, go rock climbing along the coast and explore tidal pools and grottos, visit an excellent Indian museum, have tea and popovers at an extraordinary and beautiful place accessible by road, trail, or carriage path. At night we'd either return to our tent to make supper or splurge and eat in Bar Harbor, a busy tourist town full of interesting places and shops to browse through. We spent two weeks at this park — a long time for us to camp in one place. Our campsite cost a few dollars per night, while the cheapest housekeeping cottage in the area costs well over $100 per week.

Camping is hard work, so if you are looking for a total physical rest this type of vacation is not for you. Taking care of a campsite will provide you with more exercise than a neighborhood health spa. There is smoke in the eyes, and more dirt than many of us are used to, but if you love to camp you eventually come to terms with and come to love the aspects of camping that at first are uncomfortable and annoying. All the exercise is good for you and free. It makes you feel healthy, and sometimes tired, so you climb into your sleeping bag early and get a good night's sleep. The dirt comes off with soap and water. We are bath freaks at home and this does not change when we are camping. Bathing begins right after dinner cleanup. The fire is built up to a roaring blaze. We all haul water, in every available pail, bucket and kettle, to the fire where half of it is heated to a boil. After mixing up gallons and gallons of warm bathing water, we stand in the moonlight, pour buckets of delicious hot water over each other, soap up, and then rinse until we are all clean, warm, and tingly. Dirt is just part of clean and the whole process feels great! Bathing might take hours, but we prefer it to going to a movie.

There are books full of good advice for campers. Most likely the best way to get started is to read about camping, talk to friends who have camped, and then plunge right in. There is some equipment that you will need, and it would be untrue to try to make you think that it is inexpensive. As a base you'll need a good tent big enough for four, adult sleeping bags, good kids' bags, and mess kits. We use a propane lantern and carry a single burner that screws right into a small tank of propane. We use the stove only in campsites that have no wood or to brew up a cup of coffee on a rainy morning. If you try to make camping too much like living at home expenses will really mount up and you'll be burdened with a bunch of relatively useless contraptions that break down or wear you down as you cart them around. Get good equipment, but keep it simple. Buy your gear from a place that specializes in camping equipment and can help you find gear to suit your particular needs. Track down someone who knows which store in your area is the best, where the people are honest, knowledgeable, and really interested in

making sure that you get the most out of camping with the minimal investment. Yes, the cost of equipment is substantial, but not much compared to a week of motel and restaurant bills.

One more suggestion: Why not try out your gear in your backyard or someplace else nearby? It is a pain to arrive at the first night's campsite without knowing how to put up the tent or light the lantern. Testing equipment around the house will give everyone a chance to get comfortable with it.

There are many variables in camping and no way of anticipating all the unknowns. So — prepare yourself as well as you can, take off for the mountains and woods, and remember Joshua's advice: "If your muffler breaks off, don't cry!"

Norman Baron, who goes camping when he can with Joyce, Joshua (seven), and Liza (five), is co-Director of the Rockland Project School in Valley Cottage, New York.

BOOKS FOR GROWN-UPS ABOUT NATURE

"Adventures with Your Children — Through Nature"
Cooperative Extension Service, Iowa State University
Order from:
Publications Distribution Center, Printing and Publications Building, Iowa State University, Ames, IA 50011 (15¢)
An eloquently written brochure describing activities that parents and children can share together in learning about nature.

The Audubon Society Field Guide to North American Birds
John Bull and John Farrard, Jr.
Alfred A. Knopf, Inc., Div. of Random House, Inc., 457 Hahn Road, Westminster, MD 21157 ($7.95)
The full-color photographs of individual birds make this book the best source for teaching your children about birds. Full descriptions along with silhouettes of the birds in flight.

Backpacking with Small Children
James Stout and Ann Stout
Funk and Wagnalls Co.
Dist. by: Thomas Y. Crowell Co., 666 Fifth Avenue, New York, NY 10019 ($6.95)
The authors, who seem to enjoy the wonders of nature thoroughly, give detailed stories about their explorations with their small sons. They discuss making your own gear, packing, cooking, tenting, dealing with behavior in the wilderness, techniques for safety.

"Chickadee Nest Box" (WL24); "Four Room Martin House" (WL31); "Robin Nesting Shelter" (WL23); "Simple Bluebird House" (WL21); "Weather Vane Bird Feeder" (WL20)
Cooperative Extension Service, Iowa State University
Order from:
Publications Distribution Center, Printing and Publications Building, Iowa State University, Ames, IA 50011 (Free up to five single copies)
Instructions and patterns for making bird residences from wood.

"Diary of a Blackbird"
Hans Hvass
American Humane Education Society (A.H.E.S.), 350 South Huntington Avenue, Boston, MA 02130 (20¢)
A photographic narrative of the growth of a blackbird from the first day of hatching until it is fourteen days old. The nest and a blackbird egg are pictured. The pictures are good for young children, the words suitable for adults.

"Environmental & Outdoor Education Materials Catalog"
Environmental & Education Materials Company, Box 585, Lander, WY 82520 (75¢)
This commercial catalog in newspaper format is a source for a wide variety of nature study materials including bug cages, butterfly nets and terrarium kits. An excellent selection of books on environmental education and nature crafts, all amply described.

Green Fun
Maryanne Gjersvik
The Chatham Press, Inc.
Distributed by:
E. P. Dutton & Company, Inc., 201 Park Ave. S., New York, NY 10004 ($1.95, paperback)
In case you've forgotten! A joyful book with ample pictures to tell you how to make dandelion curl earrings, a maple leaf crown, a daisy wreath, a burr basket, and other things that grownups can share with kids in a meadow.

"Master Tree Finder"
($1.00)
"Tree Finder"
(50¢)
May Theilgaard Watts, Nature Study Guild
Available from:
G.L.E.E.P., Kellogg Bird Sanctuary of Michigan State University, 12685 C Avenue, Augusta, MI 49012
Large drawings of the leaves of the most common American trees will help you and your child learn the names of the trees in your neighborhood. The general shape of the tree is also sketched.

Nature Activities for Early Childhood
Janet Nickelsburg
Addison-Wesley Publishing Company, South Street, Reading, MA 01867 ($7.50, paperback)
An excellent guidebook for both parents and teachers of groups of young children. Detailed illustrations of insects and other things of nature. Simple, clear information about ladybugs, lizards, and toads, for example. There are forty-four projects for children to do, vocabulary lists to help young children learn the words of nature, and bibliographies at the end of each secton of the book for both adults and children.

"Nature Poetry" (Vol. 57, #3, March, 1964); "Animal Traces" (Vol. 59, #2, January, 1966); "Inviting Bird Neighbors" (Bulletin 103); "Pond Life" (Vol. 60, #2)
Cornell Science Leaflets
New York State College of Agriculture, Cornell University, Ithaca, NY 14850 (25¢ ea.)
Several titles from a whole series. Each brochure is about thirty pages long. There are black-and-white photographs of animals and nature scenes in each brochure. In most cases, the writing is more appropriate for adult reading, but would be good background material for talking about animals and insects.

The New Field Book of Nature Activities and Hobbies
William Hillcourt
G. P. Putnam's Sons, 200 Madison Avenue, New York, NY 10016 ($6.95)
If you're only buying one book to help you guide your child's appreciation of nature, this should be the one. It is packed with ideas: how to make a birdbath, take plaster casts of animal prints, construct an insect-rearing cage, how to grow wildflowers, how to make leaf prints. There are close to 1000 activities suggested, with 500 of them classified by difficulty in a special project index. Each section also suggests other books, related societies and organizations and supply sources. *Excellent!*

Snips and Snails and Walnut Whales, Nature Crafts for Children
Phyllis Fiarotta
Workman Publishing Company, 231 E. 51st Street, New York, New York 10022 ($4.95, paperback)
Over one hundred craft projects are presented ranging from simple to more complex. Some of the projects suitable for young children are: leaf rubbings, daisy chains, a carrot necklace, and a pine cone/peanut butter birdfeeder. Excellent illustrations and easy-to-follow directions.

Ten-Minute Field Trips
Helen Ross Russell
J. G. Ferguson Company, 100 Park Avenue, New York, NY 10017
($6.95, paperback)
Although primarily written for teachers, Dr. Russell's book is a magnificent guide to the hundreds of possibilities for nature learning outside your front door. For example: the book explains the origin of the name "dandelion" (*dent de lion* meaning a lion's tooth from the jagged shape of the leaf) and it tells how kids can split the stems and swish them in water to make curls. Other subjects include worms, seeds, animal tracks, and common insects.

MATERIALS FOR CHILDREN ABOUT NATURE

An Aquarium
Glenn O. Blough
Harper & Row, Pubs., Inc.
Available from:
G.L.E.E.P., Kellogg Bird Sanctuary of Michigan State University, 12685 C Avenue, Augusta, MI 49012 (60¢, paperback)
A picture book in simple language telling children how to set up an aquarium. Describes goldfish, snails, and aquatic plants, the feeding and caring for fish.

Be Kind to Animals Club
American Humane Education Society, 350 S. Huntington Avenue, Boston, MA 02130 ($1.00)
New members receive a membership card, a stick-on fabric badge, a pencil with the club's name, a ruler and a year's subscription to *Animalia*, a children's newsletter that comes four times a year with stories about animals and suggestions for constructing birdfeeders, caring for pets and the like.

Birds Eat and Eat and Eat
Roma Gans
Thomas Y. Crowell Company, 666 Fifth Avenue, New York, NY 10019 ($1.25, paperback)
Everyday birds are shown eating, with an emphasis on the tremendous volume of food that birds eat each day. Directions are given for a simple birdfeeder made from a milk carton, and a suet feeder. Easy to understand for small bird watchers.

"Birds of the Garden" (BL2)
Educational Services, National Audubon Society, 950 Third Avenue, New York, NY 10022 ($1.65)
Fourteen four-page leaflets of individual birds, including chickadee, robin, mockingbird, sparrow, and the catbird. Each folder includes a full-color print of the bird, and a second, black-and-white outline of the bird for the child to color in. The birds are described: how they make nests, what their eggs look like and other information about their activities.

The Brook Book
Doug Morse
Storyfold, Inc., Newburyport, MA 01950 ($3.95)
An accordion picture book in color that spreads out to six feet. It is the story of animals and plants that live along the brook as it meanders to the sea. On the back of the story fold-out are directions for making a water scope, how to go fishing, how to make boats from easy-to-find materials, an ecology-oriented board game, among other activities.

How to Raise Goldfish and Guppies; How to Raise a Puppy; How to Raise Mice, Rats, Hamsters and Gerbils
Sara Bonnett Stein
Random House, Inc., 457 Hahn Road, Westminster, MD 21157 ($3.95 ea.)
Although these books have been written for reading by older children, you can use them as a way of communicating to a younger child about pets. *How to Raise a Puppy*, for example, explains to a child what supplies are going to be needed, how to feed a puppy, handle him gently and clean up his messes. The phrasing of the books is simple enough that it will help to communicate to a very young child a responsible, caring attitude.

The Last Free Bird
A. Harris Stone
Prentice-Hall, Inc., Englewood Cliffs, NJ 07632 (95¢, paperback)
A magnificently simple book with the beauty of delicate water-color illustrations by Sheila Heins. What human pollution and destructiveness do to birds.

Our Book Corner
Jean Wilson
Addison-Wesley Publishing Co., 2725 Sand Hill Road, Menlo Park, CA 94025 ($2.97 per set)
This British series consists of sets of child-sized paperbacks, seven in each set, with very simple texts for the beginning reader. The books are outstanding both in their simplicity and in the exquisiteness of their artwork. *Animals of Warmer Lands* includes small books on the lion, the monkey, the giraffe, the tiger, and other wild animals. *Creatures of Cold Lands* describes the polar bear, the reindeer, the penguin, and other arctic animals with clarity and beauty.

"There Lived a Wicked Dragon"
U.S. Environmental Protection Agency
Consumer Information Center, Pueblo, CO 81009 (Free)
A pollution story in coloring book form for children. Tells of a wicked dragon who lives on pollution. The grownups finally do something about the pollution and the dragon disappears.

What Is a Tree? What Is a Bird?
Jenifer W. Day
Golden Press, Western Publishing Company, Inc., 1220 Mound Avenue, Racine, WI 53404 (95¢ ea.)
Two books in a series of books dealing with nature. Both books have beautiful illustrations of their subjects in full color, and simple, easy-to-follow wording. *What Is a Bird?* introduces children to the many exotic varieties of birds such as the cormorant, the ibis and the gallinule, all words that are fun to read and say. *What Is a Tree?* has clear close-up illustrations of trees as a child would see them and makes a good early identification book.

PRODUCTS FOR LEARNING ABOUT NATURE

Observation Bee Hive
An intriguing window into the activities of these social insects. Simple installation, no gloves, protective clothing, or smoker needed. Requires only that a ⅝-inch hole be provided to the outside. The hive is ready to go when you receive it. Simply extend the entrance tube outdoors. Complete hive includes: hive with fertile queen and worker bees, entrance tube, foundation comb, feeder, cover, and complete instructions for starting and caring for the colony. From the Nasco "Learning Fun" catalog. Nasco, 901 Janesville Avenue, Fort Atkinson, WI 53538 ($30.85. Unit complete with bees shipped parcel post, special handling FOB Michigan)

Nature Lotto
Beautiful color photographs of fruits, vegetables, and flowers useful for word-picture association learning. The object of the game is to match your picture card to the picture on the master card. A simple, colorful game that even very young children can play. From the "Vital Years" catalog ($1.00) of educational materials for early childhood and special education.
Educational Teaching Aids (ETA), A Division of A. Daigger and Co., 159 W. Kinzie Street, Chicago, IL 60610 ($6.95 + $2.50 shipping and 10% handling charge for all orders under $25.00)

Butterfly Net
A strong 30-inch wooden handle and a long nylon net for capturing insects for observation and study. From a catalog of instructional materials.
School Days, 973 North Main Street, Los Angeles, CA 90012 ($3.95 + $1.00 for shipping. $10.00 minimum order)

Wildlife Photopuzzles
Photographs of popular wildlife are laminated to ⅝-inch thick durable boards. The washable surfaces resist wear and tear. Each puzzle is carefully cut so that body parts and figure ground relationships are used in assembling them. A short narrative on each animal is provided. Puzzles available: raccoon, owl, deer, hippo, elephant, lion.
Educational Design Associates, Box 712, Waldorf, MD 20601 ($5.50 ea. + $1.00 postage and handling)

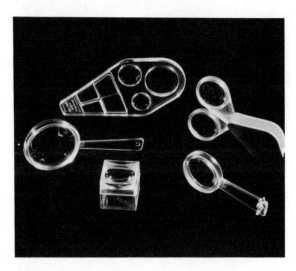

Wooden Birdfeeder Kit
All the parts of this birdfeeder are precut. The kit includes nails, screw eyes, sandpaper, a packet of wild birdseed, and a letter to the young carpenter full of fascinating facts on bird lore. Simple instructions for assembling are included. Finished overall dimensions: 8½ inches long, 7½ inches high, 6¼ inches wide. From a huge (642 pages) catalog of school supplies and equipment.
Northern Supply Co., P.O. Box 920, Bangor, ME 04401 ($2.35 + 15% shipping and insurance)

Magnifying Glass Set
Seeing things magnified stimulates and extends a child's exploration of nature. Five unbreakable magnifiers give a child the opportunity to compare the way things look through different powers of magnification. Set includes: a 1 x 1-inch box with a 4X magnifying cover, a 2 x 4-inch lucite magnifier with three different powered lenses, a plastic loupe with 2⅞-inch, 5X lens, two thermoplastic magnifiers, one with a 1-inch, 4X lens, one with a 1⅜-inch, 3X lens. From the "Special Education Materials" catalog. Price subject to change.
Childcraft Education Corp., 20 Kilmer Road, Edison, NJ 08817 ($3.50 + postage)

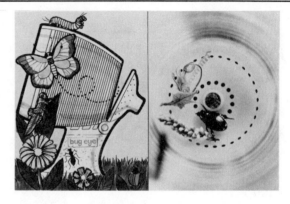

Bug Eye

A 3X lens is mounted in a molded case with a carrying grip for viewing live insects, leaves, and flowers. Bug Eye combines light amplification and magnification. The hinged-end case makes capture and release easy. A water sponge inside provides moisture for the captive. From a superb catalog of toys, educational materials, and children's furniture with each item specifying the age-level for use. ($1.00)
Novo Educational Toy and Equipment Corp., 11 Park Place, New York, NY 10007 ($3.75 + shipping. Minimum order $20.00)

Hands Free Magnifier

A giant 4-inch diameter lens, mounted in a clear lucite frame. The magnifier has a 10-inch depth of field. Doubles the size of the object or insect viewed. Fastens around the neck to free both hands or can be hand-held. Maybe you could borrow it from your child to help you remove splinters. From one of three catalogs put out by this company of inexpensive science materials and equipment.
Selective Educational Equipment (see), Inc., 3 Bridge Street, Newton, MA 02195 ($6.50 + $1.25 shipping and insurance)

Mee Too Backpack

Now your youngster can backpack right along with you. Made of waterproof material with nylon web shoulder straps. Buckles for adjusting fit. It has a large outside pocket, a covered zipper pocket and a drawstring top.
Novo Educational Toy and Equipment Corp., 11 Park Place, New York, NY 10007 ($7.45 + shipping. Minimum order $20.00)

Capturing Magnifier

A 4X magnifier featuring a clear stand that holds the lens at its optimum focal length. The sides are open to permit sliding or probing objects under the lens. If the openings are taped, the magnifier will keep insects captured while being viewed. All plastic, it measures approx. 3 x 2½ inches.
Selective Educational Equipment, Inc., 3 Bridge Street, Newton, MA 02195 ($11.25 + $1.25 shipping, insurance, and handling)

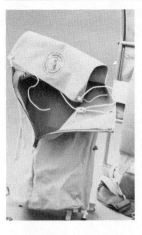
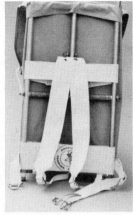

Backpack Frame and Bag
A small pack frame (Model 2000) and bag (Model 2050) suitable together for children from five to ten years of age (sold separately). The frame fits a child measuring from 9 to 12 inches shoulder to waist. The shoulder straps are adjustable. The pack bag has a 10-inch zipper and can carry up to ten pounds (if the carrier is willing and able). From a catalog of backpacking equipment (25¢).
Antelope Camping and Equipment Manufacturing Co., 21740 Granada Avenue, Cupertino, CA 95014 (Pack frame, $12.50; pack bag $8.35 + postage and handling)

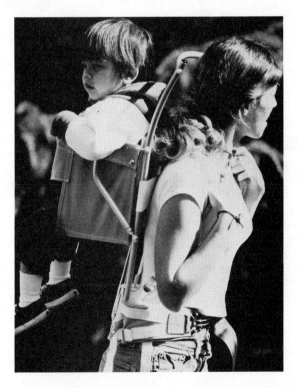

Child Carrier Attachment
An attachable seat that can be used with Antelope adult backpacking frames. The carrier accessory has a padded back and a solid seat for the child's comfort. It attaches to the frame at four screw

points. The bed roll straps at the bottom of Antelope frames can still be used with the carrier attached. Catalog shows adult frames available (25¢).
Antelope Camping and Equipment Manufacturing Co., 21740 Granada Avenue, Cupertino, CA 95014 (Approximately $14.00 + postage and handling. Carrier *only* without frame)

RECORDINGS OF BIRD SONGS

Cassettes and records of bird songs in their natural habitat have been produced by the Cornell Laboratory of Ornithology and published by Houghton Mifflin Company. The records correspond to Peterson's *A Field Guide to the Birds* also published by Houghton Mifflin Company. Being able to recognize familiar birdcalls can enrich your awareness of the birds in your neighborhood.

A Field Guide to Bird Songs
Eastern land and water birds. Two Cassettes (No. 1C, $19.95), or two records (No. 1R, $17.95).
A Field Guide to Western Bird Songs
Three cassettes (No. 2C, $23.95), or three records (No. 2R, $19.95).

Bird Songs in Your Garden
Birds commonly heard in eastern gardens. One record (No. 5R, $11.95).
Houghton Mifflin Company, Two Park Street, Boston, MA 02107

Note: Not all manufacturers and publishers will accept single orders for a product or book. Always write to them first, before sending money, to be sure that they will take your order. Make sure you've got the most recent price, including shipping and handling charges. If the company is in your state, then you may need to include state sales tax as well.

WOOD

CARPENTRY

Working with wood poses intriguing problems for a young child. Unlike clay, wood is hard and can't be molded. Constructions are limited by the shape of the wooden pieces and must be held together with glue, nails, or screws. Hammering, nailing, and sawing demand the use of new body muscles. The finished article, as heavy and cumbersome as it may appear, brings a special smile, evidence of the child's mastery of a new medium.

Your child should have a claw hammer of his own if he is to work with wood. Check to see that it weighs between 11 and 13 ounces and has a big, flat striking surface. Toy tools only frustrate a child. Choose nails that are 1½ to 2 inches long with a head on them.

A tree stump or a large board of soft wood with nailed-on block "feet" can serve as a place to hammer. Demonstrate how to hold the hammer. Plasticene clay, a wide-toothed comb or a predrilled hole will help steady the nail without the danger of the child hitting his fingers. When he's ready to hold the nail himself, remind him to use a few gentle taps to get the nail started before beginning the real "bammering," as Marcie calls it.

Wood scraps can easily be obtained at no cost from a lumberyard. See that they have no splinters or sharp edges on the ends. Look for softwoods: white pine, basswood, yellow pine, spruce, or poplar. The grain of the softwoods is further apart than that of the hardwoods and the wood is lighter in weight. Avoid hardwoods such as maple, chestnut, birch, hickory, or mahoghany since they are very difficult to nail and saw. Plywood is also unsuitable for nailing and sawing because it's hard and tends to splinter when being sawed. Discard pieces that have knots or are cross-sectioned so that the larger flat surface is the rough end of the grain rather than having the grain running lengthwise. These scraps tend to split into pieces when being nailed.

Gluing wood scraps together introduces a child to the texture and weight of wood. The result can be painted with tempera thickened with glue or milk instead of water. Scraps of cloth, pieces of styrofoam, rickrack, buttons, pipe cleaners can all be glued to the painted wood sculpture if this pleases your child. Beauty is in the eye of the beholder!

Don't invest heavily in equipment until you're sure that your child enjoys woodworking and that you enjoy being around him to supervise. The most successful woodworking experiences for a child come from the examples of an adult working on projects of her own.

A workbench, which should be a little over half the height of the child, can be made from an old wooden kitchen table with the legs cut down, or from two small sawhorses with planks nailed across them. The top should overhang on each end by about three to four inches to accommodate a vise or C-clamp. The surface your child is working on will end up with scratches, nail holes, drops of dried glue and paint, so be sure you provide a place that can get dirty with your approval.

Nailing   The hammer should be held toward the end of the handle for the best force on the nail. A child should learn to measure the nail against what is being nailed to be sure that it's neither too long nor too short.

Sawing   A hacksaw is a good beginning sawing tool because the child can put his hand on the top of the saw to help him direct it. Let your child touch the blades so that he realizes how sharp they are. A tree stump provides a good place for sawing practice, but the sides of a corrugated box can also be used. If the wood to be sawed is too high, a poor sawing action results with the saw going crosswise instead of up and down. The wood should be well secured to the bench or other surface with two nails or by vise or C-clamp. Sawing should be done close to the vise to avoid excessive vibrations. You should make grooves for your child to practice sawing. Later you can demonstrate how to begin a groove for sawing. Teach your child that sawing should be slow and rhythmical using the entire blade of the saw. The action should be "push hard and pull easy."

Teach your child how to mark for sawing with a large pencil and ruler. Caution him to ease his sawing as he gets near the end so that the wood won't break off and splinter. If he seems to be having trouble, you can gently place your hands on top of his to demonstrate an action. Be sure the wood is well secured. Don't let him try to brace it with his knee, since this is dangerous.

Using a screwdriver A child needs help in imbedding the screw into wood. You can either let him drill holes for the screw, or use a nail to make the initial hole. You can also devise a board specifically for screwing practice with well-spaced holes. The best screwdriver for a young child has a fat handle and a stubby end. Screws should fit the screwdriver and have flat heads with well-defined grooves. A little soap rubbed on the screw will help it turn easier. A child soon learns the difference between the clockwise motion used to imbed the screw and the counter-clockwise motion to remove it.

Drilling The hand drill is the easiest drill to use since it operates like an eggbeater. Bits should be thick enough to withstand the child's pressure but not so thick that they don't bite into the wood quickly. Use a stump for practice or a piece of thick wood that's been nailed down so that it won't slip out from under the drill or turn with it. Once the wood is filled with holes, your child may enjoy threading yarn through it or gluing small sticks or dowels

into the holes. A rudimentary pegboard can be constructed this way, if you specify with a marker where the holes are to go. Insert golf tees in the holes for simple games or color patterns.

Tool storage A pegboard with the shapes of the tools outlined provides an excellent way to store tools. A toolbox can also be used, though the sharp saw buried in the box may present a hazard to small hands.

Besides a hammer, a saw, a screwdriver, and a hand drill, your young carpenter will use a tape measure, a small T-square, sandpaper mounted on a wood block with thumbtacks or staples, and a variety of nails and screws.

Some ideas for first projects: a boat to float in a wading pool or bathtub; a camera with a hole in the center for the lens and a nail head for a shutter; an airplane with a crosspiece for a wing; a nail board painted in advance and then dotted with nails (bright yarn or colored rubber bands can be wrapped around the nails). A simple birdfeeder can be made with railings to keep the seed from blowing away. Mount it on a post or a windowsill. Wheels for a car or truck can be made from orange juice can tops, spools with washers to keep them on the nail, sawed-off pieces from a broom handle, or pieces of wooden dowels that you can have your lumberyard cut for you, metal jar lids, Tinkertoy centers, reels from typewriter ribbons, several pieces of cardboard cut in circles and mounted together with glue.

Other odds and ends that present interesting construction possibilities are cheese boxes; cigar boxes; leather scraps; cloth pieces; dowels; scraps of fiberboard, Cellotex, and acoustical tile; pine moldings; rubber scraps; cork; floor tile; shavings from a cabinet shop; screw eyes and hooks; washers; drawer handles, hinges, and switchplates; nuts and bolts.

BLOCK-BUILDING

Block-building and young children seem to go together! There are many different kinds of blocks: hardwood unit blocks, hollow blocks, cardboard blocks, and small plastic blocks that fit on top of each other, such as Lego sets.

Unit blocks have been carefully measured to be mathematically proportionate to each other. A child can make structures very easily because two blocks can be interchanged with one block of a larger size, and so forth. Unit blocks can usually be purchased from school supply stores. They're expensive and quite heavy since they're made of hardwood.

Make your own unit blocks by cutting up boards of white pine. One 2-inch x 2-inch x 8-foot board and two 2-inch x 4-inch x 8-foot boards will make over seventy blocks, which is more than adequate for block play. Once you establish your unit, you can cut out double, triple, and half units. You can also make large and small triangles, pillars, and cubes. Sand the blocks until they're smooth and then rub them with mineral oil. If you decide to paint them, be sure that the paint you are using is nontoxic since kids will sometimes chew on them.

Blocks are best stored on a child's level and on open shelving. There should be a smooth, uncarpeted floor area for block play. The first few times your child begins to work with blocks, you should sit down and play with him. It's valuable to demonstrate some of the possibilities of blocks to a child to get him interested. Make a bridge or two together, or make-believe farm or port for boats. Don't try to force your ideas on your child, but don't be like a mother I know who invested in a big set of blocks and couldn't understand why her child never played with them. Once you've demonstrated the possibilities blocks hold, leave your child to his own structures.

Hollow blocks are large construction blocks also sold by school supply stores. They're heavy, somewhat like vegetable crates but with a variety of shapes. They can be used to make fortresses and playhouses, to construct highways and to support seesaws and balancing boards. Their size makes them difficult to store, but a basic set would be very useful if you've got a large playroom or an outdoor area where children could set up make-believe airplanes and other structures. Some sturdy wooden crates or homemade wooden boxes and a 4-foot board or two can be used in the same manner. Be sure they're splinter-free and able to support the weight of your child jumping on them. Round off the corners so no one is injured by taking a spill.

You can make your own construction blocks by cutting off the top of a cardboard milk carton and stuffing it with crumpled newspaper. Fit a second cut-off carton over the open end to complete the block and tape it together with masking tape. Cigar boxes make good blocks. Stuff them with crumpled newspaper and tape the tops down. Bricks can also be used outside. *No throwing!* And build only up to four or five stories.

Lego blocks are small colored plastic bricks made to fit snugly together. Some sets come with wheels, windows, and other props. Teachers swear by them because their young children love them so. Parents swear *at* them because they always step on them in the middle of the night. You'll have to decide if Legos are worth having to pick up and endlessly search for pieces. I hope you'll be luckier than Jennifer's dad, who dropped a whole box of Lego blocks in the street one night while trying to carry sleeping Jennifer up to her bed.

MUD

Glorius *mud!* Time to raise your mud consciousness. Mud is the most abundant, most intriguing, and most misunderstood learning substance there is.

Maybe it was our toilet training, but something has convinced us that playing in mud is naughty and *dirty*. Think again. Soil is the substance of the earth we live on. All of the plants that make the food we eat come from the soil. Soil is made from decomposed rocks, plants, and animal matter. If anything on earth is our friend, it's soil and the mud it makes.

Marcie and her friends have a mud pit that used to be a puddle but has become a pit thanks to some plastic spoons and a pail of water. It's not particularly beautiful to look at by middle-class lawn standards, but it's the neighborhood attraction. Liquidy mud makes a lake, partially dried mud can be molded and shaped into endless pretend cakes or buildings. Of course, the children get it on themselves and their clothes.

I never took dirt too seriously, figuring it was better for them to have a good time than to try to impress people with their pristine appearances. (You'd better check with neighborhood parents to be sure it's O.K. if their children return coated with mud.)

If it's summertime, why not let your kids strip down to underpants for mud play? You'll have less to clean up. A bucket of water or a hose, an extra water bucket, and an old towel make sense for cleaning up. You can buy heavy-duty plastic spoons for mud play, or a few inexpensive stainless-steel spoons. Jell-O molds, a muffin tin, an old pot with a handle, paper cups, and other containers add variety. Sticks of various sizes are useful, too, for birthday-cake candles and for drawing figures in the mud. Cut open some paper grocery bags or lay down a piece of newspaper and let the kids try a primitive kind of finger painting. You'll find your explorers exuberant and relaxed.

SAND

Sand is a versatile material that pours when it's dry and holds shapes when it's wet. Sand play has a very soothing quality. It's particularly relaxing for grownups if they're willing to take off their shoes and make frog holes like everybody else. Sand for children's play can be purchased presterilized in 60-pound bags from toy stores or from building supply companies and companies listed under "Sand and Gravel" in the Yellow Pages. Be liberal with sand, about 12 inches deep in a homemade sandbox, since it washes away in time.

Commercially manufactured sandboxes made from molded plastic can be bought in toy stores. Less expensive alternatives are simply to pile sand in the yard or to dig a pit with boards nailed together for the sides. Railroad ties also make good sides for a sandbox. Whatever container you use for sand, you need to be sure that it has adequate drainage so that the

Equipment for Sand Play

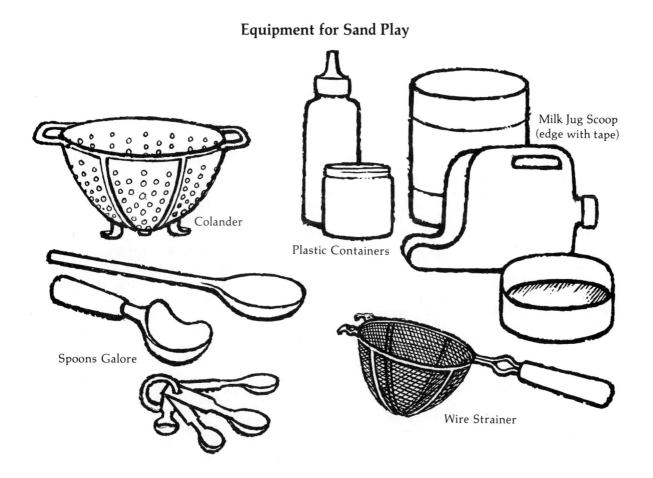

Colander

Plastic Containers

Milk Jug Scoop
(edge with tape)

Spoons Galore

Wire Strainer

sand can dry out after rain. Unmortared bricks or coarse gravel can be used for drainage.

A board across the center of the sandbox makes a good seat when the sand is wet. It can also serve as a table for unmolding cakes and sifting sand. A large concrete brick serves the same purpose. A shorter board that's not nailed down can be used by the children as a road for trucks during a sand loading job. Several large rocks will come in handy, too.

A chicken wire frame to fit over the sandbox when it's not in use will protect the box from being used as a dog and cat dumping station.

Whatever cover you have should allow sunshine and air, which act as natural purifiers, to reach the sand. Plan the placement of the box so that it will be in the shade during the hot part of the day, or children won't play in it during the summer. A canvas canopy mounted on a wooden frame with legs can provide shade when you don't have a convenient tree.

Some props for sand play are dump trucks (Tonka trucks withstand weather well); funnel; sifter; sieve; colander; scoop; shovel and pail; molds (either commercial sand molds, Jell-O molds, or containers made from the bottom of plastic gallon jugs); a large spoon; twigs or small wooden ice-cream sticks; a pail or watering can; dolls and toy animals made of wood, metal, or plastic.

WATER

Water is a most rebellious substance. If you turn your back on a pile of rocks, you can be pretty sure the rocks won't run off. In fact, rocks will sit dutifully in one place until the next geological age. Not so with water! Water will run downhill, flow over obstacles, flow under obstacles, push things out of its way, sink into the ground, or, as a last resort, it will simply evaporate. Water seems to have a headstrong mind of its own. No wonder kids enjoy it so much . . . To me, water is the most amazing stuff in the world. Try to see it and pretend it's something brand new — a new element brought back by astronauts from the moon, perhaps. You are a scientist, and you have to describe it for the first time to an eager world. Put your finger in it and describe how it feels to someone who has never felt water. Withdraw your finger and describe how the water closes up over the finger hole and instantly forms a placid surface. Pour it from one container to another and describe the sound it makes. Try to explain the riddle of how it can be both transparent and visible at the same time — how it distorts and reflects, yet how at the same time you can see through it. Watch it drip, spray, flow, turn silvery, cohere, adhere, freeze, boil and do a thousand amazing tricks. Spend ten minutes playing around with water, and you'll find it to be the most peculiar stuff imaginable. If you happen to be with a group of receptive kids, perhaps you can communicate what a wonderful substance water really is.*

Water has many properties for a child to discover: it pours, it's heavy, some things float in it, some things sink, some things dissolve, others don't. It can turn into steam or ice. Besides all of the scientific data a youngster can amass about this liquid, water is just plain fun for play.

A child's first and favorite water play place is the bathtub. It's a case of really getting into

* From *The Earth Manual* by Malcolm Margolin, Houghton Mifflin Co., 1975.

your work. Children can play in water until their fingers look like raisins — with different-sized plastic cups, sponges, corks alone or strung together in a floating armada, plastic tubing, a rubber shower hose. Remember how to fill a washcloth with air and hold the big bubble under water to squeeze the little bubbles out? Or the blast of bubbles you can make from a plastic pitcher held upside down and lowered to the bottom of the tub? How about the magic dry-hand trick, when you lower the pitcher upside down with your hand in it so the air keeps the water out? Try squashing a funnel into the water rim downward. *Voilá!* An instant fountain gushes out the other end. If these were labeled "learning experiences," they wouldn't be as much fun, yet they are teaching your child the properties of water and air.

Outdoors, you can provide your child with a wading pool for water play. Heat the water in it. Don't forget to empty the pool when you're through, particularly if there are any toddlers in the neighborhood.

A hose with an adjustable nozzle is particularly interesting to a child. He can learn to make a fine spray that doesn't go very far but makes a rainbow against the sun, and that a strong stream will travel across the yard. (He also learns that people don't like to be sprayed and that open windows are off limits, too.) A sprinkler seems very exciting to youngsters because of its unpredictability. Every sprinkling evokes new screams.

Quiet water play can take place in a washtub or baby bathtub. Here a child can float and sink objects. Plasticene clay is waterproof and can be used to make boats. Some good water play accessories are watering can; brushes (for painting walls or sidewalks); funnel; corks or Ping-Pong balls; plastic squeeze bottles; meat baster; clear plastic water pistol; small, clear plastic sandwich bag; plastic tubing; plastic containers of all sizes: measuring cups, bowls, detergent bottles with tops; clear squeeze bot-

Tools for Water Play

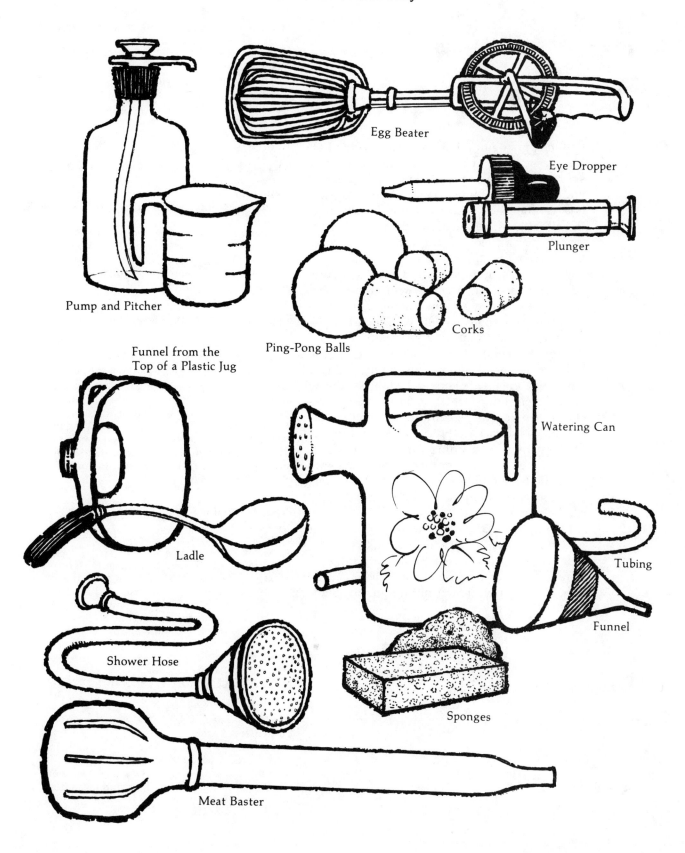

Pump and Pitcher

Egg Beater

Eye Dropper

Plunger

Ping-Pong Balls

Corks

Funnel from the Top of a Plastic Jug

Ladle

Watering Can

Tubing

Funnel

Shower Hose

Sponges

Meat Baster

tles and spray pump bottles. Boats (with a hole for passengers) can be constructed from sponges, scraps of sanded wood, flat detergent bottles, or from folded paper. A jet-propelled boat can be made from a paper milk carton cut in half with a small hole near the bottom of the rear. Inflate a balloon and put the end through the hole. Release the boat for departure.

Water and soap together add another dimension! A straw and a bowl with some warm soapy water make a giant billow of multicolored bubbles. You can make your own bubble-blowing liquid from baby shampoo or liquid detergents. Dilute them until you get good bubbles. For giant bubbles, use 1 cup of liquid detergent, ½ cup of water and 2 tablespoons of sugar or glycerine, which is available at drugstores. Mix together gently so you don't make too many surface bubbles. Make a bubble-blowing ring by bending thin wire into a 1-inch loop on one end, or by cutting a ring with a handle from the side of a gallon plastic milk jug. Use a pie pan for the liquid so that the ring can be immersed easily.

One caution: Don't buy or use bubble baths for your children. They are irritating to the genitals and can cause urinary tract infections. A pure soap, such as a castile shampoo, can be used once in a while but not frequently, since it dries the skin.

LITERATURE FOR ADULTS ON NATURAL PLAY MATERIALS

''Creating with Materials for Work and Play''
Association for Childhood Education International, 1834 Connecticut Avenue, N.W., Washington, DC 20009 ($2.00)
A collection of leaflets written for teachers of young children. Includes ideas for block play, ideas for using water and mud for play, art recipes, suggestions for working with wood, simple science equipment.

Recyclopedia: Games, Science Equipment, and Crafts from Materials
Robin Simons
Houghton Mifflin Co., Two Park Street, Boston, MA 02107 ($3.95)
A water clock, a water microscope, paper logs and newspaper dowels for construction, ideas for making wheels, axles, and car bodies from everyday materials, a water dam from a milk carton. Also includes ideas for simple games and art projects.

Soap Bubbles: And the Forces Which Mould Them
C.V. Boys
Dover Publications, Inc., 180 Varick Street, New York, NY 10014 ($2.00, paperback)
A reprint of a book based on the lectures of Sir Charles Vernon Boys, scientist, inventor, and professor. Sounds boring? It's not! This brilliant man carefully studied the nature of bubbles. Experiments abound throughout: blowing bubbles within bubbles, blowing bubbles on spirals of wire and triangular frames. Even the demonstration for making a bubble air balloon for launching a small handkerchief!

Paper Toy Making
Margaret W. Campbell
Dover Publications, Inc., 180 Varick Street, New York, NY 10014 ($1.50, paperback)
A reprint of a 1937 book that suggests eighty-two paper folding projects. Ten of the projects seem suitable for preschoolers with adult direction, including a paper boat. More complex projects are similar to origami and require the ability to match line CBA to line DVH while folding EFG to the same line.

MATERIALS FOR WORKING WITH WOOD

Carpenters' Apron
A child-sized apron for protecting clothing and for carrying tools. Made of sturdy white duck fabric with three large, 8-inch pockets. The seams are reinforced for durability. The apron measures 18 inches from bib to hem.

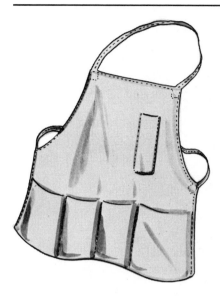

Novo Educational Toy and Equipment Corp., 11 Park Place, New York, NY 10007 ($2.25 + shipping. Minimum order accepted, $20.00)

Carry-All Tray
A plastic tray fitted with two compartmented drawers with four pockets each and two boxes with covers. Good for holding nails, screws, and odds and ends for the young carpenter. From the "Vital Years" catalog ($1.00).
Educational Teaching Aids (ETA), A Div. of A. Daigger & Co., 159 W. Kinzie Street, Chicago, IL 60610 ($7.95 + shipping and $2.50 handling charge)

Junior Hobby Bench
A sturdy workbench with a professional woodworking vise and a pegboard rack for storing tools. A handy ruler has been silk-screened on the front of the bench. The bench work area is 32½ x 16½ inches and the height is 27⅝ inches. A handy storage shelf is underneath.
Nasco, 901 Janesville Avenue, Fort Atkinson, WI 53538 ($16.35 + shipping, 24 lbs.)

Toy Patterns and Wooden Parts
Love-Built Toys and Crafts is a company specializing in toy patterns for making wooden trucks, airplanes, trains, doll cradles, and puzzles. The patterns are suitable for adults. For the young craftsman, the company carries a package of fifty wooden wheels, 1 inch in diameter, for $3.50. Other sizes are also available. The company also carries a good selection of crafts books on woodworking. Write for the brochure.
Love-Built Toys and Crafts, 418 Second Street / P.O. Box 769, Antioch, CA 94509

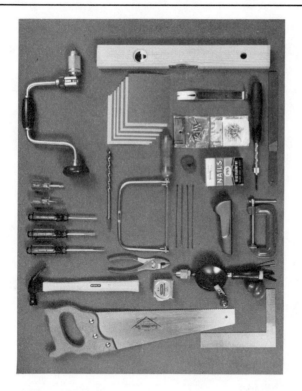

CONSTRUCTION SETS

Child-Sized Tools
Each tool has been scaled to the child's hand. All are real tools. Prices are approximate.
SY216 16" saw, $5.00
SY213 7 oz. claw hammer, $5.50
SY30064 4" screwdriver, $1.20
SY30063 3" screwdriver, $1.10
SY1721 3" Phillips screwdriver, $1.25
SY1253 10" brace, $14.50
SY12278 ½" bit, $4.00
SY61152 metric measuring tape, $3.50
SY1500 pliers, $3.30
SY104 coping saw, $3.00
SY107 four coping saw blades, $1.00
NB9077 sandpaper package, $1.00
SY68 square, $1.90
SY1220 hand drill with eight drills, $14.95
SY399 safety plane, $3.80
NB11 preschool nails, $1.70
NB37 wood screws—regular, $.75
NB2 wood screws—Phillips, $.85
SY156 3" C-clamp, $2.40
SY49 push drill, $5.60
Order from:
Lakeshore Curriculum Materials, 8888 Venice Boulevard, Los Angeles, CA 90034 (Add a 15% shipping and handling charge. CA residents add 6 or 6½% sales tax)

Take-Apart House
Children build this house with wooden tools and screws. When the house is assembled it serves as a shape sorter with holes in the roof and one side to accommodate five brightly colored blocks in a variety of shapes. From the "Vital Years" catalog ($1.00).
Educational Teaching Aids, A Div. of A. Daigger & Co., 159 W. Kinzie Street, Chicago, IL 60610 ($12.95 + shipping and a $2.50 handling charge)

Creative Wood Crafts Bag
A burlap sack filled with materials for creating with wood and glue. Included are: a bottle of glue, wood squares and shapes, small wooden sticks,

toothpicks, yarn marking pens, corks, buttons, sponges, plastic greenery for miniature landscapes and an idea-filled brochure for parents and children. Order from:
J. R. Holcomb Co., 3000 Quigley Road, Cleveland OH 44113 ($9.95 + $1.50 postage and handling)

Bolt-Tight
A real wrench and screwdriver secure nuts, bolts, and washers to predrilled hardwood blocks and wheels. Makes vehicles or other structures. Develops dexterity in the use of real tools and allows the child to build semipermanent structures. Manufactured by Creative Playthings. Order from: Drago School Equipment and Supply, P. O. Box 4868 Hialeah Lakes Station, Hialeah, FL 33014 ($7.95 + shipping and a $1.50 handling charge)

Blocks and Block Cart
These are natural, unvarnished maple unit blocks with all the edges rounded and the surfaces smoothed. The base unit is 1⅜ x 2¾ x 5½ inches. The block cart, made of solid maple with 2-inch heavy-duty casters, is a handy pickup or delivery cart for young builders, which children also love to ride in. Write for a free catalog.
Community Playthings, Rifton, NY 12471 (85 Blocks [F155], $49.50; Block Cart [A60], $32.50; Block Cart and Blocks together [70 lbs.], $79.50 + shipping)

Hollow Blocks
A set of hollow blocks that includes a mounted steering wheel for imaginary travel. Each block has rounded corners for safety. The blocks are constructed of furniture pine and are sealed inside and out with a thick coating of varnish. The large handle holes make it easy for children to move them. The set includes four 6-inch closed hollow blocks, two 12-inch open, two 12-inch closed, four 24-inch open, and one mounted steering wheel. (Closed boxes have wood on all sides. Open blocks have one open end.) Helen Brice Smith, the designer and manufacturer of these blocks, will be glad to answer questions about them or send a catalog.
Lyndon Craft Educational Equipment, P. O. Box 12, Rosemead, CA 91770 (Approx. $170.00 + shipping)

Animal Blocks

Made of Alaska yellow cedar, these cleverly
designed animals will stack on top of each other.
The blocks are finished with a nontoxic sealer to
preserve the wood and bring out its natural beauty.
The edges are rounded. Choose from: bear,
elephant, giraffe, goat, hippopotamus, horse, pig,
porcupine, rabbit, or rhinoceros. Measurements:
4¾ x 3⅛ x 1½ inches thick.
Fox Blox, 24401 Redwood Highway, Cloverdale, CA
95425 ($2.00 each + postage)

Solid Blocks

A set of fifty blocks made of Alaska yellow cedar in
a variety of sizes and shapes. There are no sharp
edges. The blocks, which have been finished in a
nontoxic sealer to preserve the wood's natural
beauty, come with a set of ten blocks with a groove
down the center for holding up the flat block pieces
like a fence.
Fox Blox, 24401 Redwood Highway, Cloverdale, CA
95425 ($10.00 + postage)

Dado Blocks

Dado blocks are made of grooved, flat plywood
pieces of wood that can be fitted together to
construct buildings, airplanes, and other creations.
A starter set consists of twelve pieces approximately
2½ x 2½ inches, four pieces 5½ x 2½ inches, four
pieces 8½ x 2½ inches, and four pieces 12 x 2½
inches. The twenty-four pieces fit neatly into a
corrugated box for storage. They're made of AA
grade ⅜-inch thick birch plywood, which has been
oil finished. Larger sets are available for schools.
Milo Products Corp. Grantham, PA 17027 (Starter
set, $24.00 + shipping)

Lego Set

This 233-piece set emphasizes building structures. It contains a wide variety of interlocking plastic pieces: platforms, movable shutters, doors, frames, roof bricks, and windows. A bright selection of colors is included. From the "Early Learning" catalog. Manufactured by: Lego Systems, Inc., 555 Taylor Road, Enfield, CT 06082 (Approximately $15.00)

Giant Blockbuster Set

A sturdy set of corrugated cardboard blocks can support up to 200 pounds. Recommended for indoor use. The blocks are packed flat for you to assemble. Each set includes twelve 12 x 6 x 4-inch blocks. These blocks are lightweight and easy for youngsters to carry. (Two sets are shown.) Lakeshore Curriculum Materials, 8888 Venice Boulevard, Los Angeles, CA 90034 ($14.95 + 15% shipping and handling charge. CA residents add 6 or 6½% sales tax)

Zig Zag

Zig Zag builds downward instead of upward! Children learn the importance of balancing. The eighty pieces are enough to build a mobile six-feet long. They are easily balanced, are lightweight, and can be suspended anywhere. From the "Vital Years" catalog ($1.00).
Educational Teaching Aids, A Div. of A. Daigger & Co., 159 W. Kinzie Street, Chicago, IL 60610 ($4.50 + $1.00 shipping and $2.50 handling charge)

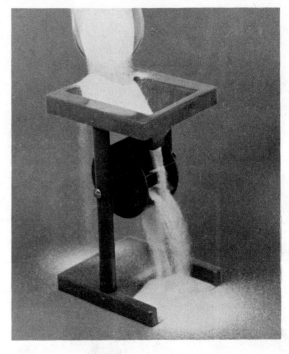

Timberloc Building Set

A children's building set with a difference — no
adult engineers are required for even the most
ambitious projects. Made of natural, unfinished
boards ¾ inch wide with slots for easy fit and
stability. The boards are from 6 to 42 inches long to
allow construction of complete kid-sized enclosures
including roofs. The set includes 160 pieces, all 3½
inches wide.
Lakeshore Curriculum Materials, 8888 Venice
Boulevard, Los Angeles, CA 90034 ($160.00 + 15%
shipping and handling. CA residents add 6 or 6½%
sales tax)

Sand and Water Wheel

The wheel goes round and round as the sand or
water filters through a funnel. Made of tough,
flexible plastic with the wheel securely attached.
Bright red with blue wheel. Height, 10½ inches.
Lakeshore Curriculum Materials, 8888 Venice
Boulevard, Los Angeles, CA 90034 (approximately
$7.50 + 15% shipping and handling charge. CA
residents add 6 or 6½% sales tax)

MATERIALS FOR SAND PLAY

Sand Sieve

A bright, indestructible sifter for the sandbox set
made of plastic with extra thick walls and a wide
brim for easy gripping. Measurements 1½ inches
deep, 10½ inches in diameter.
Lakeshore Curriculum Materials, 8888 Venice
Boulevard, Los Angeles, CA 90034 (approximately
$3.00 + 15% shipping and handling charge. CA
residents add 6 or 6½% sales tax)

WATER PLAY MATERIALS

Waterpump
A child can really learn the dynamics of hydraulics. The valve of this special pump is transparent so that your child can see the water rushing up and out of the spout as the handle is pumped. Made of red and yellow plastic, 12 inches high. From Childcraft's "Toys that Teach" catalog. Price subject to change. Childcraft Education Corp., 20 Kilmer Road, Edison, NJ 08817 ($4.95 + $1.95 shipping and handling)

WATER PLAY EQUIPMENT

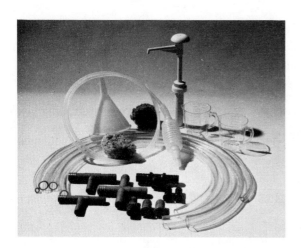

Water Play Kit
The Childcraft Water Play Kit dramatizes number and science concepts in water play with a pump, a siphon, a funnel, tubing, and connectors. Measuring pitchers and two sponges are also included. Children find endless ways to experience physical concepts, making water move by pressure, suction, and gravity. A teacher's guide is included.

From Childcraft's "Special Education Materials" catalog. Price subject to change. Childcraft Education Corp., 20 Kilmer Road, Edison, NJ 08817 ($17.95 + $2.70 shipping and handling)

Tweety Bird
A bubble bird that blows bubbles and tweets at the same time. Did you have one when you were a child? This bird is made of plastic. From the Childcraft "Toys that Teach" catalog. Price subject to change. Childcraft Education Corp., 20 Kilmer Road, Edison, NJ 08817 ($2.50 ea., 6 for $11.95 + $1.95 shipping and handling)

Note: Not all manufacturers and publishers will accept single orders for a product or book. Always write to them first, before sending money, to be sure that they will take your order. Make sure you've got the most recent price, including shipping and handling charges. If the company is in your state, then you may need to include state sales tax as well.

Music and Dance

13

ENJOYING MUSIC TOGETHER

If you love music, you'll communicate it to your child in many ways. Perhaps you hum while you work around the house or dance to the radio. No doubt you occasionally sit and enjoy music on a record player. If you're lucky, you play a musical instrument. I say lucky because this enables you to be a full participant in the world of music. Those of us who do not make music ourselves share only half of the musical experience, the listening.

What are some of the ways that parents can share music with young children? Sing if you can! I developed quite a repertoire of lullabies while rocking Marcie to sleep as a baby. I'd sing Christmas carols even in mid-July, love songs, pop tunes, whatever I could come up with. Now we make up songs together — mock operas about getting ready for bed. I hum, too, but not consciously. I was astounded to discover Marcie singing and humming in imitation of me. She could even carry a tune.

There's a whole heritage of songs suitable for adults and children to share. Most children's sections in public libraries include a shelf full of records as well as songbooks.

Singing while pushing your child on the swing is a good way to communicate the rhythm of music: "Swing high, swing low, this is the way that Sally goes. Down to the ground and up so high, like an airplane in the sky." Another is to tap two blocks together or to clap while you listen to music. Clap or use homemade drums or blocks to sound out rhythms without music and ask your child to move to the rhythm. Clap slowly, quickly, in syncopation. Play dancing school together with you as the teacher and your child the student. "And a one, two, three, one, two, three, one, two, three, hop!" The purpose of the game is for your child to try moving to the rhythm of your voice.

We've found our little portable record player to be the best toy investment we've made. Our friends Gary and Joyce revamped an old record player that a neighbor had discarded. By replacing a few tubes, they had a machine that was as good as new for their four-year-old. Children love the sense of mastery that operating the record player gives them. You need to take time to establish some basic rules. For example, it should not be plugged in or unplugged except by an adult. It won't take long for your child to master these basics if you're patient but firm from the beginning. Inexpensive children's, as well as adults', records can be found at yard and library sales.

• Clear away space in the living room or den and put a stirring march or orchestral music on your record player. Throw away your inhibitions and move to the music with your child. "Let's each do what the music tells us to do." Good movement records: "Carnival of the Animals," Saint-Saens; "The Peer Gynt Suite," Grieg; "Nutcracker Suite," Tchaikovsky. Scarves are fun to swish around while dancing.

• Buy a music box or harmonica that your child can carry around and play herself. A dime-store kazoo will inspire her to try blowing tunes.

• Make up a story while you listen to music together.

• Put a big piece of paper on the floor and draw with crayons, chalk, or marking pens as the music moves you while you listen.

• Sit very quietly outside and listen to the sounds of birds, the wind, or the city.

• Let your child feel her own and your vocal chords as you sing high and low notes.

• Find a piano that your child can use to try her hand at playing the notes. Let her look inside the piano. I've found that a very young child can learn simple piano pieces if you provide a way of distinguishing one key from another. Place a strip of cardboard coded with numbers, letters, or colors directly behind the keys. Make up sheet music of her favorite songs, using the code instead of music notations. It's important to provide a child with plenty of time just to experiment with sounds and the use of fingers, too.

• Attend parades and outdoor concerts whenever you can. It's the best way to experience music without being hassled by the squirmy, distractive nature of a young child. Children's concerts are great, too, because children are accepted as a lively, constantly moving and talking audience.

Musical Instruments for the Young Child
by Mack Perry

A baby, cooing in his crib, shakes a rattle and is filled with the wonder of its sound. The three-year old, sitting on the kitchen floor, beats a drum with happy enthusiasm and rhythmic patterns begin to emerge. A seven-year-old dances freely to music, expressing herself as she interprets it. So music happens in a child's life and progresses as the child matures.

The ages between three and eight are very significant growth years — the child goes from being self-centered into more cooperative efforts, from random to more precise behavior, from dependence to more independence. These years are significant, too, for developing basic musical understanding and for bringing a child's imagination, curiosity, and creative powers into full play.

As a parent, you can inspire a love for music in your child simply by constantly providing a musical environment for him. You will find that your child's curiosity will lead him naturally to the most accessible sound-making objects — two sticks to strike against each other, a tablespoon to strike against an old saucepan, a piece of scrap wood to clatter along a picket fence, a spoon to clang against the radiator. If you listen closely you'll recognize some of the same elements of music with which a composer works: high and low sounds, loud and soft, fast and slow, accenting one sound over another, syncopating rhythms and building sounds to a climax.

One way to help your young child to experience music is through listening to records and tapes. You should offer a variety of musical sounds, from the classics to simple pop songs composed and arranged just for children. Hap Palmer recordings are one of the many good sources for rhythmic bouncy tunes with simple directions for your child to follow.

Make music a family experience in which everyone participates. It may be fun to respond to music by clapping, tapping, moving, dancing or by playing simple rhythm, melody, or harmony instruments together.

It's valuable for a preschool child to have an opportunity to play an instrument requiring more skill than a rhythm instrument. If you have a piano, then you can encourage your child to press the keys or to press a group of keys with his open or closed hand. By pressing the lower keys with his hand, he can simulate the effects of a drum. You can guide his fingers to help him to pick out simple melodies or to establish pitch relationships. The left hand can be used for a gentle rhythmic drumming sound. It's a good time to teach respect for the instrument: being gentle while playing and learning the difference between discordant noise and a pleasing musical sound.

If you don't have a piano, a simple "xylo" for a young child to use will do. Look for one that is well-tuned and durably constructed. Another alternative is a set of resonator bells. Each note is an individual bar that can be held in one hand or placed on the table and struck with a mallet. In this way the entire family can participate in making melodic music by striking the bar when his or her note occurs in a song. Specific chords can be produced by combining three or more resonator bells and striking these bars with one or two mallets simultaneously or with multiple-headed mallets. The "xylo" can be used to play the melody of "Farmer in the Dell" and "Frère Jacques" or other simple tunes, using the resonator bars to harmonize with a single chord.

Another good instrument for a young child is the Chromoharp, Autoharp or Cytha Harp. These are zither-shaped string instruments that produce chords automatically when a child presses a button or bar and strums across the strings. The sound of a harp, banjo, guitar, or harpsichord can be simulated depending on the playing technique.

A seven- or eight-year-old will enjoy playing a simple wind instrument such as a song flute or a woodwind soprano recorder. Quality plastic recorders can be purchased for about three dollars.

This is a good age to listen to music for the purpose of recognizing the sounds of specific instruments and for recognizing pictures of musical instruments. A child at this age shouldn't be expected to tell one stringed instrument from another, for example, but he or she can differentiate the sounds of instruments from different families, such as a violin from a flute or a trumpet. Examining actual instruments can be an exciting part of the experience.

If possible, try to enroll your child in a group or class situation centered around musical creativity and development. Go to concerts together in order to hear others perform, and discuss what you have both listened to. Visiting a museum that has musical instruments of the past can be an interesting experience.

Ideally, as many instruments as possible should be made available to young children. You can introduce an instrument whenever you feel that it will enlarge your child's musical interests. If your child is given rich, varied, exploratory experience, he or she will learn to love music and to grow musically. He or she will also be in the position to make an intelligent selection of an instrument to pursue with great intensity and detail later on. You may find that your child will want to change from one instrument to another.

Pablo Casals was introduced to the piano and played it for several years as a young child. He did not like the instrument. Then he tried the violin for several more years. He didn't like that either. But from the moment he held a cello between his legs when he was about the age of twelve or thirteen, he knew that he had found *his* instrument! The rest is musical history.

As your child matures musically, he or she will learn to apply music's basic elements — melody, rhythm, timbre, harmony, and form. He or she will be able to read music and listen to it with purpose and discrimination. He or she will also be able to improvise melodies, rhythmic accompaniments, and harmonizations. He or she will be able to understand the relationship between music and other areas of human endeavor.

MATERIALS FOR TEACHING MUSIC TO YOUNG CHILDREN

Each instrument listed below is available by mail from the World of Peripole, Browns Mills, NJ 08015. Write for the free catalog of rhythm instruments, Autoharps, xylophones, recorders, and other instruments, records, and music publications for parents and teachers of young children.

Wide-Spaced Bells (P4082)
($4.50)
A well-designed one-octave diatonic "xylo" with widely spaced bars and large numbers that enable a young child to play songs before she can read music.

Songs I Can Play (PP9397)
($1.50)
A child's book of songs to play on the numbered "xylo." There are thirty-three songs in all in this gaily illustrated stand-up book with spiral binding. The large half-inch numbers match the numbers on the wide-spaced bells.

Colors and Chords for the Autoharp (PP9012)
Ludwig and Ludwig ($3.50)
By using a color code, a conventional twelve-bar Autoharp can be converted into a three-bar, "primary chord" Autoharp enabling very young children to play simple tunes. Includes a collection of songs with coordinated colored dot markings. Also describes styles of accompaniment and tells how to tune an Autoharp.

Let's Sing and Play Book (PP9073)
Peg Hoenack ($1.75)
A music book for use with recorders and small wind instruments. The unique spacing of letter notes enables young children to play sooner than they would by other methods. A stand-up book with sixty-seven songs to sing and play.

Mack Perry, M.S., is the founder and director, along with his wife, Sylvia, of the World of Peripole, Inc. He has taught in the New York City schools and at Brooklyn College. He conducts workshops for music teachers of young children all over the United States. Parts of the foregoing article were reproduced from the Peripole catalog with permission.

RHYTHM INSTRUMENTS TO MAKE

The music from a primitive instrument is no substitute for that from a real instrument, a piano, or a good collection of resonator bells, but such an instrument is fun and can help teach a child about the basic nature of music-making. Here are directions for making a number of simple instruments:

Shakers and Rattles The container: a Band-Aid box, a kitchen salt shaker, two cans taped together, a box with the lid taped down, a dried gourd. The rattles: pebbles, seeds, acorns, screws. Two stainless steel spoons suspended together by the handles with a ribbon.

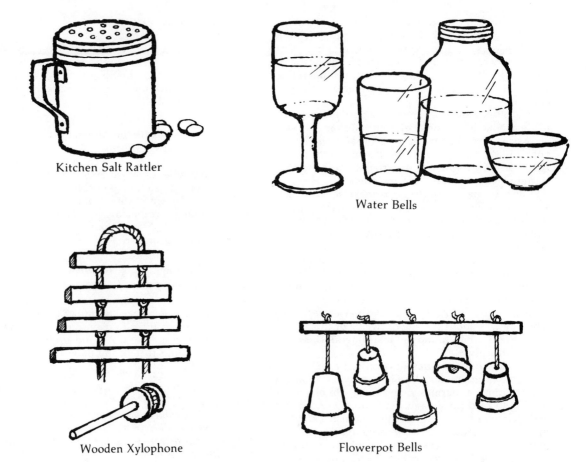

Kitchen Salt Rattler

Water Bells

Wooden Xylophone

Flowerpot Bells

Xylophone Cut a 1 x 2-inch board of redwood or pine into strips, each one one-quarter inch longer than the one before it. Nine inches is a good beginning size. Arrange the bars on the top of an open shoebox or on two fat pieces of yarn, two strips of felt, or two strips of foam rubber. Strike with an unsharpened pencil. Metal strips or electrical conduit tubing can also be used to make a "xylo."

Bells Drinking glasses filled with varying amounts of water and struck with a spoon. Wineglasses in different sizes braced upside-down by attaching dowels on both sides of the stems with string and resting the dowels on the back of dining room chairs. Different-sized clay flowerpots suspended upside-down by tying a knot around a stick and lacing the string up through the hole in the bottom of the pot. Knot the strings on a dowel or broomstick resting against two chair backs (see illustration). Spoons hung by string from a coat hanger. Venetian blind slats cut in different sizes and suspended. Other materials for suspending: pieces of electrical conduit tubing, colored glass, wooden dowels, pieces of bamboo, nails of many sizes, strips of dried potter's clay, clay in different lengths with holes at the top for

Ankle or Wrist Bells Sewn on Elastic

Bleach Bottle Banjo

Kalimba (finger piano) A ruler held on the side of a table with one hand and hit with the other. Try extending different lengths. Tongue depressors sandwiched between two blocks held together by C-clamps. Let each depressor stick out more than the one beside it.

Rhythm sticks Two dowels of different lengths and thicknesses held one in each hand and struck together. Wooden spoons struck together.

Coffee Can Drum   Spoon Castinets

suspending them. Jingle bells sewn on elastic for wearing on the ankles or wrist. Jingle bells fastened to a stick by string.

Harp Nylon fishline strung between nails or screw eyes on a board. Make each string longer than the one before. Rubber bands of different thicknesses wrapped around a shoe box or cigar box. Strips of rubber-band rubber stretched across a Y shaped branch of wood (a large slingshot frame) and tied to screw eyes so they can be tuned and tightened.

Guitar or banjo A 2½-foot flat stick threaded through flaps cut one inch from the bottom of a gallon milk jug or an empty bleach bottle (see illustration). String the guitar with fishline from one end of the stick to the other over the bottom of the jug. Use screw eyes so the string can be tuned. Use a chip of wood or a fold of cardboard to hold the strings away from the jug for better vibrations.

Drums The base can be a coffee can with both ends removed. Use well-washed inner tube rubber to cover the top and bottom. Cut the rubber 2 inches wider than the can and punch holes around the rubber about 1 inch from the side. Lace the circles onto the can zigzag fashion. Other simple drums: a trash can or stainless steel bowls turned over. A circular wooden cheese box or a wooden, metal, or ceramic bowl with damp chamois cloth (it will tighten when it dries) stretched over and tied around the rim. Strike your drum with your hands or an unsharpened pencil with a large wooden bead glued on, or a slender dowel with a tightly stuffed piece of cloth wrapped on with string.

Pie Pan Tambourine

Bathtub Tuba

Tambourine Aluminum pie plates laced together bottom out with jingle bells inside and laced on the sides. An embroidery hoop stretched with damp chamois cloth. Tie jingle bells onto the sides.

Air music A shower hose played like a tuba. A paper straw cut with a protruding "V" at one end. Blow gently into the point until you get a sound. Fold a piece of waxed paper over a comb and say "toot" into it for a homemade kazoo. Make a balloon whistle by blowing it up and pulling the rubber tightly on both sides of the neck. Blow over the rim of a Coke bottle or gallon jug while shaping your mouth as though you were going to say "two." Once you figure out how to make the sound, vary the amount of water for a change in tone.

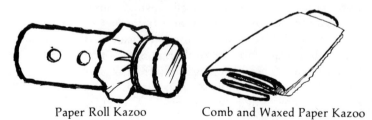

Paper Roll Kazoo

Comb and Waxed Paper Kazoo

RECORDS AND TAPES FOR YOUNG CHILDREN

The Children's Book and Music Center is an excellent mail-order source for records and tapes for young children. They issue annually a 180 page catalog, listing hundreds of records and books for children and parents as well as offering a good collection of rhythm instruments. I have asked Miriam Sherman, the manager, to select the "cream of the crop" — the sixteen best records she carries that are suitable for three- to eight-year-olds. These superb records are not just for passive listening, they encourage a response from the child. They stimulate creative activity, singing, movement, and thought. The prices on the records and cassettes will probably change, so write for the most recent catalog before ordering: Children's Book and Music Center, 5373 W. Pico Boulevard, Los Angeles, CA 90019.

"American Folk Songs for Children"
Pete Seeger
Pete sings "This Old Man," "Jim Along Josie," "All Around the Kitchen," "Clap Your Hands," "Train Is A-coming," "Frog Went A-courting," etc. One of the greatest of children's records!
($7.98 record, $7.95 cassette)

"We All Live Together," Vol. 1
Youngheart Music Group
Original and traditional songs with the rhythm and sound of today's contemporary music. Songs for rhythm and movement activity, sing-along, call-and-response and resting music. A thirty-two-page guide with the sheet music is included. Includes "ABC Rock," "Little Sir Echo," "Friendship March," and "Wiggle and Wobble."
($9.95 for record & book)

"Won't You Be My Friend?"
Marcia Berman and Patty Zeitlin
Songs for emotional and social awareness. The concepts of growing, self-confidence, and reassurance about not being alone in feelings of anger and fear. "What Makes Me Happy," "I'm Afraid," "Angry Song," "Won't You Be My Friend," and other songs in folk, rock, pop, country, and calypso styles. Booklet included.
($7.95 record)

"Everybody Cries Sometimes"
Marcia Berman and Patty Zeitlin
Songs of self-appreciation, about feelings (fear, loneliness, anger), songs about cooperation. A variety of styles — ragtime, gospel, blues, country. "Scarey Things," "I Like Myself," "Don't You Push

Me Down," "One Little Bird," "Beautiful Arms," and others. Sung with a children's chorus. Booklet included.
($7.95 record, $7.95 cassette)

"Getting to Know Myself"
Hap Palmer
An introduction to body awareness, body identification, movements, moods, and feelings. "Sammy," "Turn Around," "The Circle," "It's O.K.," and others.
($7.95 record, $7.95 tape)

"Movin' "
Hap Palmer
Music from symphony to rock, classical to pop. Original contemporary music to encourage young children to respond, move, and dance. A variety of moods and tempos, all fully orchestrated. "Funky Penguin," "Midnight Moon," "Gentle Sea," "Chickens in the Barn," and others. Instrumental.
($7.95 record, $7.95 cassette)

"You'll Sing a Song, and I'll Sing a Song"
Ella Jenkins
Ella leads the Urban Gateways Children's Chorus in fifteen finger-snapping, thigh-slapping songs and rhythm exercises. Encourages active participation. Songs from many cultures include "Shabot Shalom," "Cadima," "This Train," "Dulce, Dulce," "Mary Mack," and others.
($7.98 record, $7.95 cassette)

"Peter and the Wolf"
Prokofiev's symphonic music story for children. Tells how Peter with the help of a bird lassoed a fierce wolf in the forest.
($7.98 record)

"Tubby the Tuba"
Danny Kaye
Tubby, the generous tuba, finds a new tune that he shares with the other instruments. Narrated and sung by Danny Kaye.
($6.98 record)

"Hurray for Captain Jane"
Liberated Stories for Children
The story from the book by the same title. (The book is reviewed on p. 19.)
($7.98 record, $7.98 cassette)

"Free to Be You and Me"
Marlo Thomas and Friends
Dick Cavett, Diana Ross, Mel Brooks, Harry Belafonte, and others sing about children being themselves. "Free to Be You and Me," "Parents Are People," "It's All Right to Cry," and others. Stories are also narrated: "William's Doll," "Sisters and Brothers," "Glad to Have a Friend Like You."
($7.98 record)

"It's a Children's World"
Beautifully narrated stories from around the world. "The Boy Who Drew Cats" (Japanese), "The Bees" (Spanish), "The Raccoon" (Native American), "Little Red Riding Hood" (original version from France).
($6.98 record)

"Rhythms of Childhood"
Ella Jenkins
Songs and chants specially chosen for their rhythmic appeal. African chants, rhythms of nature, dance rhythms. Includes traditional songs, "Red River Valley," "Michael, Row Your Boat Ashore," and original pieces. Guitar, drum, banjo, and harmonica accompaniment.
($7.98 record, $7.95 cassette)

"Birds, Beasts, Bugs and Bigger Fishes"
Pete Seeger
This animal song collection by Pete includes an irresistible performance of "The Foolish Frog" complete with funny sounds to imitate. Also, "The Fox" and "Old Paint."
($7.98 record)

"It's a Happy Feeling and Other Activity Songs for Kids"
Ruth and David White
A bright new record about basic concepts. Catchy words, new music, and sound for teaching basic skills in self-concepts, spatial relations, classification, and music.
($7.98 record)

"Whoever Shall Have Peanuts"
Sam Hinton
A folksinger and folklorist who infuses traditional songs with a delightful contemporary spirit. "The Frog Song," "Barnyard Song," "All Hid?," "Ground Hog," "Green Grass Growing All Around," and, of course, "Whoever Shall Have Some Peanuts." Booklet included.
($6.98 record)

BOOKS FOR ADULTS

Two unique books deserve special mention.

Music for Fun, Music for Learning
Lois Birkenshaw
Holt, Rinehart and Winston of Canada, Ltd., 55 Horner Avenue, Toronto, ONT M8Z 4X6 Canada
($7.30)
An excellent collection of movement activities, ideas for basic rhythms and games, songs for children to sing, ways of teaching simple music skills to young children. The bibliography lists records and songs as well as books and includes a section on materials for handicapped children.

Creative Music in the Home
Satis N. Coleman
John Day and Company, (published in 1928, now out of print)
Numerous stories, historical notes on the origins of instruments, simple tunes that can be played with homemade instruments. Instructions for constructing pipes, marimbas, cigar box instruments, drums, and many other instruments. A superb old book, introducing children to music. Try getting it from a university through inter-library loan, using your own local library to request it.

MUSIC MAKERS FOR CHILDREN

Dancing Doll
An old American favorite, now made of solid black walnut by a master craftsperson. Dancing doll is a lot of fun with fast music; helps to teach rhythm. Complete with doll, stick, paddle, and instructions. Hammatt and Sons, 1441 N. Red Gum, Bldg. E, Anaheim, CA 92806 ($14.75 + shipping. Don't send money, they'll bill you.)

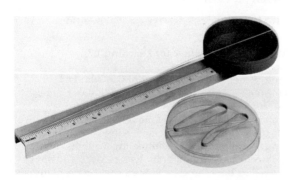

One-Stringed Instrument
A "Science in a Shoebox" kit. Your child assembles this elementary one-stringed "instrument." The basic instrument is simply a plastic bar. To experiment with sounding boards, a number of different "boxes" are provided and others are suggested. For strings, various rubber bands are used. With these rubber bands the dramatic effects of length, thickness, and tightness are discovered. Eduquip-McAllister Corp., 1085 Commonwealth Avenue, Brighton, MA 02215 ($2.95 + 20% postage and handling)

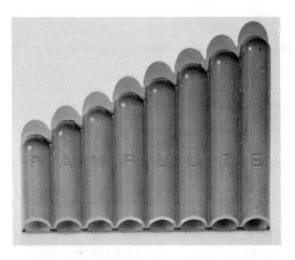

Calliope
A full-scale flute with calliope sound. Made of plastic. (Remember the sweet wax kind we used to chew at Halloween?) From the Childcraft "Toys that Teach" catalog. Prices subject to change. Childcraft Education Corp., 20 Kilmer Road, Edison, NJ 08817 ($1.00 ea.; 6 for $5.25 + $1.95 shipping and handling)

"Tiny Tympani"
A perfect drum for a preschooler! The single-bonded Lexan head measures 14 x 9 inches. With soft, bright, tympanilike tones the "Tiny Tympani"

never changes pitch. It's insensitive to temperature and climate changes. Weighs approximately 2 pounds. Strap is included.
Northern Supply Company, P.O. Box 920, Bangor, ME 04401 ($23.50 + 15% shipping and handling)

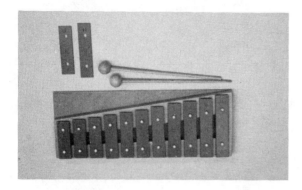

Glockenspiel, Jr.

A child-sized "xylo" mounted on a wooden base. Two wooden mallets are included. This model features C–F single row diatonic with an extra F sharp and B flat tone bar. Manufactured by M. Hohner.
Kaplan School Supply Corp., 600 Jonestown Road, Winston-Salem, NC 27103 ($10.95 + $2.75 shipping and handling charges)

Fife and Drum

A musical toy fife and a soft sounding drum for parading in our early traditions. The drum has two rubber thumpers. Drum heads and fife are made of plastic. Recommended for ages three through eight.
abc School Supply, Inc., P.O. Box 13086, Atlanta, GA 30324 ($9.50 per set + a $2.00 service charge for orders under $15.00)

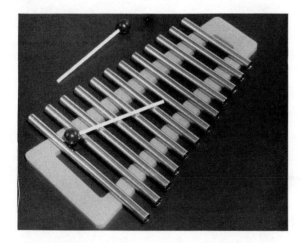

Zither

Constructed of metal, this zither includes a tuner, pick, extra strings, and ten music sheets containing twenty different songs. Overall size is 14 x 8 inches.
Kaplan School Supply Corp., 600 Jonestown Road, Winston-Salem, NC 27103 ($18.00 + $2.75 shipping and handling)

Xylopipes

Twelve graduated pipes with a 1½-octave range. These pipes have a beautiful bell-like quality. They nest on a foam base and can be rearranged at will and collected together for storage. Comes with two wooden mallets and instructions.
Lakeshore Curriculum Materials, 8888 Venice Boulevard, Los Angeles, CA 90034 ($16.95 + 15% shipping and handling charges. CA residents add 6 or 6½% sales tax)

Note: Not all manufacturers and publishers will accept single orders for a product or book. Always write to them first, before sending money, to be sure that they will take your order. Make sure you've got the most recent price, including shipping and handling charges. If the company is in your state, then you may need to include state sales tax as well.

Fantasy and Outdoor Play

14

FANTASY

To the super realistic adult a preschooler's flight into fantasy may be a bit unnerving. At one moment he is a ferocious tiger, at the next a doctor giving a baby a shot. I don't think any researcher has yet formulated a good explanation for a young child's love of fantasy. Some say that it is related to a child's frustrated longing to have power, others point to the way in which young animals are continually playing and assert that much of children's play has its origin in instinct.

There does seem to be a relationship between a child's play and the roles of the adults around him. Frequently, young children mimic the mothering and fathering roles, or the roles of doctors and other adults in their lives.

Brian and Shirley Sutton Smith in *How to Play with Your Children (And When Not To),* tell about the play of the children of Australian aborigines, who have been called a very "primitive" people. Instead of the housekeeping, fireman, and Batman roles that we see young children playing in our neighborhoods, the aborigine children play imaginative games relating to tracking, tree climbing, canoeing, spearing, and animal identification. So children's imaginative play seems to have a relationship to the future roles that they will be playing as adults.

Play sometimes seems to be a valve for letting off steam — expressing angers and fears in a way that they can be put into a safe context. After an unhappy experience with a doctor, Marcie spent a great deal of time playing doctor herself, doing operations and giving shots to a doll. A parent who senses a child's fears through imaginative play can help a child work through those fears by providing materials such as books, props, and stories. Discussions help, too. "You're really scared of doctors, aren't you?" Perhaps you can take the part of

the doll who is very afraid and who cries so that your child can be the comforter.

Children's angers are expressed through violent images, monsters, witches, tigers, and other fearsome creatures who seem to be waiting for them in the night when the lights are turned off. If you look back over the day preceding a child's nightmares and sleeping fears, you'll sometimes see your own anger toward the child, or your anxiety over some situation in your life reflected in your child's uneasiness. Punishing doesn't make the fears go away, but nurturing and close physical contact with a parent helps a great deal.

Young children seem to be in a peculiar state of animism in which simple changes can cause nonliving things to appear to have a life of their own. Marcie and I were in the bathtub together. I nonchalantly put the damp washcloth over my face and growled a deep growl. Marcie screeched, "STOP, Mommie, I don't *like* that!" It was her mother under the washcloth, but for one instant I was transformed into an unfamiliar and fearful monster. Washcloth off my face, everything was fine again. Halloween masks have the same effect, as do sheets and blankets. Anything that obscures the face has the potential for frightening a child.

Children also participate in positive imaginings. They play at caring for a baby, getting married to one another, rescuing the weak, being strong and brave. As long as group play doesn't get too destructive or clannish, so that one child is singled out and ridiculed or hurt, imaginative play seems to have a very positive effect on the outlook of the children. Side products of vigorous play of this sort are a sense of belonging to a group, an increased vocabulary, better communication, and a radiant sense of fulfillment and independence.

Dolls for play are as old as the human race. It's unfortunate that they've been labeled in our society as acceptable for girls and wrong for

Easy-to-Make Dolls

Yarn Doll

Doll from
a Stuffed Sock

Felt Gingerbread Boy

Doll from a
Rolled and Folded
Washcloth

Pipe Cleaner Doll

Beanbag Baby

boys. Dolls often come to represent the child himself in imaginary play, and can be a valuable stimulant for imagining person-to-person interaction. They also can provide a means for a child to practice nurturance.

I find the usual commercial dolls to be quite unappealing. Their bodies are hard and unyielding. Their hair soon turns to a texture like matted Brillo pads. Everything about them is quite removed from the feel of humans. They are also sexless, which must seem rather strange to a young child who has proudly established a sexual identity from the look of his or her own body. The super virile men and sexpot women dolls also are very remote from the real world of human beings and, if anything, seem grotesquely exaggerated rather than being truly attractive playthings.

Dolls should be soft, pliable, and pleasing to the touch. They should resemble real babies and people instead of Madison Avenue concoctions. They should be dressable and undressable, with the proper anatomical features. They should come in the colors and features of the races and in gray-headed versions, too.

Props for doll play are nice: a bed, or crib, a stroller, a bottle and other eating equipment, a dollhouse. But none of these things are vital. You can easily make a dollhouse from corrugated cardboard boxes, or shoe boxes stacked together. Use contact paper for the walls, spools and little jewelry boxes for making beds and tables. The furnishings needn't be letter perfect since they are only the backdrop for pretend play.

Puppets are an instant success with a young child. Most children will immediately begin to converse with a puppet the moment it's on someone's hand. Hand puppets come in a variety of styles and sizes. The most successful are those that are small enough for a preschooler's hand to operate them. Crocheted puppets are ideal because they are so flexible.

Puppets are simple to make, too. (See the illustrations on p. 196.) You can fashion the head from a variety of materials: two paper plates stapled together with a tongue depressor stick for a neck, a rubber ball with a hole cut out, crumpled newspapers tied in the toe of an old stocking, a sandwich bag stuffed with paper or cotton.

The body for your child's puppet should be made-to-measure for your child's hand so that his thumb and little finger can be the puppet's arms while the index finger serves as the neck.

Hand-puppet stages can be made from two café curtains mounted in a doorway or suspended from the ceiling by strings. A simple stage can also be made from three sides of a large carton, with a rectangle cut out of the upper half of the middle piece for the stage.

Children enjoy acting out the roles of familiar adults. It helps them, too, to become familiar with the concept of future occupations. Boys and girls ought to have equal chances to play both nurturing and professional roles, since more and more adult family members are doing both.

One way to provide props for imaginative play is through costume boxes. One mother I know has a large wicker basket just for that purpose. Inside are old shirts, crinolines, hats, scarves, big beads, ties, and other bits and pieces for putting together a "look." The box has served four children well through the dress-up preschool years and into the school play costumes.

If you have more than one child, many neighborhood children playing at your house, or you're teaching young children, you might want to make up a prop box for specific occupations.

Postal Service Worker
Pretend mailbox made from a cardboard carton
Letters and junk mail

Simple Puppets

Thumbelina

Winnie-the-Wrist

Paper Bag Puppet

Paper Plate Puppet
with a
Tongue Depressor Neck

Wooden Spoon
Puppet

Stuffed Sock
Puppet

Vegetable
Puppets with
Finger Holes

Stuffed Sandwich Bag
Puppet with Curly Paper Hair

A Styrofoam or Rubber
Ball Puppet and a Costume

Stamps (Easter Seals are good)
Envelopes
String
Boxes
Brown wrapping paper
Tape
A date stamp with an ink pad

Doctor
Tongs (in the kitchen supplies at the grocery store)
Meat basters
Rubber gloves
Small pan
Surgical mask (from drugstore)
Cotton balls
Plastic squeeze bottle with water in it
Stethoscope
Eyedropper
White shirt to wear backward for a smock
Small pad of paper for writing prescriptions
Medicine bottle with make-believe pills (raisins would be good)
Band-Aids
Doll for a patient
Tongue depressors

Nursery Worker
Wide-rimmed hat
Small plastic pots
Vermiculite
Trowel
Garden gloves
Apron
Watering can
Bag of pebbles
Seeds: watermelon, sunflower, or other large sizes
Plastic tablecloth for covering the floor
Plastic flowers and plants
(Real plants and potting soils)

T.V. Reporter
Microphone made from a paper towel tube with a foam ball on the end and a string cord

Camera made from a box with a paper towel roll for a lens
Detergent box for commercials
Tie or scarf
Mirror
(A real cassette tape recorder and mike)
A T.V. set made from an appliance box with a hole for a screen and spools for knobs

Barber/Beautician
Curlers
Brush
Comb
Shaving cream
Shaving brush
Plastic cape
Uniform made from an old shirt
An old wig or two on styrofoam stands (can be steadied with plasticene clay so they'll stand upright)
Round-tipped scissors (if you dare!)

Circus Performer
Tube of zinc oxide
Old lipstick
Jar of cold cream
Clown collar made from pleating cloth sewn onto elastic
Leotard
Tights
Ping-Pong ball with a hole cut in it, colored red with a magic marker, elastic tied on either side for a clown nose
Small rubber ball for juggling
Hoop
Rope
Wig from a yarn floor duster refill
A cardboard mustache

Plumber
Pipes and joints
Picture cards of toilets, sinks, tubs from catalogs and magazines
Faucet
Rubber boots

Monkey wrench, pliers
Plunger
Empty can of cleansing powder
Washers
Flashlight
Tool box
Hand shower and other hoses
Flotation ball and other parts of the inner
workings of a toilet

Auto Mechanic
Old license plates
Fan belt
Receipt book
Spark plugs and wires
Oil can
Flashlight
Tail light cover
Keys on a key ring
Tools
Chains
Tire pump
Windshield wiper
Old motor parts from a car repair shop
Steering wheel
Car made from cardboard cartons with pie
pans for headlights

Young children are unable to concentrate and follow the rules of most board games. They get frustrated and the other players do, too. A board game for a young child should be simple, requiring just a little counting and not reading. (From the parent's point of view, it shouldn't have a thousand tiny parts that get stepped on and lost.) Board games are valuable for young children because they help teach the all-important "wait your turn" rule. A good introduction to game playing is to invent your own board games with your child. Let him make up the rules. Use real cards, if you want, or the boards and spinners of regular games, but don't expect your child to be orderly and to follow directions: that doesn't come until school age.

A NOTE ABOUT TELEVISION

It's time that we parents stopped taking television lightly. In case you haven't given children's programming a good look lately, you'll find subtle changes in it over the past few years. Television programs that once brought beauty and fantasy to children have been overtaken by those focusing on violence, ghouls, and monsters.

Advertisers, who once aimed commercials solely at adults, now ply their trade to three- and four-year-olds. If you don't believe that commercials are successfully exploiting your young child, try passing the cereal section of the grocery store with him. We as parents are forced to tell our children that they can't watch television, or we are forced to sit and watch with them in order to attempt counteracting the commercials, or we can refuse to let our children have the objects and junk foods that they have been conned into demanding from us.

Many parents are becoming angry about the disruption that poor programming and commercials have had on their relationship with their young children. Parents have been forced into the role of no-sayers. "No, you can't watch that program." "No, you can't have Sugar Baby cereal." "No, I won't buy you a Merkin the plastic monster."

Beyond the manipulation of the minds of our children, who can only be consumers through their parents, and the stress this brings on the entire family, there is the deeper issue of our children being trained as crass materialists who believe soundly that objects are the true source of happiness and pleasure. Children are shown in a state of total joy because their parents prepare sugared drinks for them, buy them french fries, or serve them imitation foods. Toys are

treat TV with T.L.C.

T ALK ABOUT TV WITH YOUR CHILD!

TALK ABOUT PROGRAMS THAT
DELIGHT YOUR CHILD

TALK ABOUT PROGRAMS THAT
UPSET YOUR CHILD

TALK ABOUT THE DIFFERENCES
BETWEEN MAKE-BELIEVE & REAL LIFE

TALK ABOUT WAYS TV CHARACTERS
COULD SOLVE PROBLEMS WITHOUT VIOLENCE

TALK ABOUT VIOLENCE & HOW IT HURTS

TALK ABOUT TV FOODS THAT
CAN CAUSE CAVITIES

TALK ABOUT TV TOYS THAT
MAY BREAK TOO SOON

L OOK AT TV WITH YOUR CHILD!

LOOK OUT FOR TV BEHAVIOR YOUR
CHILD MIGHT IMITATE

LOOK FOR TV CHARACTERS WHO
CARE ABOUT OTHERS

LOOK FOR WOMEN WHO ARE COMPETENT
IN A VARIETY OF JOBS

LOOK FOR PEOPLE FROM A VARIETY
OF CULTURAL & ETHNIC GROUPS

LOOK FOR HEALTHY SNACKS IN THE
KITCHEN INSTEAD OF ON TV

LOOK FOR IDEAS FOR WHAT TO DO
WHEN YOU SWITCH OFF THE SET...

READ A BOOK. . DRAW A PICTURE
...PLAY A GAME

C HOOSE TV PROGRAMS WITH YOUR CHILD!

CHOOSE THE NUMBER OF PROGRAMS
YOUR CHILD CAN WATCH

CHOOSE TO TURN THE SET OFF WHEN THE
PROGRAM IS OVER

CHOOSE TO TURN ON PUBLIC TELEVISION

CHOOSE TO IMPROVE CHILDREN'S TV BY WRITING
A LETTER TO A LOCAL STATION... TO A TELEVISION
NETWORK... TO AN ADVERTISER...
TO ACTION FOR CHILDREN'S TELEVISION

TENDER
LOVING
CARE

ACTION FOR
CHILDREN'S TELEVISION
46 AUSTIN ST., NEWTONVILLE
MASS., 02160

shown as the sole means to having friends, security, and love. Children-puppets, who are paid a great deal of money by advertisers, dutifully pretend to be deeply in love with lifeless plastic dolls. If misleading the minds and hearts of our children isn't corruption, then what is?

What to do about it? Write the companies and tell them what you think about their approach. Write the producers of the children's television program with offensive advertising and tell them that you are no longer permitting your child to watch it. Better yet, write Michael Pertschuk, Chairman of the Federal Trade Commission, which regulates television advertising (see below for the address) and ask that candies, sugared cereals, and violent toys be banned from advertising during children's programs. Finally, support Action for Children's Television (ACT), a parent's organization that is fighting the commercial exploitation of children by television advertisers. Among the remarkable successes of ACT has been the reduction by 40 percent of advertising during children's programs. The group is working to tone down television violence and to remove candy and sugared cereals from children's commercials. Send fifteen dollars for a year's membership, which includes an informative newsletter.

Federal Trade Commission, Pennsylvania Avenue at 6th Street, N.W., Washington, DC 20001
Action for Children's Television (ACT), 46 Austin Street, Newtonville, MA 02160

OUTDOOR PLAY

Americans don't seem to appreciate the value of outdoor play as much as the people of other countries. In Sweden, for example, young children are kept outside as much as possible. Their rosy cheeks and bright eyes are a reminder of the tremendous value of rigorous play, sunshine, and fresh air.

Why do we keep our kids indoors so much?

Is it because we're suffering from the stresses of cities? Are we afraid that our children are not safe outdoors? I think automobiles are a big threat to parents who want to let their children outside to play.

I never really thought much about how intimidating cars are until I lived in Charlottesville, Virginia. Downtown Charlottesville was drying up — people were selling their stores. The city decided to do something about it. They bricked in Main Street, planted trees, put in benches and fountains, and made the cars stay out. The downtown area came alive with people more than it had in years. Smiling parents strolled down the center mall, their children running free without danger. Elderly people sat on the benches and talked together. There was a collective sigh of relief for having one place in the city free from those fuming metal machines of ours.

Architects of apartment buildings seldom think about the needs of children. One apartment complex we lived in had buildings jammed together with no outdoor living space in between. As a concession, children were given a tiny blacktopped area with a set of swings, a sliding board and a sandbox. It seems true in America that if you have money you can have space, the less money you have the more crowded your conditions are in the city. I look to the day when we'll care enough about all of our children to provide adequate, safe outdoor space for them to explore, to climb in, and where they can develop their bodies to the fullest.

The U.S. Consumer Product Safety Commission estimates that not only are the usual swing sets and playground equipment unimaginative, but they're also unsafe. Each year 100,000 children are raced to emergency rooms for treatment from injuries associated with public and home playground equipment. Most of the kids injured are under ten years old.

The Commission suggests the following precautions for those of you who are seeking playground equipment for your youngster:

• Stability is very important. The legs of swing sets should be set in concrete in the ground. If pegs are used, they should be well below ground level rather than sticking up. There should be no slack in the chain or cable.

• Any exposed screws or bolts should be covered with caps. If you can't find a set with protective caps, then cover them with duct tape.

• Don't buy equipment with open-ended hooks, such as "S" hooks.

• Avoid equipment with parts that might pinch or crush fingers and equipment that has sharp edges or rough surfaces.

• Don't buy a set with hanging rings that are less than 5 inches or more than 10 inches in diameter since children can get their limbs or heads entrapped in them.

• Choose lightweight, flexible seats over hard, heavy seats.

• Don't put playground equipment on concrete or asphalt.

• Put the set at least 6 feet from fences, walks, or other obstructions or protrusions.

• Inspect the set frequently and replace all nuts and bolts or swing chains that are rusty. Sand and repaint rusty spots on the metal tubing right away.

• Make hard and fast rules for your children for play around the swing set and see that they are enforced:

No rough play around the equipment.

Sit in the center of the swing, not to the side.

No twisting around and then untwisting.

Never swing empty seats or walk in front of moving swings.

Never play on a sliding board wearing a poncho or wool neck scarf. Children have been accidentally strangulated in both cases by getting their garments caught as they headed down the slide.

THINGS TO DO TOGETHER OUTDOORS

• Draw pictures in the dirt with a stick.

• Stage a neighborhood play from a familiar tale. Use the clothesline to hang the stage curtain.

• Make a lei by stringing blossoms with a blunt needle and thread.

• Make a flower necklace out of braided clover and a knotted clover ring for your finger.

• Blow dandelion seedlings on a glue-spotted piece of paper to see the pattern that emerges.

• Split dandelion stems and put them in cold water to watch them curl.

• Sculpt with garden clay.

• Make a picture from pebbles.

• Take a walk in the rain.

• Float paper boats on puddles.

• Fill balloons with water and have a water battle.

• Put on bathing suits to splash under the hose and frolic under the sprinkler. Make a rainbow by spraying the water between you and the sun.

• Fill a pan with water and paint the sidewalk, the walls, wherever you wish with a big brush.

• Blow bubbles.

• Set up a bowling alley on the sidewalk, or other flat, smooth surface by using ten half-gallon milk cartons and rolling a ball or unopened soup can into them.

• Make a walkie-talkie with two empty cans or paper cups and a string. Punch a hole in the center of the end of the cans. Pull a string through and knot it.

• Have a watermelon eating contest (no forks allowed) and then see who can spit the seeds the farthest.

• Play newspaper stepping stones, spreading the sheets farther and farther apart. "Don't fall off or the alligators will get you!"

- Play limbo by trying to go under a broomstick held lower and lower to the ground.
- Have a wheelbarrow race. Two people are wheelbarrows, walking on their hands. Two are farmers, holding on to the wheelbarrows' feet.
- Take a blind man's walk — one person blindfolded, the other leading and presenting objects for the blindfolded person to identify.
- Try walking a tightrope — a broom handle — without falling off.
- Have a tug of war with an old bicycle inner tube.
- Play Sardines. One person hides. After counting to ten — "coming, ready or not" — the others begin to look. When you find the hider, join him. Keep quiet until everybody's hiding in the same place. The first one to find the hider is "it" the next time.
- Pretend that you are imaginary animals waking up one morning in the jungle. First very quiet and sleeping, then noisier and noisier.
- Play games like Simon Says, Mother May I? and Red Light, Green Light.
- Go on a collecting walk. Collect leaves, acorns, pebbles, or flower blossoms. Iron the leaves and blossoms between two sheets of waxed paper and hang them in the window.
- Use the garden hose or a piece of rope to make the imaginary walls of a house or a fort, to make imaginary rivers to jump across, or to make a snail-shaped spiral to run in and out of.
- Play hopscotch.
- Find big corrugated boxes and make a train, a plane, a house.
- Have an impromptu picnic in the yard or a park.
- Make a tent from a rope tied between two trees with a blanket or sheet hung over it. (The rope must be low enough to the ground so that the tent will stay open.)
- Make a parachute from a 12-inch circle cut from a plastic garbage bag. Tape four 9-inch pieces of string to the chute and the other end of the strings to a stick, a small stone or a doll.
- Rake leaves into a giant pile and jump into them.

Helping Your Child to Develop Body Skills
by Raymond Stinar

Being a physical educator, I have always said that I was not going to force my children to become involved in any specific "movement experiences." But to my surprise, I didn't have to force anything. Children love to play. It's natural. My children were no exception. By just being willing to take the time to play with my three children when they wanted me to I exposed them to the all-important body skills essential for good physical ability and coordination.

I remember when Robbie was just a little over two years old, one of her favorite things to do was to play "Up in the Sky." I would take her in my hands, hold her under her arms and toss her up into the air. She would cry "Up in the sky, Daddy! Up in the sky!" Pam, my wife, would hold her breath, but Robbie loved it, and I never dropped her. Another favorite thing was to just get down on the floor and roll around together. We played circus. Robbie would crawl up on top of me, stand on my hands and I would lift her over my head. We had a great routine. We did handstands, flying angels, and a toss from my feet to my knee as I lay flat on my back.

The real player in the family proved to be my son, Brad. From about the time he was two, he always wanted to play with me. We would roughhouse on the living room floor and do all the things I used to do with Robbie. Brad really liked to be outdoors, and we spent many afternoons rolling in the grass and up and down hills. As soon as Brad could hold something in his hand, he was always trying to hit a ball with it. His first big ball venture proved to be golf. I bought him a set of plastic clubs, about two feet long, and we would go outside and hit balls in the back yard. I would take out a few of my golf clubs, and we would play together. He was amazing! He would hit big plastic balls straighter and farther than I could with my smaller ones.

I was always careful not to play any longer than he wanted to, but did we play! From golf, Brad progressed to his own style of baseball. He would hit any type of plastic ball I would roll, bounce, or throw to him. He started out by using an oversized plastic bat we got from a toy store and quickly progressed to a regulation-sized bat. He loved to bat so much that I ended up always chasing balls that went over my head but never getting to bat.

Brad was three, his sister, Robbie, was almost seven when we moved into an apartment that had a community swimming pool. Robbie knew how to swim as a result of lessons. Brad and his little brother, Brent, twenty months old, were really afraid of the water. They felt much safer playing in the water in the shallow kiddie pool. I would sit for hours in the kiddie pool and splash around with them, until I became quite bored with it. I decided that if they wanted to play, it had to be in the big pool. To my surprise, just by playing around in the water, Brad learned to swim in about six weeks and his brother, Brent, a few weeks after that.

We would play "Up in the Sky" in the water (I suppose I really enjoy throwing my children in the air.) Sometimes on purpose I would forget to catch Brad. In a couple of days Brad found out that I didn't need to catch him anymore. Then he began to jump off the side of the pool. He would come up and dog paddle over to the side and crawl out. In no time at all by just playing around in the water, Brad was paddling into the deep end of the pool and finally jumping off the diving board under my watchful eye.

Brent became mad that I wasn't playing with him enough. So I began to do the same things with him that I had done with his older brother. To my surprise, in just a short while, little twenty-month-old Brent was jumping off the side of the pool and dog paddling back over to the side. He really loved jumping in with me, but it was hard for me to keep us afloat. It's too bad that so many parents miss the opportunity to enjoy their children.

People around the pool would watch my children swimming and would ask me if I would teach their children to swim. I would always reply that "all you have to do is get out of your lounge chair, get into the water and play with your child," but no one seemed to want to take the trouble to become involved with their own children.

As a physical educator working with young children over the past twelve years, I've noticed that many parents encourage their children's learning by providing them with books, crayons, paints, and other learning materials while neglecting the all-important business of helping them master their bodies. Many of us wait until our children come to us years later wanting to go out for Little League or gymnastics. By then, the prime time for learning to run, jump, climb, hang, swing, and other body skills has already passed.

Studies on the motor development of young children point out that after the age of five or six, no new basic body skills appear in a child's movement repertoire, but rather the quality of performance continues to improve. The motor development area has a critically important period for development during these early years. Some fortunate children have a rich background of physical movement because of play with their brothers, sisters, and other children in their age group. Other children lead very sterile lives in regard to their body experiences, perhaps because of the tendency to keep children indoors and an undue emphasis on developing the child's intellect at the expense of engaging in vigorous physical activity.

Something should be said at this point about standard playground equipment. The problem with swings, seesaws, and sliding boards is that they force children into passive roles that require little balance, strength, or imagination. Ideally, children should have equipment that they can hang on with their arms or legs, that they can climb on and jump from. This kind of equipment need not be elaborate or expensive — monkey bars are good, as are large domes made of metal tubing. Even a single wooden dowel supported by side posts can offer ample opportunities for strengthening muscles and improving coordination. If you decide to make your own equipment, make sure it will allow your children the freedom to be able to climb from all directions and hang and swing freely from it.

How can you help to develop the strength and coordination of your child? I've made up a list of simple activities so that you can see the great variety of things that you and your child can do together to foster body skills. You will notice that I've broken down the skills from the simplest to the most complex — the easiest to the most difficult. Please follow two simple rules: don't force your child to do anything he or she doesn't want to do, and don't be concerned about the quality of your child's performance. The important thing is that both of you have a good time together free from the pressure of having to compete, or perform well.

BALL HANDLING

HITTING A BALL

For beginners, large, slow balls are best, followed later by smaller balls. Examples of beginners' balls: a yarn "puff" ball that you can easily make yourself, a Nerf foam ball, large beach balls, balloons, a variety

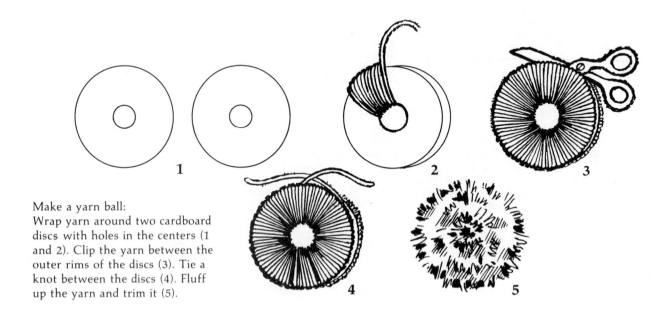

Make a yarn ball:
Wrap yarn around two cardboard
discs with holes in the centers (1
and 2). Clip the yarn between the
outer rims of the discs (3). Tie a
knot between the discs (4). Fluff
up the yarn and trim it (5).

of smaller balls of different sizes and weights. The first skill in ball handling is to simply hit the ball with some part of the body. Here are some alternative ways of ball-hitting (I've phrased my suggestions for the child):

• Keep the ball still and hit it with a fist, a foot, an elbow, or any other part of the body.

• Hit the ball very hard so that it goes far. Hit it very softly so that it stays near. Make it go high, bounce, hit the wall, or go back to someone else.

• Try hitting different places on the ball, on the bottom so that it goes up, on the sides so that it goes away, on the top so that it goes down.

• Try hitting the ball as it rolls toward you. Hit one that is thrown up in the air by you, or is thrown to you by someone else.

BATTING A BALL

After having mastered making contact with the ball by using the body, your child is ready to try batting. The best way to begin is with a large-surfaced paddle. (See Kadima paddle, p. 220.) Next comes rackets, preferably with a short handle, such as a badminton racket, or a racket you can make yourself by stretching a pair of pantyhose over a wire coat hanger bent into a circle. You can bend the hook portion into a handle and then wrap it well with adhesive tape to provide a firm grip. A fat plastic toy bat, the shorter the better, is excellent for gaining batting skills. As in learning to hit a ball, it is best to begin with a large ball first and then to progress to smaller balls from different types of materials, such as plastic, fleece, and rubber.

• Strike the ball while it is stationary.

• Strike it while it is rolling.

• Try striking a bouncing ball.

• Try to hit a ball as it is tossed in the air by you, or tossed to you by someone else.

THROWING AND CATCHING BALLS

The best size ball for these activities is one that will fit easily into one hand. You can use a small rubber ball, a tennis ball, a yarn ball, or a ball you make yourself by stuffing the end of an old sock with crumpled newspaper and sewing it up or wrapping the newspaper around and around with adhesive tape. Here are some throwing possibilities:

• Throw the ball just for the sake of throwing while standing still.

• Throw the ball as far as you possibly can.

• Try throwing the ball overhand, underhand, or side arm.

• Try throwing the ball at a large target — a wall, a

Plywood Paddle

Coat-Hanger Paddle Made
from Pantyhose

fence, the back of a building. Now try hitting a
smaller target.
● Throw the ball in any of the above ways while you
are moving.
● Throw the ball to someone else.
   Learning to catch requires a large soft ball made of
plastic, rubber, or out of a sock, progressing to
smaller balls as skills are gained. At later stages your
child can learn to catch a ball in a scoop made from a
bleach bottle.
● Have someone else roll the ball to you. Have them
roll it to the left or to the right of you.
● Have someone roll the ball to you while you are
moving.
● Bounce the ball to yourself. Now try bouncing it to
yourself while you move around the room.
● Toss the ball into the air and catch it as it bounces.
Try letting it bounce various numbers of times before
you catch it — one, two, or three times.
● Have someone else bounce the ball to you. Now
both of you try moving while bouncing the ball back
and forth.
● Have someone toss the ball to you in an arc while
you stand. Try varying the size of the ball.
● Try catching the ball while you're on the move.
Now both of you move as you toss and catch.
● Try catching the ball with a scoop, first standing
still and then moving. Try catching balls with a baseball glove.

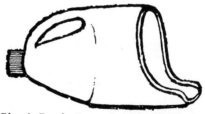

Bleach Bottle Scoop (edge with tape)

DRIBBLING A BALL

The rule is the same as before: begin with larger balls
and progress to a variety of sizes.
● Bounce the ball with two hands — don't catch it,
just hit it. Do this while you're standing still.
● Bounce the ball with one hand and then the other.
● Now try different-sized balls.
● Move around while bouncing the ball with two
hands, one hand, and then the opposite hand. Try to
see if you can go faster.
● Try moving the ball around by kicking it with your
feet. Try different parts of your feet for kicking the
ball — your toes, your heels, the inside or the outside of your feet.
● Try going faster as you kick the ball forward with
your feet.

LEARNING HOW TO MOVE AND RUN

There are all kinds of ways of getting from one place to another! With a little imagination you can help your child to gain a better understanding and control of his body.

- Walk forward, sideways, and backward. Walk to a specific place and back using one of these methods. Start walking and then have someone tell you to go in a different direction.
- Walk with someone else matching your steps. Now try to walk just the opposite of someone else.
- Run slowly and then gradually go faster. Try running forward, backward, and sideways.
- Run and then change directions when someone tells you to.
- Try playing tag by catching someone else and vice versa.
- Try running with a ball in your hands. Try running around obstacles that have been put on the ground.

JUMPING, GALLOPING, AND ROLLING

There are lots of ways of jumping: on one foot, from one foot to the other (leaping), hopping on both feet from one place to another, and a running long jump as you leap into the air and land on both feet.

- Jump around the room using the different kinds of jumps. Try jumping forward, backward, and sideways while hopping.
- Try jumping or leaping over a small hurdle or obstacle. Try to jump as far as you can, going from two feet and landing on two feet.
- Play tag while jumping with someone else. Try doing different things with your body as you jump — stretch high, curl up, twist around.
- Try skipping (step-hop on one foot, then step-hop on the other).
- Gallop like a horse with one foot always leading.
- Gallop or skip to a specific place and back. Go around in a circle, try playing tag, or imitating someone else's galloping or skipping.

Children love to roll down hills! There are lots of ways to do it. Try rolling forward in a somersault, or rolling like a log with your arms at your side, or rolling with your arms over your head.

- Roll slowly, roll quickly, roll forward, roll backward.
- Roll down the hill, but also roll *up* the hill!
- Try rolling with your eyes closed.
- Try rolling down the hill beside someone else. Now try rolling down with someone else as though you were one person.

MOVEMENT GAMES

Help your child become acquainted with the abilities and skills of his body that he isn't even aware of. Point out the body parts — arms, legs, head, elbows, knees, seat, then try these exercises:

- Use three, four, or five body parts and move slowly. Now move faster.
- Use three, four, or five body parts and move while staying very low to the ground. Play "copy cat" with each other. Now try playing tag together using a specified number of body parts for locomotion.
- Try moving like animals — a cat, a bear, a dog, an elephant, a duck, a kangaroo.
- Try moving like a machine does — a car, a tractor, an airplane, a boat, a bicycle.
- Pretend that you are carrying a large box, walking in mud, walking in snow, swimming.

BALANCING

Your child will learn first to balance using the body, then he will learn to do stunts with balance and on outdoor play equipment.

- Balance on tiptoe with your arms at your side. Now try putting your arms above your head. Stretch way up high and then squat down low.
- Try balancing with your eyes closed. Now try balancing on one foot. Hold your arms out to the side, put them down, put them over your head.
- Balance on one foot with your arms crossed in front of you. Try balancing on one foot with your eyes closed.
- See if you can find ways to balance on body parts other than your feet and still stay upright — on your knees, your seat, your back.
- Try balancing with your feet over your head. Balance on just your hands with your body squatting, with your knees on your elbows.
- Try balancing on just your hands while someone else holds your feet. Try standing on your hands while you do a mule kick.
- Do a headstand while someone watches your feet for you.

SIMPLE BALANCING EQUIPMENT

There are three pieces of equipment that you can make or buy to help develop your child's balancing skills. A balance beam is a long plank of sanded wood that has been propped on its side by wooden stands on either end (see Balance Beam, p. 223). A

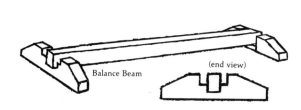

Balance Beam   (end view)

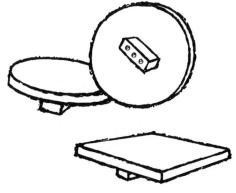

Plywood Balance Boards

balance board is a thick plywood circle or square to stand on with a small bottom stand that causes the board to pivot backward, forward, or sideways (see illustration, p. 222). Stilts are old-fashioned pieces of balancing equipment. They can be made from two planks of wood with a wooden block nailed to each piece to serve as a footrest (see illustration, p. 221). Coffee can stilts can be made easily from two one-pound coffee cans with thin rope looped through them to hold onto. (The plastic lids are good for using on both the top and the bottom of the cans to prevent marring the floor.) Here are some stunts to do on a balance beam:
• Walk forward, backward, and sideways on the beam. Walk slowly. Walk fast.
• Step over an obstacle placed on the beam. Walk to the middle of the beam and then turn around and walk back.
• Try walking across the beam while holding a ball, a hoop, or a beanbag.

Things to do on coffee can stilts:
• Walk in different directions on the cans. Go slowly. Go fast.
• Walk to a specific place and then come back moving backward.
• Step over different objects while you are walking on the cans.
• Try walking on the cans while holding the ropes in one hand only.
• Try jumping forward and backward on the cans.

HANGING, SWINGING, AND CLIMBING

The best way to teach your child coordination and balance is by using your own body. Not only is body play good exercise for both of you, it also helps to develop a sense of closeness between you. Here are some suggestions of things to do on the floor with your child while roughhousing.
• Let your child try to jump over you.
• Let your child try to balance on you, sit on you, stand on you.
• Have your child hang on to you and the two of you roll on the ground together.
• Let your child find different ways to go around you and ways of crawling over you — you try to do the same.
• Try to find different ways to support your child in various balanced positions — on your feet, on your knees, hands, back, etc. Have a mock wrestling match allowing for all kinds of body contact. The point is to try to pin you down.

Activities for a bar, a tree limb, or a Jungle gym:
• Find as many ways as you can to climb up and down.
• Hang by your hands, by your knees, with both your hands and feet. Find as many ways as you can to swing.
• Try to find ways of balancing — on two feet, on one foot, with the whole body lying down.
• You and someone else try matching movements together on the bar, then try moving in opposite directions — if you're high, the other person must be low, and vice versa.

Raymond Stinar is Assistant Professor of Physical Education, Towson State University in Baltimore, Maryland. He has taught physical education to children ages three through sixteen for the past twelve years and he is a specialist in early childhood and elementary physical education.

MAKING A PLAYGROUND FROM SCROUNGED THINGS

With a little imagination and planning, you can make a play area for your child or for a play group from materials that you can get free for the asking or very inexpensively. Who says playgrounds have to always look the same? It's what the children *do* that counts — running, jumping, swinging — vigorous things that help them to develop their arm and leg muscles.

Straw and hay   From local fields in the fall or from a feed store. For jumping in or using for a thatched roof.

Railroad ties   From railroad companies and crews. For an imbedded balance beam, the sides of a sandbox, or a make-believe car with a mounted steering wheel.

Large rocks   From road construction sites, gravel pits, or the woods. For damming up a stream to make a pool or making stepping stones.

Bricks   Use culled, or seconds from a brick-yard or construction company. For building forts or pretend swimming pools. For constructing a climbing wall with concrete.

Concrete culverting and clay tile pipes   From concrete companies, the city sewerage system, the telephone company. For making tunnels and bridges. Be sure they're well embedded in the ground.

Tree sections and tree trunks with limbs   From the city electric company, neighbors, or a lumber mill. For climbing and practicing hammering, sawing, and other woodworking skills.

Sand   From the beach, a construction company, or a sand and gravel pit. For making a sandbox. (Should have drainage bricks underneath and a cover to keep cats and dogs out.)

Wooden blocks and pieces of lumber   Discards from lumber companies and the city utility company. For building structures with hammers and nails, for stacking and other structures.

Ropes, rope ladders and cargo nets   From hardware stores and shipyards. For climbing and swinging.

Barrels   From a hardward store or a distillery. For rolling in, making houses and tunnels. (Be sure to sand away the splinters.)

Large, rectangular plastic containers   From textile mills — used for fabric storage. To make play houses and for stacking.

Large wooden electric wire spools   From the electric company. For making tables, stools.

Discarded Rowboat   Ask around piers and docks. Use for imaginary voyages, or drill holes for drainage and use as a sandbox.

Automobile tires   From auto junkyards and service stations. Clean them up and paint them bright colors with paint made especially for rubber. Use to roll, to stack, to climb on, as swings.

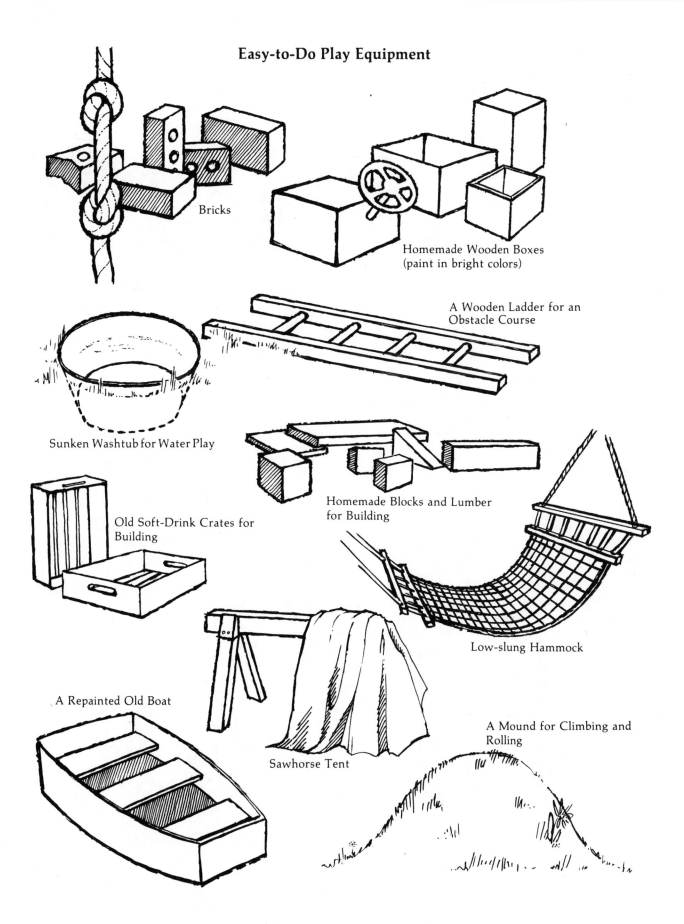

Easy-to-Do Play Equipment

Bricks

Homemade Wooden Boxes
(paint in bright colors)

A Wooden Ladder for an
Obstacle Course

Sunken Washtub for Water Play

Homemade Blocks and Lumber
for Building

Old Soft-Drink Crates for
Building

Low-slung Hammock

A Repainted Old Boat

Sawhorse Tent

A Mound for Climbing and
Rolling

Tires

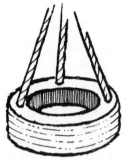
Swing Made with Rope

Obstacle Course

Tunnel

Spin-around Swing

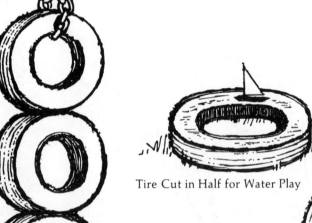
A Suspended Climber
(tires are bolted together)

Tire Cut in Half for Water Play

Ride'm Horsey Tire

BOOKS ON DEVELOPING THE PHYSICAL SKILLS OF CHILDREN

Be a Frog, a Bird or a Tree
Rachel Carr
Doubleday and Co., Inc., 501 Franklin Avenue, Garden City, NY 11530 ($5.95)
Photographs illustrate simple yoga exercises with drawings of the animals that children are imitating. Simple wording. Notes to parents on how to help children in doing the exercises.

Yoga for Children
Eve Diskin
Arco Publishing Co., Inc., 219 Park Avenue S., New York, NY 10003 ($8.95)
Yoga exercises are divided into beginning, intermediate, and advanced levels. Lots of photographs and drawings. The exercises are very simple and well named for young children: "Rag Doll," "Kitty Cat," "Elephant Trunk." Children can develop a clear understanding of their bodies, breathing, and relaxation.

Skiing with Kids
Christi Mueller Northrop
The Chatham Press, 143 Sound Beach Avenue, Old Greenwich, CT 06870 ($5.95, paperback)
If you want your child to learn to ski, or even if you're just planning a ski vacation and wonder what to do with your kids, you'll find this book indispensable. It reviews the child care and children's ski instructions available at all the major ski slopes in the United States. Gives specific suggestions for purchasing brand name clothing and ski equipment. Directions on how to teach a child to ski. A wealth of information from a former ski instructor and racer who has instructed her own children in the art.

See What I Can Do! A Book of Creative Movement
Maya B. Doray
Prentice-Hall, Inc., Englewood Cliffs, NJ 07632 ($4.95)
An excellent book of simple, well-illustrated movements for a young child to imitate. Walking on one leg, hopping, other movements perfectly fitted to four- and five-year-olds.

"Families Play to Grow"
The Joseph P. Kennedy, Jr., Foundation, 1701 K Street, N.W., Washington, DC 20006 (Single copies free)
An excellent guide for parents of young children or children needing help in developing physical skills. Includes leaflets on movement activities, ideas for rhythm and dance, techniques for teaching a young child ball throwing and batting, and a myriad of other activities for families to do together. Large posters are included so that family members can record their participation in activities.

BOOKS ON OUTDOOR PLAY EQUIPMENT

"Idea Exchange: Playgrounds"
LINC Publications
Order from:
Idea Exchange, 800 Silver Avenue, Greensboro, NC 27403 ($1.25)
Directions for making a climbing structure that includes a sandbox, a deck with storage, and a ladder. Also has plans for a water-play table, a Jungle gym made from plumbing pipe, a sliding board using vertical tires as steps, a tire swing.

"A Priceless Playground for Exceptional Children"
Patricia G. Adkins
Learning Resources Press, 609 La Cruz Drive, El Paso, TX 79902 ($1.50 + 35¢ postage)
Directions for mounting a cargo net, a walking trough, a tire swing, a sandbox, a walking beam, a balance board and other easy playground constructions.

Homemade Innovative Play Equipment
American Association for Health, Physical Education, and Recreation
Order from:
The Council for Exceptional Children, 1920 Association Drive, Reston, VA 22091 ($3.65)
Directions for making a target toss, an overhead ladder, adjustable monkey bars, a climbing tower, balance beams and boards, and a "Buckin' Broncho" made from a metal barrel mounted on two trees by ropes, horsey style. Originally intended for handicapped children, the ideas are useful for parents and teachers of normal young children, too.

Build Your Own Playground!
Jeremy Joan Hewes
Houghton Mifflin Company, Two Park Street, Boston, MA 02107 ($7.95, paperback)
A myriad of ideas for designing elaborate play structures from wood and tires. Probably more than a parent would want to tackle, but a good sourcebook if you're in a parent co-op and planning a playground for a group.

"Building with Tires"
Early Childhood Education Study of Advisory for Open Education
Education Development Center (EDC), Distribution Center, 39 Chapel Street, Newton, MA 02160 ($1.50)
How to make climbing constructions and swings from tires bolted together and hung from ropes. A single tire swing on a swivel, a tire bridge, a tunnel, and multitire swings.

BOOKS ON TOY MAKING

Professor Hammerfinger's Indestructible Toys
Steve Ross
Oliver Press, 1400 Ryan Creek Road, Willits, CA
95490 ($3.95)
A do-it-yourself guide to making seventy-five
simple wooden toys. An airplane, a car, a boat, a
train, a teeter-totter, a sandbox, a small farm and
gas station to name a few. Patterns for a simple doll
and hand puppet.

Learning Materials Handbook
Karen Hewitt
The Vermont Crossroads Press, Waitsfield, VT 05404
($2.00)
Designs and instructions for making Montessori-
type toys, a variety of wooden puzzles, a Geoboard
made from nails, mounted posts for stacking beads,
a peg board, a board with nuts and bolts to screw
on and off, dominoes, and simple wheeled toys.

Things to Make for Children
The Editors of Sunset Books and Sunset Magazine
Lane Publishing Co., Willow and Middlefield
Roads, Menlo Park, CA 94025 ($1.95)
Directions for making a variety of small wooden
toys, a jigsaw puzzle, a portable drawing table, a
dollhouse, and a child-sized couch among other
interesting ideas.

Puppets for All the Grades
Louise Binder Scott, Marion E. May, Mildred S.
Shaw
The Instructor Publications, Inc., Dansville, NY
14437 ($1.95)
A great puppet ideabook! How to make wigs,
hands, and garments. Puppets made from socks,
vegetables, paper bags. How to make a stage and
light it. The most idea-packed puppet book that I
have found.

GAMES AND IMAGINATIVE PLAY

Tiddlywinks
An old-fashioned game that's fun for youngsters!
Chips come in a bright red mushroom cup. First
player to flip all of the chips in the mushroom cup
wins. Two to six players. This company produces a
superb catalog of toys and games with each toy
listed by the appropriate age and grade level of the
child (catalog, $1.00). Order from:
Novo Educational Toy and Equipment Corp., 11
Park Place, New York, NY 10007 ($2.25. $20.00
minimum order)

Giant Pic-Up-Stix
Children try to pick up a stick without disturbing
the others. The one with the most sticks at the end
of the game wins. Sticks are brightly colored wood.
Order from:
Novo Educational Toy and Equipment Corp., 11
Park Place, New York, NY 10007 ($1.45. $20.00
minimum order. Write for catalog, $1.00.)

The Vegimals
Soft, huggable vegetables, each with a unique
personality! Shown here: Corn with Velcro fasteners
to make it "shuckable," in lime green and yellow.
Peas in pea green, of course! A nylon zipper keeps
the "Pea Brothers" in their pod. Tomato is red and
green velour. Order from:
The Vegimill, Bristol, VT 05443 ($18.90 ea.,
postpaid)

Bucket and Mop
Mop has a thick, absorbent 7-inch-wide sponge.
The handle is 32 inches long. Durable, child-sized
bucket included. From the "Growing Years"
catalog. Prices subject to change.
Childcraft Education Corp., 20 Kilmer Road,
Edison, NJ 08817 ($2.95 + $2.00 shipping and
handling charge)

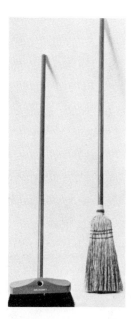

Brooms
The large push broom has a 36-inch red wooden
handle. The corn broom has a total length of 38
inches. From the "Growing Years" catalog. Prices
subject to change.
Childcraft Education Corp., 20 Kilmer Road,
Edison, NJ 08817 (Push broom, $3.95; corn broom,
$2.95 + $2.00 shipping and handling per order)

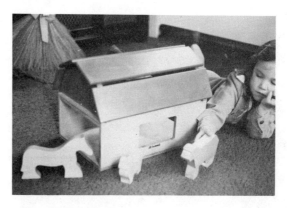

Barn and Animals
A red-topped barn with a removable roof. The barn
measures 18 inches long, 12 inches high and 12
inches wide. The Farm Animal Set is made of solid
hardwood with a clear lacquer finish. Three
animals: a horse, a sheep, and a cow. An excellent
catalog of wooden toys and handmade hand
puppets. Order from:
Artwood, P.O. Drawer A, Highway 41 at Valley
Road, Woodland, GA 31836 (Barn, $22.70; Farm
Animal Set, $8.55 + shipping)

Dollhouse

A birch laminate dollhouse with a birch floor. Clear finish with a painted hardboard detachable roof. Measurements: 12 inches wide, 16 inches long, and 8 inches high, plus roof. Individual house units can be stacked together to make a two- or three-story house. A catalog of wooden toys and climbing equipment. Order from:

Holbrook-Patterson, Inc., 170 S. Monroe Street, Coldwater, MI 49036 ($25.00 + shipping)

Puppet Stage

A hardwood-framed puppet stage with a colorful curtain that rolls up and down. The washable vinyl backdrop can be painted for changing the scenery. Rubber tips on the base protect the floor. Measurements: 27 inches long x 26 inches high, with two 12½-inch side panels to hide the puppeteer. Catalog of educational toys and games available. Order from:

Lakeshore Curriculum Materials, 8888 Venice Boulevard, Los Angeles, CA 90034 ($29.50 + 15% shipping and handling charge. CA residents add 6 or 6½% sales tax)

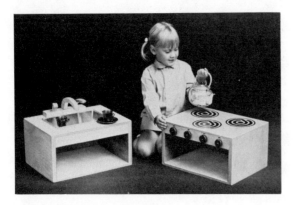

Table-Top Sink and Stove

The sink is lightweight and portable with a removable aluminum sink pan and solid maple faucets that turn. The stove has simulated burners with knobs that turn. Both of birch laminate construction with each one measuring 16 inches wide, 12 inches deep, and 8¼ inches high. Order from:

Holbrook-Patterson, Inc., 170 S. Monroe Street, Coldwater, MI 49036 ($23.50 ea., + shipping)

Puppets and a Doorway Theatre

Made specially for hand puppets, this washable poplin stage measures 29" x 62". It hangs in a standard doorway on its own adjustable tension rod, and folds away quickly for storage. Bright red. Also available are a variety of bright, whimsical "Poppets." Shown here are Clown (908), Roby Rabbit (902), and Julie (905). A full color brochure is available. Order from:

Poppets, 1800 E. Olive Way, Seattle, WA 98102, (Theatre, $21.50. Puppets, $9.75. Both are postpaid)

Animal Puzzles
Color photographs of eight different animals are
die-cut to separate the animal's body into its
principal parts. Each puzzle measures 8½ x 11
inches. The animals are: dog, cat, horse, cow,
rooster, deer, squirrel, and chipmunk. Mounted on
heavy durable board, which has been varnished.
Instruction leaflet included.
Developmental Learning Materials, 7440 Natchez
Avenue, Niles, IL 60648 ($5.50)

People in Motion Puzzle
A puzzle designed to help a child gain a better
understanding of the parts of the body and the
concepts of "left" and "right." The roller skater
comes in fourteen pieces, and is carefully divided
by left, right, and parts of the body. From the
Childcraft "Special Education Materials" catalog.
Price subject to change.
Childcraft Education Corp., 20 Kilmer Road,
Edison, NJ 08817 ($3.95 + $1.95 shipping and
handling charge)

Play Scenes Lotto
Color photographs of children at play in familiar
settings. The game was developed in cooperation
with the Women's Action Alliance. The object of the
game is to match cards with the same photograph
on a master card. Easy enough for a very young
child to play. From a catalog of games and colorful
toys for children.
Milton Bradley Co., Springfield, MA 01101 ($3.50 +
$1.00 shipping)

DOLLS AND PUPPETS

Doll Pattern

One pattern of many from a catalog of adorable dolls
of all sizes and shapes. This tot with a gingham
dress is 19 inches tall. For a catalog of doll patterns,
send 75¢ to:
Carolee Creations, 144 N. Clinton Avenue,
Elmhurst, IL 60126 ($2.35 pattern only)

Tooth Fairy

Lisa Drumm has created a limited edition of this
fantasy character. She's made of cotton and stuffed
with polyester fiber. She wears a felt and satin
crown that unzips to disclose a chain of gold coins.
She wears a cameo made from felt with little
mother-of-pearl teeth embroidered on it. Her wand
is removable and she has sheer wings in the back
for flitting around to the bedrooms of six-year olds.
Other soft sculpture fantasies are shown on a free
leaflet.
Don Drumm Studios and Gallery, 437 Crouse Street,
Akron, OH 44311 ($42.00)

Asian Dolls

The dolls are 13 inches tall with movable arms, legs,
and head. The boy is dressed in a numbered
teeshirt and shorts. The girl has rooted hair and is
dressed in a colorful jumper set. Similar dolls
available in white, black, and Hispanic versions,
each with characteristic features and coloring. From
an excellent catalog of early learning materials.
Kaplan School Supply Corp., 600 Jonestown Road,
Winston-Salem, NC 27103 (Boys $10.00; girls $12.00)

Hound Dog Hand Puppet

A large furry friend with big flappy ears, hound dog
can help you tell nighttime stories and encourage
your child to use his imagination. He fits adult-
sized hands but is cuddly enough to be hugged.
Measurements: 13 x 6 inches. From a beautiful, full-
colored catalog of learning materials, many tailored
specifically for children with learning disabilities.
Minimum $10.00 order required.
Developmental Learning Materials (D.L.M.), 7440
Natchez Avenue, Niles, IL 60648 ($9.00 + 60¢
shipping)

Anything Muppet ™

This soft, felt puppet comes with a blank head and a
bagful of accessories that stick on with Velcro: two
pairs of eyes, glasses, a big red nose, a colorful wig,
and two hairpieces that can be eyebrows,
sideburns, mustaches, or beards. Children can use
yarn, paper, and tape to make an endless variety of
faces and costumes. Minimum order $20.00; catalog
available, $1.00.
Novo Educational Toy and Equipment Corp., 11
Park Place, New York, NY 10007 ($7.95 + shipping)

Hand Puppet Idea Bag

A burlap sack filled with materials that inspire
children to make puppets using their own ideas.
Included are a bottle of glue, marking pens, a soft
sock, tongue depressors, wooden clothespins, glue-
on eyes, yarn for hair, fabric, a hand puppet
pattern, and an excellent ideabook that gives
suggestions for constructing the puppets. The
possibilities are limitless! Order from:
J. R. Holcomb Co., 3000 Quigley Road, Cleveland,
OH 44113 ($9.95 + $1.50 postage and handling)

WHEELED TOYS

Steering Wheel

A handsomely made real steering wheel that adds
dramatic scope to imitative play. Two nesting chair
blocks — one as the hood and the other as the
driver's seat to recreate the family car or a bus. From
the "Growing Years" catalog. Price subject to
change.
Childcraft Education Corp., 20 Kilmer Road,
Edison, NJ 08817 (Steering wheel and two Childcraft
nesting chair blocks $44.95 + shipping and
handling charge)

Steering Truck

A ride-on truck with loading space and removable seat. The chassis is made of beech wood in a natural finish. The front bumper is padded against collisions. Silent, strong rubber tires. Measurements: 28¾ inches long. From ''Vital Years,'' a catalog of educational materials for early childhood and special education ($1.00) Educational Teaching Aids (ETA), 159 W. Kinzie Street, Chicago, IL 60610 ($48.50 + shipping)

Thingamabobbin

An open-ended toy that can be made into a car, a boat, a rocket, or a gear machine. The center core is made of spruce. The kit also contains hardwood bobbins, dowels, and rubber bands. All can be used interchangeably for a variety of structures. Available in a natural or a painted finish. Order from: Karen Hewitt, Box 45A, East Corinth, VT 05040 ($8.50 painted finish; $7.50 natural finish + $1.40 postage and handling)

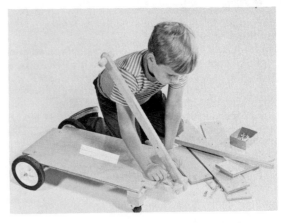

Wooden Hand Car

This roll n' play car is 7½ inches long and is made entirely of smooth wood. The window makes a good handle for chugging the car around in the sandbox or up the wall. Order from: Handcraft Designs, Div. of Bill Muller Wooden Toys, Inc., Rockhill Industrial Park, 87 Commerce Drive, Telford, PA 18969 ($4.95 + $1.00 postage and handling)

Wheeled Construction Set

The Construction Set offers a real challenge to young mechanics. It comes with a variety of parts, four picture ''blueprints,'' and includes wrenches, bolts, a handle, two end pieces, two side pieces, one bottom piece, an axle with two 2-inch swivel casters and another axle with 6-inch wheels. Makes a scooter, a coaster, and a wagon. A supplementary set enables a child to bolt together a doll bed, a wagon, a doll buggy, a high and a low wheelbarrow. From a catalog of wooden educational toys and blocks. Order from: Jonti-Craft Educational Play Equipment, Div. of Rapids Sash and Millwork, Inc., Sauk Rapids, MN 56379 (Basic set, $42.50; supplementary set, $23.24; complete set, $63.35 + shipping)

Swedish Variplay Set
Versatile, relatively unstructured building pieces.
Consists of: two chair pieces, one flat piece with
two sides, four 8-inch rubber wheels, two
hardwood axles with plastic fastening swivels on
the ends. It can be used to make a chair, a table, a
wheeled toy, and as building blocks. From a catalog
of carefully designed preschool wooden toys and
educational equipment.
Community Playthings, Rifton, NY 12471 ($68.50 +
shipping)

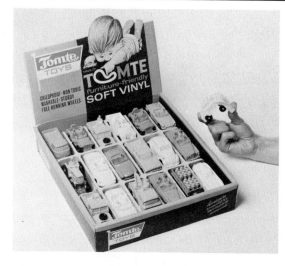

Vinyl Vehicles
A fleet of soft vinyl cars that won't harm the
furniture. Your child can twist them, stomp on
them, chew them — they're practically
indestructible. From their large catalog of toys and
educational materials.
Kaplan School Supply Corp., 600 Jonestown Road,
Winston-Salem, NC 27103 (12 cars for $7.00)

OUTDOOR PLAY EQUIPMENT

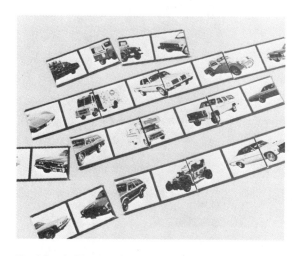

Car Match-Up Puzzles
Twenty-eight dominolike cards are placed end-to-
end to reassemble twenty-seven color photographs
of cars. The length of the complete train is more
than 8 feet. From the catalog. No orders under
$10.00 accepted. Order from:
Developmental Learning Materials, 7440 Natchez
Avenue, Niles, IL 60648 ($3.25 + 60¢ shipping and
handling)

All Ball Tennis
A child-sized tennis game with short rackets, a net
that ties onto the back of two chairs or can be put
up in the driveway, the playroom, or outdoors and
two spongy, bouncing, yellow foam balls that are
light enough to be safe for indoor play. Order from:
Tennis Resources, Inc., West, 2563 Greer Road, Palo
Alto, CA 94303 ($17.98 for the complete set; $2.98 for
three balls)

Nerf Ball
The Super Nerf (tm) is a large 7-inch foam ball for catching, batting, kicking, and throwing. Quite a bathtub toy, too! From a catalog of educational equipment and supplies.
Playtime Equipment Co., 808 Howard Street, Omaha, NE 68102 ($2.95 + postage and handling)

Kadima
Large, hollow-core rackets that are just right for the youngster learning to hit a ball. A small soft rubber ball is designed for use by adults playing Kadima, a noncompetitive game in which players work together to keep the ball up in the air. Tennis-ball-sized, foam balls are also available for indoor use or as a training ball. Order from:
Drybranch, Inc., 60 E. Jericho Turnpike, Minneola, NY 11501 (Kadima set: two rackets and one small rubber ball, $8.00 + $1.50 shipping and handling; tennis-ball-sized foam balls, 3 for $3.00 + $1.00 shipping and handling if ordered separately from the Kadima set.)

Blooper Ball
An extra safe ball with a soft-textured surface. It can be used in place of a softball for family fun. Rules for playing softball with it are included. Size: 4 inches in diameter. Order from:
Hammatt and Sons, 1441 N. Red Gum, Bldg. E, Anaheim, CA 92806 ($7.75 + shipping charges. You will be billed for your order)

Deluxe Playground Ball
A bright yellow ball made with nylon windings and a laminated rubber bladder for rugged durability. A self-sealing valve. Good for kickball and traditional ball games as well as for beginning catching and throwing practice for preschoolers. From a catalog of family-style recreation equipment.
Hammatt and Sons, 1441 N. Red Gum, Bldg. E, Anaheim, CA 92806 ($7.50 + shipping charges. You will be billed for your order)

Giant Balloons
Four brightly colored balloons of heavy-duty
rubber. They inflate to a whopping 3-foot diameter.
From a catalog of scientific and pseudoscientific
gadgets.
Edmund Scientific Co., 300 Edscorp Building,
Barrington, NJ 08007 ($3.95 postpaid)

Junior Stilts
Made of fine hardwood with smooth, beveled
edges. The foot opening is 8½ inches off the
ground. A firm hand grip for stability. High
adventure for the young beginner. From the "Toys
That Teach" catalog. Price subject to change.
Childcraft Education Corp., 20 Kilmer Road,
Edison, NJ 08817 ($10.95 + $1.95 shipping and
handling)

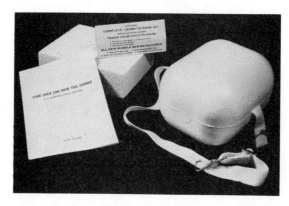

Plastic Kites
Choose a hawk or a butterfly! Constructed of heavy-
duty plastic with brilliant colors. Sturdy and easy to
fly. Excellent for the beginning kite-flyer. From a
full-color catalog of kites from around the world.
Go Fly a Kite, Inc., 1434 Third Avenue, New York,
NY 10028 (Hawk, approx. $5.00; butterfly, approx.
$4.00)

Swim-Aid
The complete Learn-to-Swim kit includes an
instruction book by an experienced teacher, a
polystyrene foam bubble with rugged straps and a
safety lock that won't open accidentally, extra foam
for constructing a smaller bubble to provide less
support as your child learns to swim. For children
eighteen months and older. (Not to be used as a life
preserver, but as an aid to learning to swim.) Order
from:
Mrs. Janet Rogers, P.O. Box 933, Dunedin, FL 33528
($6.00 postpaid)

EQUIPMENT FOR PHYSICAL PLAY

Home Exercise Mat
Give your youngsters a safe place to exercise, wrestle, and roughhouse with abandon. Ideal for placement under indoor swings. A 2-inch-thick mat filled with firm, density-bonded polyfoam and covered with a vinyl-coated nylon fabric. Random solid colors. From a catalog filled with innovative, wooden outdoor play equipment.
Child Life Play Specialties, Inc., 55 Whitney Street, Holliston, MA 01746 ($37.00 + shipping)

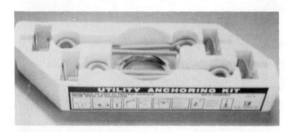

Playground Equipment Designs
A kit with step-by-step instructions for assembly and list of materials for making a wideslide, a tiretree (both pictured), a ropetree and a kid klimber. The kit includes four plans, suggestions for total development of a playground for children and the analysis report of a structural engineer. Order the kit from:
Learning Stuff, P.O. Box 4123, Modesto, CA 95352 ($12.50)

Swing Set Anchor
Keep-stake anchors give maximum, convenient anchoring to prevent swing sets from tipping over. Each kit contains four anchors, fifty feet of cable and instructions for construction. Be sure that the anchor is buried so that no sharp edges or cables protrude to trip youngsters. From the "Catalog of Child Safety," a free catalog filled with safety equipment designed for youngsters. Order from:
Safety Now Co., Inc., Box 567, 202 York Road, Jenkintown, PA 19046 ($9.50 + $1.75 postage and handling)

Balance Board
A birch plywood platform covered with a nonslip rubber mat, 16 x 16 inches. The four-sided balance point underneath has a broad surface that rests on the ground so that the user can remain upright easily.
abc School Supply, Inc., P.O. Box 13086, Atlanta, GA 30324 ($15.95 + $2.00 handling charge and shipping)

Balance Beam

A 6-foot long beam that has an edge 6 inches from the ground. Your child can either use the 2¾-inch-wide side or the 1⅜-inch side for perfecting balance.
Community Playthings, Rifton, NY 12471 ($24.50 + shipping)

two sets of rings for fastening it into a door jamb or beam. Children can adjust the height of the ropes themselves.
Child Life Play Specialties, 55 Whitney Street, Holliston, MA 01746 ($24.00 postpaid)

Vari-Balance Boards

A set of balance boards made of solid maple with maple bases. The boards fit on pegs on the stands and can be arranged in any number of patterns from a circle to zigzags. The boards are 48 inches long x 4 inches wide. Prices subject to change.
Holbrook-Patterson, Inc., 170 S. Monroe Street, Coldwater, MI 49036 ($29.00 each + shipping)

Doorway Gym

Ideal for apartments and for active play indoors. Includes a flexible belt swing, a trapeze bar, steel trapeze rings with comfortable plastic grips, a climbing rope with wooden blocks going up it, and

See-Sawhorse

A triangle sawhorse with three rungs on each of two sides making it possible to adjust the height of the cleated board. The cleats on the board make it useful as a slide, a balance board or a seesaw. The board is 60 inches long; the sawhorse, 13 inches high.
Creative Educational Distributor (CED), 159–163 East Lancaster Avenue, Wayne, PA 19087 ($31.00 + shipping)

Right-Angle Climber and Slide

A sturdy climber for young children. The platform is 36 inches high. The aluminum rails go 12 inches above the platform. A tunnel underneath for hiding. Excellent for two- to four-year-olds.
Community Playthings, Rifton, NY 12471 ($79.50 + shipping)

Jolly Gym

Portable, versatile, strong, and stable — everything you could want in an indoor-outdoor gym! The fifteen components slide together in five minutes. The sturdy plastic compound cannot rust, chip, or crack. The bars are 2 inches in diameter. The entire unit stores in one 21 x 21 x 12-inch carton and weighs only 30 pounds. (Smaller set than pictured.) Recommended for eighteen months to four years of age. From the "Toys that Teach" catalog. Price subject to change.
Childcraft Education Corp., 20 Kilmer Road, Edison, NJ 08817 ($99.99 + $5.25 shipping and handling charge)

Junior Gym-Pla Trainer

A set of components that offer maximum versatility for indoor and outdoor play. Set includes: two 36-inch horses, three 8-foot horizontal beams, an 8-foot hardwood ladder, and a reinforced Masonite slide 76 inches long.
Holbrook-Patterson, Inc., 170 S. Monroe Street, Coldwater, MI 49036 ($295.00 + shipping)

Ladder Exerciser

A safe, nontipping ladder gym. Rungs, ladders, and uprights are scaled for secure climbing. Good for large muscle development. All wood construction with metal hardware. Instructions for assembly included. Recommended for three- to eight-year-olds. Measurements: 59½ x 41 x 42¼ inches. From a general school supply catalog. Manufactured by Creative Playthings. Order from:
William G. Johnston Co., P.O. Box 6759, Pittsburgh, PA 15212 ($76.00 + shipping)

Junior Gym
Backyard adventures begin here! This simple
structure with lots of inviting climbing rungs, two
movable platforms, a crawl-through door and a 6-
foot slide makes a good arena for imaginative play.
The slide is made of galvanized steel. The entire
unit is 4 feet tall. Folds flat for storage.
Recommended for three- to seven-year-olds. Price
subject to change. Express only.
Childcraft Education Corp., 20 Kilmer Road,
Edison, NJ 08817 ($181.95 + shipping)

Variplay Triangle Set
A versatile set that offers a number of constructions.
The set consists of a large triangle 30 inches long
and 15 inches high; two small triangles 10 inches
wide with wheels; a board 72 inches long; and a
short board 44 inches long. Can be made into a
sliding board, a seesaw, a four-wheeled vehicle, a
climber.
Community Playthings, Rifton, NY 12471 ($85.50 for
the set + shipping. Pieces can be ordered
individually)

Firefighter Gym Kit
An 8-foot-tall wooden gym set with rungs going up
on all sides. Two cleated boards can be moved
inside the gym to make a table, a roof, or steps.
Includes a polyfiber rope net and a climbing rope.
The optional 8-foot slide can be attached anywhere
on the gym. The kit form can be assembled in three
to four hours plus time for sanding, painting, and
drying. All you need are a hammer, pliers, a
screwdriver, and a paintbrush. Paint is provided,
holes predrilled. Prices subject to change.
Child Life Play Specialties, Inc., 55 Whitney Street,
Holliston, MA 01746 (Partially assembled, $235.00;
in kit form, $204.00; sliding board, $37.00)

Note: Not all manufacturers and publishers will
accept single orders for a product or book. Always write to them first, before sending
money, to be sure that they will take your
order. Make sure you've got the most recent
price, including shipping and handling
charges. If the company is in your state, then
you may need to include state sales tax as well.

Index

20884

372.24 Jones, Sandy
JON
        Learning for little
        kids

DATE			
OCT 17 '80	.